HAṬHA-YOGA
Its Context, Theory and Practice

Haṭha-Yoga

Its Context, Theory and Practice

MIKEL BURLEY

With a Foreword by

DR. DAVID FRAWLEY, O.M.D.

MOTILAL BANARSIDASS PUBLISHERS
PRIVATE LIMITED • DELHI

First Edition: Delhi, 2000

ISBN: 81-208-1705-2 (Cloth)
ISBN: 81-208-1706-0 (Paper)

Also available at:
MOTILAL BANARSIDASS
236 Sri Ranga 9th Main III Block, Jayanagar, Bangalore 560 011
41 U.A. Bungalow Road, Jawahar Nagar, Delhi 110 007
8 Mahalaxmi Chamber, Warden Road, Mumbai 400 026
120 Royapettah High Road, Mylapore, Chennai 600 004
Sanas Plaza, 1302 Baji Rao Road, Pune 411 002
8 Camac Street, Calcutta 700 017
Ashok Rajpath, Patna 800 004
Chowk, Varanasi 221 001

Printed in India
BY JAINENDRA PRAKASH JAIN AT SHRI JAINENDRA PRESS,
A-45 NARAINA INDUSTRIAL AREA, PHASE-I, NEW DELHI 110 028
AND PUBLISHED BY NARENDRA PRAKASH JAIN FOR
MOTILAL BANARSIDASS PUBLISHERS PRIVATE LIMITED,
BUNGALOW ROAD, DELHI 110 007

Contents

Part Two:
THEORETICAL ASPECTS OF HAṬHA-YOGA

Part Three:
PRACTICAL ASPECTS OF HAṬHA-YOGA

Foreword

by Dr David Frawley, O.M.D.

(Director of the American Institute of Vedic Studies. Author of *Ayurveda and the Mind*; *Yoga and Ayurveda*; *Gods, Sages and Kings*; etc.)

Haṭha Yoga is probably the most commonly known of the different branches of Yoga, but it is also, for the same reason, perhaps the most misunderstood. Yoga practice in the west is now defined mainly in terms of āsanas or physical postures, which are the easiest aspect of yoga for the outward-looking western mind to grasp. As these are most elaborately described in Haṭha Yoga texts, this modern western āsana-based yoga often calls itself Haṭha Yoga as well.

However, Haṭha Yoga is much more than āsana. It is a complete and integral system of spiritual development for body, mind and soul. It is not only a sophisticated physical system but contains in-depth knowledge about the subtle body, its nāḍīs and cakras, as well. It goes into great detail not only regarding āsana, but also prāṇāyāma, mantra and meditation.

The goal of āsana practice in traditional Haṭha Yoga also differs from that of most modern groups. Haṭha Yoga does not aim merely at making us feel better on a physical level, it contains intense ascetic practices for physical and psychic purification, which require specific instruction from a teacher on an individual basis. It is a path to full enlightenment or Self-realization, not a preliminary or bodily-based system only. Classical Haṭha Yoga therefore contains but goes far beyond the usual idea of modern yoga approaches and their exercise/therapy orientation.

If we look at Haṭha Yoga in its original and broader sense we see that few people are really practising it today and few really understand what it is, including many professional yoga teachers. A greater examination of the subject is therefore essential in order to understand what yoga was originally meant to be and what its greater parameters have always been.

Another misconception is that Haṭha Yoga is something relatively new in the Indian tradition. This is because most Haṭha Yoga texts that describe āsanas in detail appear to be only about a thousand years old. However, we can find many seals of figures in yoga postures from the Harappan (or, as it is now called, the Indus-Sarasvatī) culture going back to 2500 B.C.E. This shows that classical Haṭha Yoga practices rest upon much older traditions. Indeed, disciplines of āsana, prāṇāyāma and meditation can be found in all aspects of the Indic tradition and all layers of its literature, Tantric, Purāṇic and Vedic. One could call classical Indic culture 'yogic,' extending a yogic approach even to literature, music and dance.

Haṭha Yoga comes in for some criticism for its fixation on the physical body. This is truer of modern āsana yoga than of classical Haṭha. The Haṭha yogi views the body as a multilayered system of which the physical is only the outer rung, inseparable from inner levels of prāṇa, mind and consciousness. The Haṭha yogi is not concerned with the physical in itself but only as a means to access the deeper levels of body and mind. Haṭha Yoga is in fact more concerned with prāṇa than with the body, and looks at the body as a prāṇic or energy system, not as a mere physiological structure or set of biochemical reactions.

Prāṇa itself is an important subject in the Upaniṣads and Brāhmaṇas, where it is often identified with the ātman or supreme Self. The determination that the human being breathes 21,600 times a day (10,800 by day and by night or about one breath every four seconds) occurs first in the *Śatapatha Brāhmaṇa*, a very old text from before the Upaniṣadic period, showing that the Vedic rishis examined the subject with great attention. It can be argued that the main deity of the *Ṛg Veda*, Indra, is a symbol for the awakened prāṇa. He is a deity of the atmosphere or region of air, and wields the lightning or power of transformative insight. More specifically he is the prāṇa or energy of seeing (*dṛg-śakti*). Haṭha Yoga develops from such an energetic worldview, not from a simple fixation on physical forms and structure.

There are very few good books on Haṭha Yoga available today despite the plethora of titles in the field. Most are modern āsana books aimed at a mass audience, with little understanding of classical Yoga. Some are scholarly works done as museum pieces by those who have never practised the system, and who may be unaware of the living aspects of the tradition.

In contrast to these one-sided and potentially misleading approaches, Mikel Burley presents a work that is both scholarly and reflects the understanding of a practitioner in the field. His approach is not merely academic but experiential. The author possesses both a good intuition and sound reasoning so that his views reflect both spiritual and intellectual truth. He is sensitive to the deeper basis of the yoga tradition but at the same time free of the fantasy, illusion and wishful thinking that often characterizes new age explorations.

Most notably the author has assimilated new data on ancient India that show that the old model of the Āryan invasion of 1500 B.C.E. is incorrect. A new archaeological model has arisen showing a continuous development of civilization in India from the earliest times (Mehrgarh 7000 B.C.E.) not defined by any outside invasions or intrusive populations. The ending of the Harappan culture came about not through Āryan hordes but through a drying up of the river systems, most notably the Sarasvatī river of Vedic fame, on the banks of which most Harappan and pre-Harappan sites have been located. This occurred around 1900 B.C.E. and is described in the Vedic and Purāṇic texts that speak of the shift from the Sarasvatī to the Gaṅgā as the center of civilization in India. This information necessitates a rethinking of the yoga tradition as well, both making it older and connecting it more to Vedic roots.

Many previous scholars, perceiving the long history of yoga in India, have looked for a pre-Vedic basis for the yoga tradition, as it clearly existed before the 1500 B.C.E. date of the proposed Āryan invasion. However, now that that invasion has been disproved, one has to move back the dates of Vedic texts, which reflect the Sarasvatī culture, to 3000 B.C.E., if not earlier. This gives an adequate time for the development of the yoga tradition in an Indian context such as is reflected in Vedic texts, which was the idea of great yogis like Sri Aurobindo and Paramahansa Yogananda.

Indeed, the ancient Europeans may have been migrants out of India, or culturally influenced by Indic groups, rather than migrants into the country, as most scholars today still believe. Ancient India according to the new model possessed a great civilization based upon Sanskrit as well as a large population that could result in either migrations or cultural diffusion. This means that a yogic element probably existed in ancient European culture, such as appears in the Gundestrop cauldron and in pagan deities like Cernunos, a kind of European Śiva figure who sat in yoga postures. It raises the probability that yoga is something inherent in the European psyche as well, and that in taking up yoga Europeans are not doing something exotic but are returning to their more ancient roots.

The demise of the Āryan invasion theory opens the door for a new scholarship on India and a rethinking of the entire yoga tradition. Burley has pioneered important new work in this area that other scholars should follow up and work out in detail.

The new model is of yoga (āsana, prāṇāyāma, mantra and meditation) as an integral part of the Vedic tradition, representing its more practical or experiential side. The Vedas project a view of the universe as the cosmic person (puruṣa). This seeing of the universe in one's own body is the basis of all yogic practice. *Haṭha-Yoga: Its Context, Theory and Practice* is important reading for all serious practitioners of yoga, as well as all real scholars in the field, both traditional and modern. Burley's is a real yogic scholarship about yoga.

DAVID FRAWLEY (VAMADEVA SHASTRI)
Santa Fe, New Mexico
April 1999

Acknowledgements

I wish to express my sincere gratitude to those individuals and institutions that have assisted me during the course of my research. Special thanks go to David Frawley, director of the American Institute of Vedic Studies, for his encouragement and for contributing the excellent foreword to this book. Other individuals who have offered helpful comments upon the manuscript at various stages of its progress include: Isabelle Glover (Mary Ward Centre, London), James Santucci (Uni. of California), Richard King (Uni. of Stirling), Ian Whicher (Uni. of Cambridge), Clodomir ('Miro') B. Andrade, Sue Pomfrett, Adrian Driscoll, Peter Glover, Mary Scott, and Nicky Richardson. Their well-considered opinions have helped me to carry the work forward; though, of course, it is I who accept final responsibility for the material presented here.

Since I have, in the present work (especially Chapter 5), drawn upon some of the research I carried out for my Master of Arts degree at the University of Nottingham (1996-97), I would like to thank members of the Philosophy Department there, most notably Brian Carr and Jonardon Ganeri. I am appreciative of the library staff at the University of Nottingham, the University of Exeter, Exeter Central Library, and the Theosophical Society (London) for their help in acquiring books and journal articles, and of staff at the Inner Bookshop in Oxford, who were also very cooperative in this regard.

Duncan Hulin, Director of the Devon School of Yoga, has provided practical guidance and friendship, and I am grateful to him, along with fellow teachers and students of the School, for the encouragement and support I have received. Thanks are due to a fellow Devon yoga teacher, Sally Ornellas, who took the photograph that appears on the front cover of this book. They are due also to *Yoga and Health* magazine for publishing many of my articles on yoga and Indian philosophy, and its readers who have supplied intelligent comments thereon. For the publication of the book, I am grateful to Narendra Prakash Jain and others who were involved at Motilal Banarsidass.

The loving support of my parents, Roger and Stephanie Burley, has been invaluable, and I am deeply appreciative of all that they have done, and continue to do, for me. And to Sue Pomfrett I offer thanks beyond measure, not only for the immense practical assistance that she has provided, and for her stimulating thoughts and observations during our many conversations together, but, most of all, for her unfailing love and companionship. I am truly grateful.

Finally, I wish to acknowledge my indebtedness to the many teachers who have guided, encouraged, pushed and cajoled me along the path of yoga, and especially to Rām Kṛṣṇa Dās of Rām Mandir, Pāśupatināth, Kathmandu, whose mantra stays with me always.

MIKEL BURLEY (GYĀN DĀS)
Exeter, England
April 1999

Abbreviations

The following abbreviations appear where the relevant text is referred to in parentheses or in a footnote. Elsewhere, the full title will be given, with the exception of the *Haṭha-Yoga-Pradīpikā*, whose title has been abbreviated to *HYP* more often due to its length and the frequency of its occurrence.

Vedas

AV	*Atharva-Veda*
ṚV	*Ṛg-Veda*

Upaniṣads

KU	*Kaṭha-* (a.k.a. *Kāṭhaka-*) *Upaniṣad*
MU	*Maitri-* (a.k.a. *Maitrāyaṇīya-*) *Upaniṣad*
ŚU	*Śvetāśvatara-Upaniṣad*

Classical Sāṃkhya and Yoga texts (and commentaries)

SK	*Sāṃkhya-Kārikā* of Īśvara Kṛṣṇa
TV	*Tattva-Vaiśāradī* of Vācaspati Miśra
YB	*Yoga-Bhāṣya* of Vyāsa
YS	*Yoga-Sūtra* of Patañjali

Haṭha-yoga and other Tāntrika texts

GS	*Gheraṇḍa-Saṃhitā*
GoŚ	*Gorakṣa-Śataka*
HYP	*Haṭha-Yoga-Pradīpikā*
J	*Jyotsnā* of Brahmānanda
ṢCN	*Ṣaṭ-Cakra-Nirūpaṇa* of Pūrṇānanda
ṢCNC	Kālīcaraṇa's commentary on the *ṢCN*

ŚS	*Śiva-Saṃhitā*
ŚSv	*Śiva-Svarodaya*

Other texts

BG	*Bhagavad-Gītā*
MS	*Manu-Smṛti* (a.k.a. *Mānava-Dharma-Śāstra*, *Manu-Saṃhitā*)
VSB	*Vedānta-Sūtra-Bhāṣya* of Śaṅkara
YV	*Yoga-Vāsiṣṭha(-Mahā-Rāmāyaṇa)* of Vālmīki

Introduction

What is haṭha-yoga?[1]

Haṭha-yoga—which may also be referred to as haṭha-vidyā[2] or simply haṭha—is a branch of Indian soteriology;[3] that is, a technical system whose purpose is to achieve 'freedom', 'release', or 'salvation' for its practitioners. There are many Sanskrit terms for this goal, and several of these will be discussed during the course of this work. The English term that I most frequently use to denote the goal of haṭha-yoga, and of yoga in a broader sense, is 'Self-realisation', which is really an abbreviated way of saying 'the realisation of one's true identity as the Self', the Self (with a capital initial) being the *param-ātman* (the 'highest' or 'supreme' Self), who, according to yoga philosophy, is identical to *Brahman* ('the Absolute').

Outside of India, and especially in the West, the term *haṭha-yoga* has come to be most closely associated with physical posture work and relaxation techniques, but it should be made clear right away that, in its traditional form, haṭha-yoga offers far more than a fitness regime and a method of stress-relief management. The use of haṭha practices to build stamina and agility, and to sooth the nervous system after a stressful day at

---

[1] *Haṭha-yoga* should be pronounced roughly 'hut-huh yo-guh'. The dot beneath the 't' in *haṭha* indicates that the letter should be pronounced with the tip of the tongue turned back on the hard palate (see Appendix B for further guidance on pronunciation of Sanskrit terms).

[2] *Vidyā*: 'knowledge', 'vision', 'wisdom', 'science'.

[3] *Soteriology* derives from the Greek term *soteria* (salvation), and may refer to the study of (the means to attain) salvation. In the Indian context, 'salvation' should be understood in the sense of Self-realisation, and not as merely an 'after-life' in heaven.

work, are perfectly valid on their own level, but a gross injustice is done to a noble tradition when such narrow uses are equated with haṭha-yoga *per se*. While not wishing to undervalue the importance of postural training and relaxation, it should be stressed that, in the opulent palace of haṭha-yoga, these aspects constitute merely the gates at the entrance. It should also be noted that the degree of dedication required of a traditional Indian haṭha initiate is likely to far exceed that of a typical practitioner of westernised 'postural' yoga. While the latter may be content to attend a weekly class, and perhaps to incorporate a short routine into daily life, the former will be expected to make a serious life commitment—involving sustained, rigorous and devoted practice—and to orient his or her whole being towards the spiritual goal.

The popular identification of haṭha-yoga with 'postural' yoga has often led to haṭha's being falsely contrasted with what are perceived to be more 'mental' or 'meditative' forms of yoga. It is true that there have traditionally existed different approaches to yoga, and that one of the defining features of the haṭha approach is the emphasis that it gives to postural work, but to draw rigid distinctions on this point is misleading. In this study I shall endeavour to draw attention to the integrity of haṭha-yoga and to its comprehensiveness as a soteriological discipline. I shall show that what distinguishes it from other systems is not so much its underlying philosophy—for this has elements in common with many other Indian traditions—but, as intimated already, the *emphasis* it gives to a particular set of techniques. These include postural techniques, but also, and perhaps more importantly, techniques concerned with the alteration of breathing rhythms, the retention of 'vital force' (see below), and the training of the mind.

The principal objective of haṭha-yoga practice is to engender the retention and 'union' (*yoga*) of two modes of *prāṇa*, the subtle 'vital force' which is held to permeate the human bodily complex.[4] The practitioner closes off various orifices through

---

[4] *Prāṇa* may also be rendered as 'organisational principle'. See Chapter 7

which prāṇa might escape, doing so chiefly by means of muscular contractions called 'seals' (*mudrā*) or 'locks' (*bandha*), and endeavours to cause the ordinarily upward-flowing and downward-flowing prāṇas to move in contrary directions, thereby effecting their 'union' within the central channel of vital force known as *suṣumnā-nāḍī*.[5] The 'heat' (*tapas*) or 'fire' (*agni*) which results from this forceful union is held to arouse the still more refined—and still more potent—force known as *Kuṇḍalinī-śakti*, which is characterised as the Goddess (*Devī*) and represented as a coiled serpent. This 'serpent power' is said to then rise up through the suṣumnā channel, 'piercing' and 'opening' several vital centres (*cakra*s) as she does so, and eventually 'joining with' Brahman (personified as Śiva) in the *sahasrāra-padma* ('thousand-petalled lotus') at the crown of the head.

On one level, the word *haṭha* is an adjective meaning 'forceful', 'firm', 'persistent', 'strenuous', 'aggressive', or 'violent', and hence a literal rendering of *haṭha-yoga* would be something like 'forceful yoga'. Such a translation is accurate insofar as the discipline utilises relatively forceful techniques, but it provides only a partial understanding. To explain haṭha's deeper significance, haṭha-yogins often employ a kind of 'folk etymology',[6] which consists in breaking the word down into its two component syllables. *Ha* is said to stand for 'sun' and *ṭha* for 'moon', and this gives us 'union of "sun" and "moon"' as a translation of *haṭha-yoga*.[7] 'Sun' (*Sūrya*) and 'moon' (*Candra* or *Soma*), along with 'fire' (*Agni*), are potent symbols within Indian mythology generally, and in the symbology of haṭha in particular. In the latter, they have several associations or correspondences, the most important being the following: 'Sun' stands for (a) the upward-flowing prāṇa that travels along

for a fuller discussion.

[5] The 'downward-flowing prāṇa' should, strictly speaking, be referred to as *apāna*.

[6] Thanks are due to James Santucci for suggesting this phrase.

[7] Cf. e.g. Vasu's Foreword to his translation of the *Gheraṇḍa-Saṃhitā* (1976: viii).

piṅgalā-nāḍī (situated to the right of suṣumnā), (b) piṅgalā-nāḍī itself, and (c) the subtle 'female' and 'heating' energy known as *rajas* (lit. 'space' or 'void'), which must be unified or integrated with the 'male' 'cooling' energy, *bindu*. 'Moon' stands for (a) the downward-flowing prāṇa, called *apāna*, which travels along *iḍā-nāḍī* (to the left of suṣumnā), (b) iḍā-nāḍī itself, and (c) bindu (lit. 'point', 'spot' or 'seed'), the subtle essence of 'male' energy, which manifests on the gross physical level as semen (*śukra* or *śukla*). 'Fire' stands for (a) the transmuting force of 'inner combustion' brought about by the 'union' of prāṇa and apāna in suṣumnā-nāḍī, (b) suṣumnā-nāḍī itself, and (c) Kuṇḍalinī-śakti, who is stirred from her 'sleep' by means of haṭha-yoga.

Purpose and structure of the study

As its subtitle intimates, the purpose of the present study is to explore haṭha theory and practice within their proper context. Only by taking account of this context can we hope to make any headway in understanding the complex praxis associated with haṭha-yoga. The 'context' or 'background setting' I have in mind is broadly philosophical—comprising epistemological and metaphysical aspects, and including the crucial notion of self-identity—but it also encompasses the fields of mythology, cosmology, history and physiology. As has been noted, the major themes which colour the mosaic of haṭha philosophy are shared by many other streams of Indian thought, and thus haṭha cannot be studied in isolation. My approach has involved examining and bringing together material from a wide range of sources, carefully appraising that material, and drawing out its significance in relation to the haṭha tradition.

The study is divided into three parts. Part 1, comprising chapters 1-4, deals with the context out of which haṭha-yoga has grown, and within which it remains firmly rooted. The aim of this first part is to set forth a clear and concise overview of those aspects of the Indian spiritual and religious tradition that are relevant to an understanding of haṭha-yoga, a task that involves examining (a) the seminal texts and principal *darśana*s[8] of Indian philosophy (chapters 1 and 2), (b) the pedagogical relationship between *guru* (teacher) and *śiṣya* (student) (Chapter 3), and (c) some of the mythological and symbolic associations that underly much of the terminology used in haṭha treatises (Chapter 4).

Parts 2 and 3, comprising chapters 5-7 and 8 and 9 respectively, focus more sharply upon haṭha-yoga itself, Part 2 dealing with its important theoretical concepts, and Part 3 with its practical techniques (Chapter 8) and some of the effects of those techniques (Chapter 9).

Although a substantial amount of literature already exists on haṭha-yoga, I hope the reader will find that I have made a useful and novel contribution to this field of enquiry. Indeed, while a profusion of books have been published, and continue to be published, on haṭha, relatively few of these display more than a superficial appreciation of the subject matter. Publications can be found—often occupying space in the 'health' sections of bookshops and libraries—that provide guidelines about the cleansing procedures, breathing techniques, and multifarious postures which form an integral part of haṭha practice, but rarely is such practice closely examined in relation to philosophy. The amount of attention that has been given to the more gymnastic and 'aesthetic' aspects of haṭha-yoga—in popular books, magazines, and other media—has tended to further ingrain upon the western mind the view of this discipline as primarily postural and fitness-oriented. Haṭha-yoga has, to a large degree, become 'secularised' in the West, but to remove the spirit from haṭha is to leave a husk. It is therefore essential that some effort is made to redress the balance.

It is also, unfortunately, necessary that the kind of 'spiritual snobbery' exhibited towards haṭha by certain practitioners of other mind-training disciplines be shown to be wildly misdirected. By 'spiritual snobbery' I mean the opinion that haṭha is a 'low', or even a 'decadent', form of yoga simply because it

---

[8] *Darśana*: 'vision', 'viewpoint', 'philosophical branch or school'.

pays attention to, and works with, the body rather than ignoring the physical level and concentrating exclusively on 'higher', more 'lofty' (supposedly more 'spiritual') things. In the present study I attempt to shed some light upon the far-from-decadent ideas that underpin all haṭha practices, to step beyond, as it were, the threshold of the palace gates.

Textual sources

The textual sources I have drawn upon are many and varied, and a complete list of these can be found in the Bibliography. There are, however, a far smaller number of texts which have formed the backbone of my research, some of these being among the earliest known systematic manuals of haṭha-yoga. Below are brief sketches of the key texts referred to, including details of the specific editions used.

Haṭha-Yoga-Pradīpikā and *Jyotsnā*

The *Haṭha-Yoga-Pradīpikā*, for which the abbreviation *HYP* is used throughout most of the study, is one of the best known and most widely available treatises on haṭha-yoga. *Pradīpikā* means 'that which sheds light', and hence the title of this work translates as 'Light on, or illumination of, haṭha-yoga'. Its authorship is attributed to Svātmārāma Yogin (or Yogīndra), who is believed to have lived in the fourteenth-century C.E., and whose name is mentioned in the second *śloka* (stanza); however, much of its material resembles, or even precisely duplicates, passages from other haṭha manuals, notably certain works attributed to Gorakṣa, and thus it is perhaps more accurate to regard the *HYP* as a compilation from earlier sources rather than an original work.

Several English translations of the *HYP* exist, of which I have found the Adyar Library and Research Centre edition to be most useful. It was first published in 1893, with a translation by Srinivasa Iyangar, and this was followed by a second (revised) edition in 1933. A third edition was published in 1972, in which the translation was revised by Radha Burnier and A. A. Ramanathan. Although currently out of print, this edition is particularly useful to practitioners and scholars who possess a knowledge of Sanskrit, as it includes an unabridged version of both the *HYP* and *Jyotsnā* (see below) in the original *devanāgarī* script.[9]

The *HYP* comprises a total of 389 *śloka*s, a śloka being a Sanskrit verse usually consisting of two pithily composed lines. The work is divided into four *upadeśa*s (lessons or chapters), containing 67, 78, 130 and 114 ślokas respectively. The 'first' or 'principal' chapter (*prathamopadeśa*) deals, amongst other things, with the right environment for haṭha practice, certain ethical requirements, and the yoga-*āsana*s or 'postures'. The *dvirtāyopadeśa* (second lesson) principally concerns prāṇā-yāma—the 'harnessing' of vital energy through various modes of 'retention' (*kumbhaka*)—but also discusses the *ṣaṭ-karmāṇi* (six [cleansing] acts) which are required to aid the purification of vital channels (*nāḍī*s).[10] In the *tṛtīyopadeśa* (third lesson), the subject of *mudrā* (sealing) is addressed; and the *caturtho-padeśa* (fourth lesson) discusses the state of *samādhi*, which in its highest form is the ultimate goal of yoga, and the practice of *nāda-anusandhāna* (meditation upon the inner sound) which leads to that goal.

Several Sanskrit commentaries are known to have been written on the *HYP*, including those by Umāpati, Mahādeva, Rāmānanda Tīrtha, and Vrajabhūṣana. The best known, however, is the *Jyotsnā* ('Light', 'Illumination') of Brahmānanda, which itself quotes extensively from other works of Indian philosophy. A notable feature of Brahmānanda's commentary is his endeavour to show how Svātmārāma's text relates to the broader context of yoga, and to the *aṣṭāṅga-* ('eight-limbed') yoga system of Patañjali in particular (see below).

---

[9] *Devanāgarī* (lit. 'divine city') is the name of the script in which Sanskrit is traditionally written.

[10] The six cleansing acts or procedures are discussed in Chapter 8 below (pp. 192ff.).

Gheraṇḍa-Saṃhitā

The *Gheraṇḍa-Saṃhitā* ('Collection of Gheraṇḍa'), is a work of 351 ślokas, divided into seven upadeśas. Each upadeśa deals with an aspect of the sevenfold system (*sapta-sādhana*) dictated by the sage Gheraṇḍa to his disciple, Caṇḍakāpāli. The seven aspects are: (1) ṣaṭ-karmāṇi, (2) āsana, (3) mudrā, (4) pratyāhāra (sense-withdrawal), (5) prāṇāyāma, (6) dhyāna (meditation), and (7) samādhi. Georg Feuerstein dates the work to the 'late seventeenth-century',[11] and it is generally agreed to be later than the *HYP*, from which several ślokas are borrowed. It is worth noting that when, in the second śloka, Caṇḍakāpāli asks Gheraṇḍa to teach him the way to achieve the knowledge of truth (*tattva-jñāna*), he uses the term *ghaṭastha-yoga*. Since *ghaṭa* means 'vessel', 'pot' or 'container', this may be translated as 'yoga of the vessel (of the Self)', the 'vessel' being not simply the gross physical body but the whole psychophysical organism through which the Self (ātman, puruṣa) experiences the world.

I have used the Theosophical Publishing House's version of the *Gheraṇḍa Saṃhitā*, the third edition of which was published in 1976. It contains both the original Sanskrit text in devanāgarī and an English translation by Śrīś Chandra Vasu.

Gorakṣa-Śataka

Gorakṣa, also known as Gorakṣanātha (*nātha*: 'lord', 'master') or in Hindī as Gorakhnāth, is one of the principal gurus named in haṭha-yoga lineages. His status is legendary, and numerous myths are associated with his name, which literally means 'cow-protector' and is also one of the titles of Śiva.[12] Numerous works on haṭha-yoga are attributed to Gorakṣa, although several of these are merely slightly different versions of the same text. They include the *Siddha-Siddhānta-Paddhati* ('Path of the adepts' doctrine'), *Gorakṣa-Siddhānta-Saṃgraha* ('Compendium of Gorakṣa's perfect doctrine'), *Gorakṣa-Vacana-*

---

[11] Feuerstein 1990a: 116.

[12] For a useful summary of myths about Gorakṣa, see Briggs 1973: 228-250.

Saṃgraha ('Compendium of Gorakṣa's instruction'), *Gorakṣa-Vijaya* ('Gorakṣa's victory'), *Amaraugha-Prabodha* ('Undying flood of wisdom'), as well as many others. In the present study, I have made use of the *Gorakṣa-Śataka* ('One hundred [verses] of Gorakṣa') published as Chapter 14 of G. W. Briggs' *Gorakhnāth and the Kānphaṭa Yogīs*, which includes the Sanskrit text in Roman script along with English translation. The *Gorakṣa-Śataka* actually comprises 101 ślokas, which outline the practices of āsana, *prāṇa-saṃrodha* (= prāṇāyāma), mudrā, and *japedoṃkāra* (repetition of the syllable *om*), as well as mentioning certain concepts relating to yoga's subtle physiology, such as the *kanda*, *nāḍī*s, *cakra*s, *Kuṇḍalinī*, etc. (cf. Chapter 7 below).

Śiva-Saṃhitā

The *Śiva-Saṃhitā* ('Collection of [the knowledge of] Śiva') is presented as though directly spoken by the deity Śiva himself, and is likely to date from a similar period to the *Gheraṇḍa-Saṃhitā*, although the ideas contained within it extend back much farther. Its author propounds a *yoga-śāstra* (yoga doctrine) which is influenced both by the *Advaita* (non-dualist) school of Vedānta and by later Tāntrika material. Its five chapters together comprise 645 ślokas, making it far longer than the other main texts considered here. The first chapter provides an introduction to advaita metaphysics, and states that it is the yogin's task to realise the unity of the individual self and the universal Self (*ŚS* 1.62)—to perceive the true nature of reality by 'dissolving' the veil of *māyā* (phenomenal existence) (*ŚS* 1.67). Its second chapter describes certain aspects of the human subtle bodily matrix, while Chapter 3 includes some discussion of prāṇāyāma and āsana. The fourth chapter is concerned with mudrā, and the fifth, being by far the longest chapter, includes further descriptions of the six major cakras as well as discussing four varieties (or aspects) of yoga, namely *mantra-*, *haṭha-*, *laya-* and *rāja*-yoga.[13]

---

[13] The various 'yogas' will be discussed in Chapter 5 below.

The edition of the *Śiva-Saṃhitā* that I have used is the one first produced by the Panini Office, Allahabad, in 1914-15 and republished in 1996 by Munshiram Manoharlal. This contains the devanāgarī text plus an English translation by Rai Bahadur Srisa Chandra Vasu, who, under a shorter version of his name, also translated the edition of the *Gheraṇḍa-Saṃhitā* mentioned above.

Yoga-Sūtra and *Yoga-Bhāṣya*

The *Yoga-Sūtra* is not strictly speaking a work of haṭha-yoga, but provides, rather, a systematic codification of yoga *per se*, which may be drawn upon by yogins of various schools and traditions. Due to its being attributed to the sage Patañjali, the text is sometimes referred to as the *Pātañjala-Sūtra*, and its doctrine characterised as *Pātañjala-yoga*. Its principal practical doctrine revolves around an 'eight-limbed' (*aṣṭāṅga*) system, those limbs being: (1) yama (restraint), (2) niyama (secondary restraint), (3) āsana, (4) prāṇāyāma, (5) pratyāhāra, (6) dhāraṇā (concentration), (7) dhyāna, and (8) samādhi. Such a system is broadly adhered to by haṭha-yoga treatises, albeit with a far greater emphasis on the third and fourth limbs. Indeed, in haṭha-yoga, prāṇāyāma is regarded as the key practice, with successive limbs coinciding with prolongations of prāṇa-retention. No mention is made in the *Yoga-Sūtra* of mudrā, nor of the notion of Kuṇḍalinī-śakti's ascension along suṣumnā-nāḍī, while many more objects of meditation are suggested than in the haṭha texts. Despite these qualifications, haṭha- and Pātañjala-yoga are complementary in all major respects, and hence it may be useful to refer to the *Yoga-Sūtra* for clarification on certain technical points—especially those concerning the various 'levels' of samādhi—as I have done, most notably in Chapter 5. (More is said about the relation between Pātañjala- and haṭha-yoga in Chapter 2.)

As is the case with many yoga texts, the *Yoga-Sūtra*'s year of composition is unknown. Some scholars have estimated it to be as early as the fourth century B.C.E.,[14] while others have placed it as late as the third century C.E.,[15] but the evidence for any precise date is thin. The text itself comprises 196 *sūtra*s distributed over four *pāda*s ('steps', i.e. parts or chapters). The meanings of the word *sūtra* include 'thread' and 'that which sews', and in a literary context it refers to a particularly terse form of composition, the intelligibility of which usually requires an accompanying commentary. Probably the earliest and best known commentary on the *Yoga-Sūtra* is that ascribed to the sage Vyāsa,[16] which dates from around the fifth century C.E. It is most commonly referred to as the *Yoga-Bhāṣya*, a *bhāṣya* being an explanatory composition which 'fills out' or 'unpacks' information contained in a sūtra text, but which itself may require further commentaries. Other names for Vyāsa's commentary include the *Vyāsa-Bhāṣya* and the *Sāṃkhya-Pravacana-Bhāṣya* ('Instructive exposition of Sāṃkhya'), Sāṃkhya being a particular Indian philosophical tradition which provides the metaphysical basis for Patañjali's system (although the terminology may differ to some extent).

For the devanāgarī text of the *Yoga-Sūtra* I have used *The Yoga Sutras of Patanjali* by Sri Swami Satchidananda,[17] and the *Yoga-Bhāṣya* I have obtained from Bangali Baba's *Yoga-sūtra of Patañjali with the Commentary of Vyāsa.*[18]

Ṣaṭ-Cakra-Nirūpaṇa

Finally in this list of principal source texts, the *Ṣaṭ-Cakra-Nirūpaṇa* ('Exposition of the six cakras') should be mentioned. This has been most useful with regard to Chapter 7 of the present work, and especially the section on cakras. The text constitutes the sixth chapter of the 16th-century work, *Śrī-Tattva-Cintāmaṇī* ('Thought-gem of supreme truth'), by Pūrṇānanda

---

[14] E.g. Raju 1985.

[15] E.g. B. S. Miller 1996: 6.

[16] *Vyāsa* means 'arranger' or 'compiler' and may thus be an honorific title rather than the name of an individual author.

[17] Integral Yoga Publications, 1990.

[18] Motilal Banarsidass, 1976.

Svāmī, the bulk of which work remains unpublished. The *Ṣaṭ-Cakra-Nirūpaṇa* comprises 55 ślokas plus a preliminary śloka, and provides elaborate descriptions of the six main cakras of the human 'subtle body' (*sūkṣma-śarīra*) plus the *sahasrāra-padma* ('thousand-petalled lotus') at the crown of the head. An excellent English translation, presented along with the Sanskrit text in Roman script, appears in *The Serpent Power* by Arthur Avalon (an alias of Sir John Woodroffe).

Where the above texts are quoted, the translation may be assumed to be my own unless otherwise stated. Only in the case of the *Ṣaṭ-Cakra-Nirūpaṇa* did I consider the existing translation (i.e. Avalon's) to be satisfactory. There is a sense in which any translation from Sanskrit into English will remain imperfect, since many Sanskrit terms are multivalent, and their inherent meanings are piled one upon another in the pithy verses of philosophical treatises. It is not so much the case that a line of Sanskrit may have one dominant signification and several auxiliary ones, as that several significations may be present *simultaneously*. This fact makes it virtually impossible to capture the whole meaning of a Sanskrit sentence in a single line of English; and hence, to some extent, any translation already contains within it an interpretation. To avoid distortion as much as possible, when I provide quotations they will often include a liberal scattering of Sanskrit terms in parentheses, so that the reader is aware of which technical terms are being used. This can have the effect of interrupting the flow of a sentence, but facilitates, I think, a clearer understanding of the subject.

In addition to textual sources, I have, of course, also drawn upon my own *experience* of haṭha-yoga, having studied with teachers in Britain, Australia, India and Nepal. Although far from extensive, this practical familiarity with the subject has, I feel, furnished a useful complement to the intellectual research skills required for a study such as this. I hope that the qualities of clear thinking and passionate commitment have been fruitfully combined herein.

Part One

CONTEXTUAL ASPECTS OF HAṬHA-YOGA

1

Early Sources

The full history of the haṭha-yoga tradition has yet to be written, and such a project is, unfortunately, far beyond the scope of the present work. The intention here—in the first part of this book—is far more modest: it is simply to 'set the scene' for a more detailed exploration of haṭha in Parts 2 and 3—to provide, as it were, a topographical sketch of the philosophical landscape out of which haṭha could and did emerge.

Haṭha is generally assumed to have developed in the so-called 'post-classical' era of Indian yoga, i.e. some few hundred years following the composition of the principal 'classical' work on yoga known as the *Yoga-Sūtra* of Patañjali. As is often the case in discussions of Indian philosophical, or soteriological, traditions, however, the lack of accurate chronological evidence leads to inevitable vagueness concerning dates. Even if the composition dates of critical epoch-defining works could be agreed upon—which they frequently cannot—the fact that treatises in the field of yoga almost invariably borrow material from earlier sources, including oral sources never before written down, means that the ideas themselves could derive from the intangible depths of pre-history. While many scholars prefer to locate haṭha-yoga's formative years somewhere between the ninth and tenth centuries C.E., coinciding with the estimated flourishing of the great *siddha*s (adepts) Matsyendra and Gorakṣa,[1] other researchers and practitioners of yoga look

---

[1] Feuerstein, for example, says of Matsyendra that he 'probably lived at the beginning of the tenth century A.D.' (1990a: 216) and that Gorakṣa's

much farther back in time. The Indian Sanskritist and haṭha-yogin, Śrīmān T. Krishnamāchārya, for example, views haṭha-yoga as a tradition whose roots extend back at least several thousand years, with its earliest known authentic text being the *Yoga-Korunta*[2] attributed to Vamana Ṛṣi. Krishnamāchārya claims to have come across a 1,500-year-old manuscript of this text, 'the style of language [being] derived from an oral tradition predating classical Sanskrit, and possibly going back as far as 5,000 years.'[3]

While, then, adherents of the tradition may regard haṭha as a vehicle for a form of practical liberatory knowledge that is in fact timeless, its best known treatises—such as the *Haṭha-Yoga-Pradīpikā*, *Gheraṇḍa-Saṃhitā* and *Śiva-Saṃhitā*—fall within a particular Indian literary category known as *Tantra*. It is for this reason that haṭha-yoga is sometimes referred to as a variety of 'Tantrism'. It should be noted, though, that the Tantras constitute a very broad category indeed, and thus being designated as *Tāntrika* (or Tantric) tells us little about the content of a work. As Feuerstein points out, the Hindu Tantras alone 'contain accounts of psychocosmology and the history of the world (divided into ages, or *yugas*), descriptions of the deities and their appropriate rituals of worship, and of rites for the acquisition of a battery of magical powers.' 'There are also', continues Feuerstein, 'instructions about the esoteric process of activating the psychospiritual power called *kundalinī-shakti*,'

'probable date is the ninth or tenth century A.D.' (*ib.*: 118). P. C. Bagchi, on the other hand, states that he is 'inclined to believe that the Ms. of [a text widely attributed to Matsyendra known as] the Kaulajñānanirṇaya was written towards the middle of the 11th Century A.D.' (1986: 6). Such proclamations are based entirely on linguistic evidence, which is notoriously imprecise, and hence they remain highly tentative.

[2] *Korunta* is, presumably, an alternative transliteration of *kuruṇṭha* (or *kuruṇṭa*), which Monier-Williams defines as 'yellow amaranth or Barleria' (1963: 294).

[3] Birch 1995: 20. The *Yoga-Korunta* has not been published, and information about it remains sketchy, although Krishnamāchārya (now deceased) and his disciple, Pattabhi Jois, claim that the system of *aṣṭāṅga-vinyāsa-yoga* ('eight-limbed moving yoga') which they promote is faithful to its teaching.

and it is this set of processes which has most to do with haṭha-yoga. The 'northern' or *Mahāyāṇa* ('greater vehicle') Buddhist schools also have treatises known as Tantras, hence the term 'Tantric Buddhism'; and, as André Padoux has noted, 'there is also a Jain Tantrism, or Tantric elements in Jainism'.[4]

The verbal root of *tantra* is *tan*, whose meanings include, as Monier-Williams notes, 'to extend, spread, be diffused (as light) over, shine,...to continue, endure,...to put forth, manifest, display, augment'.[5] Of the word *tantra* itself, Ernest Payne writes that it 'has various meanings; starting from that of web or warp, it came gradually to stand for an uninterrupted series, orderly ritual, the doctrinal theory or system itself, and finally its literary exposition.'[6] The *particular* doctrinal theory or system being expounded is not specified by the term *tantra*, although since, within the Hindu context, so many of the works known as Tantras subscribe to a cosmological schematic in which the Absolute is personified as the deity Śiva, Tantra or 'Tantrism' has come to be most closely connected with the Śaiva and Śākta traditions.[7] Nevertheless, it would be wrong to assume that haṭha-yoga is exclusively Śaiva, for there are many practitioners of the discipline who honour the supreme Self or Godhead in the form of Viṣṇu or one of his two principal *avatāra*s, Rāma and Kṛṣṇa;[8] and, besides, the most enlightened of yogins whom I have had the privilege of meeting have been non-sectarian, and have emphasised the ultimate unity of the Divine.

While haṭha-yoga has, from time to time, been frowned up-

---

[4] Padoux in Eliade 1987: 274.

[5] Monier-Williams 1963: 435.

[6] Payne 1933: 49.

[7] *Śaiva* means 'of, or associated with, Śiva' and *Śākta* means 'of, or associated with, Śakti', Śakti being the 'power-aspect' of Śiva, personified as his female consort (cf. Chapter 4 below). There are also Vaiṣṇava tantras—i.e. tantras in which the divine principle is personified as Viṣṇu—but these are less prevalent.

[8] *Avatāra*: 'descended one', i.e. the Lord incarnated in human form.

on by supposedly 'orthcdox' brāhmaṇas[9] and even by practitioners of more predominantly 'mental' forms of yoga (because of haṭha's explicitly body-affirmative approach), its basic metaphysical tenets are continuous with those of *śruti*, i.e. the 'heard' revelations of the Vedas and Upaniṣads. Differences lie not so much in the underlying doctrine of the identity of *jīvātman* (living self) and *paramātman* (supreme Self) as in the more explicit nature of the methodological material contained in the haṭha texts, and in the greater emphasis given to postural and breathing techniques therein. Although such techniques do not receive systematic literary attention until the Tāntrika period, enough references to similar methods appear in certain of the early major Upaniṣads to suggest that haṭha practice, as well as its theoretical basis, is *Vaidika* (Vedic) in origin. It is therefore appropriate that something be said about the most ancient of Indian scriptures—the Vedas—and about the Upaniṣads which form their latter part.

Vedas

> [T]he Yogic tradition is originally the Vedic tradition. (Frawley 1993: 211)

Veda means 'knowledge' in the sense of an immediate disclosure of truth (as opposed to the mere learning of facts). The four earliest existent compilations of Indian spiritual yearning are collectively known as the Veda, and are individually referred to as the *Ṛg-*, *Sāma-*, *Yajur-* and *Atharva-Veda*. These are believed by followers of the *Sanātana-dharma* (Eternal Law), which may be approximately described as 'orthodox Hinduism',[10] to be infallible revealed knowledge or śruti—directly intuited, rather than composed, by great *ṛṣi*s (seers) in the ancient past. Indeed, according to this belief, no date can be

---

[9] A brāhmaṇa (often incorrectly spelt 'brāhmin') is someone who belongs to the Vedic 'priestly' caste.

[10] For a useful discussion of the term *Sanātana-dharma* in relation to Hinduism, see Lipner 1998: 12-13.

placed upon the Vedas, for they are held to be timeless documents whose words embody eternal truth. These four mighty works—which, prior to being written down, are likely to have been transmitted in oral form from *guru* (spiritual preceptor) to *śiṣya* (disciple) for hundreds, possibly thousands, of years—constitute the very roots of spirituality, religiosity, mythology, law, ethics, art and science in India, as well as further afield. They are recited in, and have come to be written in, Sanskrit, which has evolved over time, but is still, contrary to the opinion of some scholars, a living language in India.[11] There are said to be four styles of literary expression in the Vedas, and these are first mentioned in *Ṛg-Veda* 10.90.9. They are *ṛc*, *sāman*, *yajus* and *chandas*, the first three of which respectively give us the titles of the first three Vedas, while *chandas* is a general term indicating 'metre'. *Ṛc* (which, for reasons of euphony, becomes *Ṛg* when followed by *Veda*) denotes a 'hymn' or sacred verse in praise of a deity, and thus the *Ṛg-Veda* is 'the revelatory book of hymns'. *Sāman* refers to 'a metrical hymn or song of praise,' *Sāma-Veda* being 'the Veda of chants'.[12] *Yajus* is a form of prose intended to be recited in a ritual or sacrificial context, and hence the *Yajur-Veda* is 'the sacrificial Veda'.[13] The fourth Veda, the *Atharva*, does not take its name from any literary or oratorical style, but from Atharvan, the mythic son of the creator-god Brahmā. In this Veda can be found the knowledge believed to have been breathed from the mouth of Brahmā to his son, including many mantras for the healing of diseases and other purposes.

---

[11] P. U. Arya notes (1986: 19n.) that some 'two thousand people...register Sanskrit as their first language in the census of India', and that it 'is still the language of traditionally learned assemblies, used to more or less a degree by hundreds of thousands of people throughout that country, and is one of the fifteen official languages of India.'

[12] Monier-Williams 1963: 1205.

[13] Much of the content of the *Yajur-* and *Sāma-Veda* overlaps with that of the *Ṛg-Veda*. In the case of the *Yajur-Veda* many of the *Ṛg-Vedic* hymns have been rearranged for ritual purposes.

Each of the four Vedas can itself be divided into four parts or categories of material, namely: (1) *Saṃhitā* (lit. 'collection' or 'compilation'), comprising hymns and litanies, often to be recited as part of a ritual;[14] (2) *Brāhmaṇa*s ('relating to or given by a brāhmaṇa'), technical treatises dealing with the performance of sacrificial rites and ceremonies; (3) *Āraṇyaka*s (forest texts), which give accounts of the spiritual philosophy of renunciant forest-dwellers; and (4) *Upaniṣad*s (secret teachings),[15] which form a broader category of cosmological and soteriological exposition. Strictly speaking, the Saṃhitās alone constitute the true Veda, with the other three categories being later appendages, but all four varieties of text come under the heading of śruti.

In the later *śāstra*s (doctrinal treatises) of Hinduism, a connection is made between the four textual divisions of śruti on the one hand and the four *āśrama*s or 'stages of life', stipulated for 'twice-born' males, on the other.[16] The four āśramas are: (1) *brahmacārin* (student),[17] one of the chief duties of whom is to learn by rote many of the Vedic hymns (hence the correspondence with Saṃhitā); (2) *gṛhastha* (householder), who, while raising a family and following a suitable profession, must

---

[14] The Saṃhitā portion of the *Yajur-Veda* is divided into the *Taittirīya-* or *Kṛṣṇa-* (black, dark) *Saṃhitā*, and the *Vājasaneyi-* or *Śukla-* (white, pure) *Saṃhitā*. The former division is so-called because the Saṃhitā and Brāhmaṇa sections are confused (and hence 'dark'), while in the latter the Saṃhitā has been more clearly distinguished ('pure'). The word *Saṃhitā* also applies to later texts which do not fall within the Vedic canon, including specifically haṭha works such as the *Gheraṇḍa-* and *Śiva-Saṃhitā*.

[15] *Upaniṣad* literally translates as 'to sit down near', in the sense of sitting at the feet of one's guru, from whom the esoteric knowledge is received. The verbal root *sad* (from which *ṣad* is derived) also means 'to destroy', which gives us 'that which destroys (ignorance)' as another possible signification of *upaniṣad*.

[16] The term 'twice-born' (*dvija*) applies to members of the first three 'castes' of Hinduism who have undergone initiation into Vedic study (see Lipner 1998, esp. Ch. 4). Cf. Deussen 1906: 4-5.

[17] *Brahmacārin* literally translates as 'one who moves in Brahman', i.e. one who is intent upon the study and service of the Divine.

not neglect his duty to perform the rituals set forth in the Brāhmaṇa texts; (3) *vānaprastha* (forest-dweller), who, after having fulfilled familial responsibilities, retires to the forest or other secluded location for the purpose of spiritual contemplation; and (4) *saṃnyāsin* (renunciant),[18] who symbolically gives up all possessions and, living as a wandering mendicant, dedicates his remaining years to realising the truth declared in the Upaniṣads, i.e. the identity of oneself (ātman) as the Absolute (Brahman).

The above-mentioned portions of śruti may be more broadly grouped into two categories: the Saṃhitās and Brāhmaṇas together form the *karma-kāṇḍa* (section on [ritual] action), while the Āraṇyakas and Upaniṣads constitute the *jñāna-kāṇḍa* (section on knowledge). Alternative names for these two broad categories are *pūrva-* and *uttara-mīmāṃsā*, meaning 'early or prior investigation' and 'later investigation' respectively, and these same titles have been adopted by certain branches of Indian philosophy which specialise in interpreting one or the other field (see pp. 48-49 below). These categories suffice as traditional terms of reference, although they are somewhat less than clear-cut. Certain of the Āraṇyakas, for example, may be included in the Brāhmaṇas; and the divisions break down still further when one takes into account the possibility of *esoteric* interpretations of early mantras and benedictions. When, for instance, a passage directed towards Sūrya (sun) or Soma (moon or nectar) is considered literally, as a eulogy to that particular solar or lunar deity, then it may justifiably be regarded as the oratorial component in an exoteric ritual (*karma*). When, on the other hand, the terms are interpreted esoterically, as representing aspects of the human being's 'inner' or psychic nature, then it is jñāna—gnosis or Self-knowledge—that is the subject-matter.

Despite the earnest scholarship of certain early (i.e. late 18th century C.E.) western researchers of ancient Sanskrit litera-

---

[18] Also called *bhikṣu* (monk) or *parivrājaha* (wanderer).

ture,[19] a tendency developed during the 19th century to ignore possible esoteric interpretations of the Vedas, and to represent them principally as the ejaculations of a primitive and warlike race, whose spirituality had yet to progress beyond the worship of personifications of meteorological and astronomical phenomena. Notwithstanding the inherent subtlety of Vedic Sanskrit, which cannot but recommend itself to multi-layered interpretation, a comparable subtlety of exegesis has frequently been lacking.

The profound significance of the Vedic hymns will inevitably be overlooked unless the crucial distinction between *exoteric* and *esoteric* levels of interpretation is recognised and respected. At face value, much of the Vedic literature comprises devotional verses lauding the power of any of innumerable deities, and it is because this literal surface has so rarely been penetrated that the spurious notion of Hinduism as a polytheistic religion has developed. Beneath this surface, however, lies an esoteric—i.e. an 'inner', 'spiritual' or 'psychological'—meaning, pregnant with the essence of later Indian soteriology; and it is through uncovering these deeper layers that the yogic nature of the Vedas is revealed.

The philosopher-yogin Śrī Aurobindo points out that, as the ancient ṛṣis believed true self-knowledge to be sacred and liable to be misused if imparted to immature ears, they purposely clothed their arcane utterances in the garb of ritual worship.[20] Hence, when the Vedas are recited, (at least) two messages are conveyed: one for the majority of hearers, who wish to worship the Divine in external concrete form, and another for the 'elect', who have been initiated into the inner teaching and who understand the deeper meaning underlying the words and forms; who recognise, for example, that Agni stands not merely for the physical sacrificial fire, but for the inner fire of spiritual

---

[19] Among whom may be counted J. Z. Holwell, Alexander Dow, N. B. Halhed, Charles Wilkins (who produced the first English translation of the *Bhagavad-Gītā* in 1785), and William Jones. Cf. Marshall 1970.
[20] Aurobindo 1956: 8-9.

zeal (*tapas*) or, as David Frawley speculates, for Kuṇḍalinī, 'the flame at the base of the spine.' Soma, continues Frawley, 'is the immortal nectar or ānanda in the head.' Sūrya is not just the sun at the centre of our solar system, but 'the consciousness of the Self (ātman) in the heart', and 'Indra is the awakened life-force or perceiver who facilitates the practice [of yoga].'[21] The initiates will also appreciate that, when Indra slays the serpent Vṛtra at the foot of Mount Arbuda, thereby releasing the 'seven rivers' (*ṚV* 10.67.12), this is not some historical event being described, but is a symbolic account of the struggle to overcome spiritual ignorance. Frawley contends that Vṛtra may also represent Kuṇḍalinī, and that the seven rivers, whose waters are held captive by Vṛtra, may stand for the six principal *cakra*s or centres of vital force plus the crowning *sahasrāra-padma* (thousand-petalled lotus), which are deemed to be 'opened' or 'activated' as Kuṇḍalinī ascends through the central spinal *nāḍī* (subtle channel).[22]

While, then, the Vedas rarely mention the term *yoga* directly—and even where it does appear, it is not always in the sense of spiritual discipline[23]—their verses are nevertheless imbued with symbolism that evokes the psychophysical practices associated with later yoga. Indeed, if we are prepared to search beyond the ritualistic outer flesh, we find an inner core in the Vedas of what Feuerstein refers to as 'the proto-Yoga of the [ṛṣis]', which itself

> contains many elements characteristic of later Yoga: concentration, watchfulness, austerities, regulation of the breath in connection with the recitation of sacred hymns during the ritual, painstakingly accurate recitation (foreshadowing the later Mantra-Yoga), vision-

---

[21] Frawley 1993: 219 (diacritical marks have been added). David Frawley is one of the few westerners recognised in India as a *Vedācārya* (teacher of the Veda).

[22] *Ib.*: 216-17.

[23] Other meanings of *yoga* include 'work' (as contrasted with *kṣema*, 'rest'), and the 'yoking' of animals.

> ary experience, the idea of self-sacrifice (or surrender of the ego), and the encounter with a Reality larger than the ego-personality.[24]

The notion of surrendering the ego-personality to a higher reality which Feuerstein mentions is symbolically embodied in, for example, the Vedic fire sacrifice (*homa* or *agni-hotra*), in which food or ghee (clarified butter) is offered to the consuming flame.

The potent employment of sound in Vedic ritual is emphasised by the Vedicist Jeanine Miller, who writes that 'The practice of meditative absorption (*dhyāna*) as the crux of yoga goes back to Ṛgvedic times when the *ṛsis* had already achieved mastery in the wielding of thought as an instrument of power and consequently the *word* [*śabda*] as a means of creative activity.' 'The Vedic bards', continues Miller, 'were *seers* who *saw* the *Veda* and sang what they saw. With them vision and sound, seership and singing are intimately connected and this linking of the two sense functions forms the basis of Vedic prayer.'[25] As has already been suggested, amongst the subjects orated by the ancient ṛsis were those concerned with the subtle forces and structures beneath the gross exterior of the human bodily complex. Behind a web of geographical terminology it is possible to decipher oblique references to the vital centres later known as cakras, and to the 'streams' connecting them known as nāḍīs, both of which concepts are central to haṭha-yoga. A suitable illustration is the following passage from the *Ṛg-Veda*, in which the Sarasvatī river—to whom the hymn is dedicated—can be seen to symbolise the suṣumnā-nāḍī, into which it is the task of haṭha-yogins to channel their vital energy:

> Whose infinite, unencompassed, brilliant and mobile flood impetuously continues to roar. Bearing truth, may she take us beyond all opposition, beyond her other sisters and extend the days like the Sun. Who has filled the earthly realms and the broad atmospheric region, [Sarasvatī] should be adored. Who has three stations and

---

[24] Feuerstein 1990b: 103-4.
[25] J. Miller 1974: 45.

> seven levels, who increases the five births of men, in all encounters she should be worshipped. (*ṚV* 6.61.8, 9, 11, 12)[26]

The 'seven levels' are the seven vital centres, which are associated with levels of consciousness or self-identity; and the 'three stations' may be understood as the three 'knots' (*granthi*s)—situated at the base-, heart- and brow-cakras respectively[27] —through which Kuṇḍalinī must break. It is unclear what 'the five births' refers to, although Frawley proffers 'the five senses' as a possibility.[28]

The use of symbolic imagery to signify yogic processes and aspects of the subtle bodily matrix are not unique to the Vedas, as we shall see in subsequent chapters (esp. 4, 6 and 7), but due to these texts' antiquity it takes a sharp eye and mind to pinpoint particular references. Nevertheless, as Frawley again asserts, verses such as 5.81.1 of the *Ṛg-Veda*—which reads 'Seers of the vast illumined seer yogically [*yuñjante*] control their minds and their intelligence'[29] —show that 'at least the seed of the entire Yoga teaching is contained in this most ancient Aryan text.'[30] Unfortunately, however, not only have the Vedic texts been subjected to simplistic and misleading interpretations by scholars unfamiliar with the intricacies of yoga praxis and literary expression, but this bias has tended to be consolidated by a mistaken theory about ancient Indian history. The theory to which I refer posits the āryans as having been, not indigenous inhabitants of the Indian subcontinent, but a tribe of foreign invaders who imposed Vedic culture upon the existent Drāviḍian civilisation sometime between 1500 and 1000 B.C.E.; and, although widely and convincingly discredited, the 'Āryan invasion' theory—or some watered-down version of it—still manages to pollute a considerable amount of the debate around

---

26 Trans. Frawley 1993: 219.

27 Or, according to some texts (e.g. *HYP* 4.70ff.), in the heart, throat and brow cakras.

28 Frawley *op.cit.*.: 220.

29 Trans. *ib.*: 210.

30 *Ib.*

Indian philosophy and culture. For this reason it is worth briefly outlining the main arguments against it.

The 'Āryan invasion' myth

> To lift the veil of the past, we must first lift the veil of our own minds. (Feuerstein et al 1995: 4)

The 'Āryan invasion' hypothesis has been subscribed to in one form or another by the majority of western Indologists ever since it became popular in the 19th century; and, despite the lack of strong evidence in its favour, only relatively recently has the balance of opinion begun to shift. The theory initially came to prominence due to its apparent ability to explain the remarkable phonetic and grammatical similarities between Sanskrit and other Indo-European languages, including Persian, Greek and Latin. After these similarities were first noticed in 1786 by the British judge and Sanskritist William Jones, researchers in comparative linguistics began to speculate about an original 'proto-Indo-European' language which may have spawned later tongues, and the idea was proposed that a nomadic race of people, situated somewhere in central Asia, must have spread out in various directions, invading regions of Europe, the Middle East, and what is now the Indian subcontinent, and taking their language with them. Scholars gave to this hypothetical race the label 'Āryan', from the Sanskrit word *ārya* which appears in the *Ṛg-Veda* and elsewhere, and claimed that the presence of the Sanskrit language and of Vedic civilisation in India was due to a forceful invasion—or, according to later versions of the theory, a more gradual migration—by this central Asian race. This theory—which places the nation of India in the role of 'victim' and denies an autochthonous origin to Vedic language and religion—is rapidly crumbling beneath the weight of new evidence from the fields of archaeology and textual analysis, but it is nevertheless important to at least mention some of the refuting arguments here, so that the subject of Indian soteriology, and of haṭha-yoga in particular, may be clearly appraised and remain undarkened by the long shadow of a false hypothesis.

The first point to mention is that, in Vedic literature, the term *ārya* does not in fact refer to a racial type or to a language, but is, as Frawley remarks, 'a title of honor and respect given to certain groups for good or noble behavior.'[31] To support the invasion theory, passages of the Vedas that speak of a conflict between 'light' and 'dark' powers had been interpreted as references to a literal battle between fair-skinned 'Āryans' and darker-skinned 'Dasyus', the latter term being (wrongly) supposed to denote the Drāviḍian people most prominent today in South India. As Aurobindo makes clear, however, the conflict being described is a moral and spiritual, not a physical, one:

> The Aryan is he who does the work of sacrifice, finds the sacred word of illumination, desires the Gods and increases them and is increased by them into the largeness of the true existence; he is the warrior of the light and the traveller to the Truth. The Dasyu is the undivine being who does no sacrifice, amasses a wealth he cannot rightly use because he cannot speak the word or mentalise the superconscient Truth, hates the Word, the gods and the sacrifice and gives nothing of himself to the higher existences but robs and withholds his wealth from the Aryan.[32]

Secondly, it should be remembered that there is no hard evidence for the invasion theory, only conjectures based on 'soft' linguistic evidence, and this soft evidence is completely overridden by archaeological discoveries made during the 20th century. These discoveries include not only the well-known sites such as Harappā and Mohenjo-Daro located along the banks of the Indus river, but also over *five hundred* ancient sites associated with the Sarasvatī river, some of which are far larger than any Indus valley settlements. *Sarasvatī* ('she who flows') is the name given to the major river described in the Vedas, and also to a Vedic goddess. Geological research has indicated that

[31] Frawley 1994: 12-13.
[32] Aurobindo 1956: 281.

such a river used to flow from the Tibetan Himālaya down to the Arabian Sea, but that 'major tectonic shifts...possibly accompanied by volcanic eruptions' led to changes of the river's course and its eventual drying up sometime around 1900 B.C.E.[33] What was once a fertile valley now forms part of the Thar desert of north-west India and eastern Pakistan. Evidence gleaned from excavations of sites long hidden by the Thar sands suggests the existence of a culturally-advanced civilisation throughout the Sarasvatī-Indus region stretching back to 6500 B.C.E., long before even the earliest proposed dates for an invasion from the north. Artefacts found at Sarasvatī-Indus settlements show signs of a culture bearing a marked resemblance to that revealed in the Vedas, as well as a strong continuity with Hindu society thereafter. 'This continuity', remark Feuerstein et al, 'is evident in the religious ideas, arts, crafts, architecture, writing style, and the system of weights and measures', facts that are hard to explain if one supposes the Āryans to have been 'foreign invaders who leveled the native civilization of the Indus Valley'.[34]

Thirdly, textual analysis of the Vedas shows that a close correspondence exists between geographical and climatic features described therein and those of northern India as it would have been before the Sarasvatī dried up, a correspondence which also applies to the flaura and fauna.[35] Furthermore, a comparative study of the Vedic Saṃhitās and the later Brāhmaṇas and Purāṇas[36] suggests that a large migration took place around 1900 B.C.E. away from the Indus-Sarasvatī region and towards the Gangetic plane to the east, not to escape the violence inflicted by some invading hoard, but because the rivers to the west had been 'burned out' by the blazing heat of Agni (the fire deity, perhaps in this case representing the heat of the

[33] Feuerstein et al 1995: 91.
[34] *Ib.*: 156.
[35] Cf. *Ib.*
[36] The Purāṇas are post-Vedic texts covering an encyclopedic range of material.

sun).[37] Thus a plausible explanation exists for the abandonment of the Indus-Sarasvatī settlements which is supported by textual and geological data and does not rely on the invasion myth, for which textual and archaeological evidence is conspicuous by its absence.[38]

Whereas, on the Āryan invasion hypothesis, the introduction of Vedic religion and culture into India had been assumed to have taken place sometime after 2500 B.C.E.,[39] interpreters of the new evidence propose a steady development *within the Indian subcontinent* along the following chronological lines:

ca. 6500-3100 B.C.E.: Early Indus-Sarasvatī civilisation, early *Ṛg-Veda*;
ca. 3100-1900 B.C.E.: Mature Indus-Sarasvatī civilisation; period of the four Vedas;
ca. 1900-1000 B.C.E.: Migration of Indus-Sarasvatī civilisation to the region of the Gaṅgā river; late Vedic and Brāhmaṇa period.

While additional significant archaeological finds no doubt remain to be made, the likelihood is that these will serve only to push the tentative dates proposed above back still farther into the ancient past, and not to undermine the the basis of the new schematic. Whatever future research throws up, the Āryan invasion myth can safely be consigned to the dustbin of history.

Yoga in the Upaniṣads

So now, after the above brief historical excursion, let us turn our attention to what are perhaps the most recognisably 'yogic' of Vedic texts—the Upaniṣads. As already mentioned, the word

---

[37] See, e.g. the *Śatapatha-Brāhmaṇa*, cited in Feuerstein et al 1995: 94.

[38] For a fuller account of the arguments against the Āryan invasion hypothesis, see, e.g. Feuerstein et al 1995, Frawley 1993 and 1994, and Rajaram 1993.

[39] The General Introduction to Radhakrishnan and Moore's highly respected *Sourcebook in Indian Philosophy*, for example, locates the 'Vedic Period' 'approximately between 2500 and 600 B.C.' (1957: xvii).

upaniṣad translates as 'secret teaching' or 'esoteric doctrine', and denotes a variety of text which is intended to expound the spiritual philosophy of the Vedas. The earliest Upaniṣads were attached to one of the first three Vedas—namely the *Ṛg-*, *Sāma-* and *Yajur-Veda*—and of these there are eleven in number, which are listed in the table below:

Veda	**Associated Upaniṣads**
Ṛg-Veda	*Aitareya-*, *Kauṣītaki-Upaniṣad*
Sāma-Veda	*Chāndogya-*, *Kena-Upaniṣad*
Yajur-Veda ('Black')[40]	*Taittirīya-*, *Mahānārāyaṇa-*, *Kaṭha-*, *Śvetāśvatara-*, *Maitri-Upaniṣad*
Yajur-Veda ('White')	*Bṛhadāraṇyaka-*, *Īśā-Upaniṣad*

These are regarded as the major or principal Upaniṣads, to which list may be added the *Praśna-*, *Muṇḍaka-* and *Māṇḍūkya-Upaniṣad*, whose authority was firmly established by their having had full commentaries written upon them by the medieval exponent of Advaita Vedānta, Śaṅkarācārya. It is from this set of fourteen major Upaniṣads that quotations are most often taken and to which reference is most often made in later Indian philosophical treatises; and thus this set may be justifiably described as the foundation of Indian soteriological thought.

In addition to the 'major' Upaniṣads, there are numerous 'minor' ones. In fact, although the total number of Upaniṣads is traditionally set at 108 (an auspicious number, signifying completeness), there are known to be over 200.[41] The term 'minor Upaniṣad' should not be thought to imply inferiority, although there have been disputes over precisely which Upaniṣads rightfully belong to the category of śruti or 'revealed knowledge'. The minor Upaniṣads are usually attached to the

---

[40] For the reason why the *Yajur-Veda* is divided into two versions, see footnote 14 (p. 20) above.

[41] Radhakrishnan and Moore 1957: 37.

Atharva-Veda, which, according to Paul Deussen, due to its having been compiled later than the other three Vedas, avoided strict guardianship by certain *śākhā*s (lit. 'branches', i.e. schools) of Vedic interpreters, and was thus more susceptible to interpolation.[42] While the number of Upaniṣads associated with the *Atharva-Veda* varies according to the source,[43] Deussen himself identifies thirty-nine, and divides these into the following five categories: (1) 'pure Vedānta-', (2) 'Yoga-', (3) 'Saṃnyāsa-', (4) 'Śiva-', and (5) 'Viṣṇu-Upaniṣads'.[44] These classifications are based on the primary content or philosophical persuasion of the texts concerned, and are therefore valid and helpful up to a point, but they should not be regarded too rigidly. It is potentially misleading, for example, to specify 'Yoga' as a distinct category of Upaniṣad, for in truth the central theme of *all* Upaniṣads is yoga, if, that is, we understand *yoga* to mean the union and identity of ātman and Brahman, and the path to attaining the realisation of this fact. Nevertheless, 'Yoga-Upaniṣad' is a convenient and abbreviated way of referring to those minor Upaniṣads which deal most explicitly with the energy channels (nāḍīs) and centres (cakras) of the human subtle body, repetition (*japa*) of and meditation upon the sacred syllable *om*, and such practices as āsana (posture) and prāṇāyāma (control of 'vital force'). These texts thus represent some of the earliest treatments of subjects which have come to be most directly associated with haṭha-yoga, these subjects having been only obliquely or fragmentarily touched upon in the major Upaniṣads. Deussen mentions eleven Yoga-Upaniṣads, namely: the *Brahmavidyā-*, *Kṣurikā-*, *Cūlikā-*, *Nādabindu-*, *Brahmabindu-*, *Amṛtabindu-*, *Dhyānabindu-*, *Tejobindu-*, *Yogaśikhā-*, *Yogatattva-*, and *Haṁsa-Upaniṣad.* Feuerstein, on the other hand, provides a more comprehensive

---

[42] Deussen 1906: 33.

[43] E.g. Fifty-two are listed by both Colebrooke and Nārāyaṇa and 108 titles appear in the *Muktikā* collection of South India (Deussen 1906: 33-35).

[44] Deussen: 9.

list, including some twenty-one titles,[45] and also notes that the Yoga-Upaniṣads 'were composed after the *Yoga-Sūtra*', Feuerstein's favoured date for this latter text being 'the early post-Christian era'.[46] As always, however, one should bear in mind the conjectural nature of dating texts which are based on an ancient oral tradition.

As is the case with the Upaniṣads generally—as well as with other material on yoga—the Yoga-Upaniṣads are of limited value with regard to giving detailed instruction in yoga techniques. They provide, rather, a skeletal framework which would then be fleshed out by the teachings of a guru, the pedagogical institution of discipleship being so integral a part of Indian soteriological traditions as to be taken for granted. This also applies to the later treatises of haṭha-yoga, which, though constituting more systematic compendiums of the information contained in the Yoga-Upaniṣads, nevertheless remain incomplete when divorced from personal guidance.

It is not my intention here to enter into a detailed discussion of the content of the Yoga-Upaniṣads, since this would take us prematurely into the sphere of haṭha praxis, which is to be examined in later chapters; however, in order to support my contention that yoga generally, and haṭha-yoga in particular, is fully rooted in the Vedic tradition, it is worth noting a few examples of references to such disciplines in the major Upaniṣads.

Although each of the major Upaniṣads has much to offer for our understanding of yoga, I shall restrict the discussion here to three in particular, each of which has traditionally been associated with the *Kṛṣṇa-* ('Black') *Yajur-Veda*. The first is the *Kaṭha-Upaniṣad*, sometimes referred to as the *Kāṭhaka-Upaniṣad*. *Kaṭha* is the name of an ancient branch or school of yoga, and *Kāṭhaka* simply means 'of or belonging to the Kaṭha'. While in the Vedic Saṃhitās, yoga tends to be spoken of only in highly elaborate analogical terms, with the Upaniṣads

---

[45] These are listed in Appendix C.

[46] Feuerstein 1990a: 418.

we begin to see a more direct exposition of what yoga involves. The *Kaṭha-Upaniṣad* revolves around a dialogue between a spiritual aspirant called Naciketas and Yama, the guardian of the after-death world. Of three wishes that Naciketas has been granted, his third wish is to know the secret of what happens to a person after physical death. Yama is initially very reluctant to reveal the answer, and offers his questioner any number of material benefits instead; but Naciketas, remaining resolute in his rejection of material pleasures in favour of Self-knowledge, eventually persuades Yama to speak forth. A person's true self (ātman), says Yama, is analogous to a man riding in a chariot, the chariot representing the human body, the chariot-driver being the higher intellect (*buddhi*), the reins being the cognitive principle (*manas*), the horses being the senses, and what they range over standing for the objects of sense (*KU* 3.3-4).[47] The conditional self of one who is unable to discriminate between the true source of his identity and the vehicle in which he rides (i.e. the mind, senses, body, etc.) will, according to Yama, fail to reach the goal and will continue to wander through cycles of birth and death (*saṃsāra*) (*KU* 3.7), whereas one who does possess those powers of discernment transcends such wandering (*KU* 3.8). Yama defines yoga as 'the steady holding [*dhāraṇā*] of the senses' (*KU* 6.11),[48] i.e. fixing the mind's attention upon a single point without its being pulled in multifarious directions by unruly 'steeds'. This sets the ground for the realisation of oneself as Brahman (*KU* 6.15).

The notion of purifying the relationship between mind and senses is echoed in the title of the second major Upaniṣad to be considered here, namely the *Śvetāśvatara-Upaniṣad*. *Śveta* means 'white' or 'pure' and *aśva* means 'horse', hence, if we bear in mind the chariot analogy mentioned above, *śvetāśvatara*

---

[47] The analogy of the chariot is common to later Indian philosophy and appears, for example, in the well-known Buddhist dialogue between King Milinda and the sage Nāgasena (see Warren 1915: 129-33). It is also used by Plato.

[48] Trans. Feuerstein 1990b: 152.

refers to one 'whose senses are purified and under control.'[49] With regard to studying the earliest descriptions of yoga practice, some of the most pertinent stanzas in the whole Upaniṣadic canon occur in the second chapter of the *Śvetāśvatara-Upaniṣad*. Included there, for example, are basic instructions on the correct bodily posture for prāṇāyāma and meditation:

> Holding the body straight with head, neck and chest in line,
> With senses and mind withdrawn into the heart,
> Let a wise man on Brahman's raft cross over
> All the rivers [of this life] so fraught with peril. (*ŚU* 2.8)
>
> Restraining here his breath, his movements well controlled,
> Let a wise man breathe in through the nostrils, his breath
> reduced;
> Free from distraction, let him hold his mind in check
> Like a chariot harnessed to vicious steeds. (*ŚU* 2.9)[50]

Also stipulated are the ideal environmental conditions in which to practise:

> Let the place be pure, and free also from boulders and sand,
> Free from fire, smoke, and pools of water,
> Here where nothing distracts the mind or offends the eye,
> In a hollow protected from the wind a man should compose
> himself. (*ŚU* 2.10)[51]

Similar advice is given in the *Haṭha-Yoga-Pradīpikā*, which states that haṭha-yogins should live alone in a small hermitage (*maṭhikā*), no less than a 'bow's measure' (*dhanuḥ-pramāṇa*)—i.e. the distance covered by an arrow fired from a bow—from (falling) rocks, fire and water (i.e. dampness) (*HYP* 1.12).[52]

---

[49] Feuerstein *ib.*

[50] Trans. Zaehner 1966: 206.

[51] Trans. Deussen 1906: 387.

[52] The same śloka notes that the land should be governed by a just ruler and should be abundant in provisions.

Just as in the later haṭha treatises, the author of the *Śvetāśvatara-Upaniṣad* draws attention to the bodily transformation which results from intense yoga practice:

> He knows nothing further of sickness, old age, or suffering,
> Who gains a body out of the fire of yoga.
> Activity, health, freedom from desire,
> A fair countenance, beauty of voice,
> A pleasant odour, fewness of secretions,
> Therein at first the yoga displays its power. (*ŚU* 2.12-13)[53]

Again the passage is close to one found in the *HYP*, wherein the signs of success in haṭha-yoga are said to include: 'beauty, slimness of physique, eloquent speech, radiant complexion,...clear eyes (or vision), freedom from illness, [and] control over vital fluid (bindu)' (*HYP* 2.78). These are, of course, only the external indications of yogic attainment, the ultimate goal being the internal realisation of the Self, referred to in the *Śvetāśvatara-Upaniṣad* as *puruṣa* (e.g. *ŚU* 3.8).

Before discussing the next Upaniṣad, the *Maitri*, we need briefly to mention the *aṣṭāṅga-* or 'eight-limbed' system of yoga practice outlined in the highly authoritative *Yoga-Sūtra* of Patañjali (*YS* 2.29-3.3). This comprises: (1) yama (restraint), (2) niyama (observances), (3) āsana (posture), (4) prāṇāyāma (prāṇa-retention), (5) pratyāhāra (sense-withdrawal), (6) dhāraṇā (concentration), (7) dhyāna (meditation) and (8) samādhi (identification).[54] Although, in texts other than the *Yoga-Sūtra*, certain of these 'limbs' may be strongly emphasised and others barely referred to, the eightfold schematic is basic to most schools or traditions of yoga. In the haṭha manuals, it is common for substantial attention to be given to the third, fourth and eighth limbs, with less being said about the others, but this should not be taken to indicate that haṭha somehow lacks the comprehensiveness or holistic nature of other approaches to spiritual development. It is not that the other components are

---

[53] Trans. Deussen 1906: 395.

[54] These terms will receive fuller attention below, especially in Chapter 8.

overlooked, only that āsana and prāṇāyāma are—with considerable justification—held to constitute the basis of yoga discipline, out of which the other limbs can grow and flourish, and in the absence of which all effort is misplaced.

The importance of the *Maitri-Upaniṣad* with regard to aṣṭāṅga-yoga is that it is probably the earliest extant source of a very similar methodological system. The *Maitri-* is also sometimes known as the *Maitrāyaṇīya-Upaniṣad*, Maitri being the name of a sage, and Maitrāyaṇīya ('of Maitri') being the school which followed his teachings. It is in *Maitri-Upaniṣad* 6.18 that a *ṣaḍaṅga* ('six-limbed') yoga system is expounded, the six components being: (1) prāṇāyāma, (2) pratyāhāra, (3) dhyāna, (4) dhāraṇā, (5) tarka, and (6) samādhi. The first major difference between this schema and that of classical aṣṭāṅga-yoga is the absence from the former of yama, niyama and āsana. *Yama* translates as 'restraint', 'observance' or 'rule of social conduct', and *niyama* as 'lesser restraint' or 'observance without external restraint' (i.e. self-discipline), these two limbs combining to form the ethical catechism of yoga.[55] Little detailed instruction pertaining to moral conduct is given in any of the Upaniṣads, but it should not be concluded from this that the sphere of ethics was of no concern to the Upaniṣadic authors; far more likely is that the notion of moral discipline as a prerequisite and counterpart to spiritual development was such common knowledge as to be implicitly assumed.[56] Similarly, the fact that āsana is not mentioned in the *Maitri-Upaniṣad* probably means that the importance of a correct sitting posture

---

[55] In the *Yoga-Sūtra* (2.30-45), five yamas and five niyamas are listed. The five yamas are: (1) *ahiṃsā* (non-harming), *satya* (truth[fulness]), *asteya* (non-stealing), *brahmacarya* (continence), and (5) *aparigraha* ('non-grasping', i.e. non-covetousness); and the five niyamas are: (1) *śauca* (purity), (2) *saṃtoṣa* (contentment), (3) *tapas* ([spiritual] heat), (4) *svādhyāya* (study [of the scriptures]), and (5) *Īśvara-praṇidhāna* (devotion to 'the Lord'). Certain haṭha texts (e.g. *HYP* 1.16) mention ten yamas and ten niyamas (see pp. 190-92 below).

[56] Cf. Deussen 1906: 387.

has been taken for granted, and not that it has been considered irrelevant. Other ways in which the *Maitri* system appears to be at variance to that of the *Yoga-Sūtra* are that: (a) the order of *dhāraṇā* ('holding' or 'fixing' the mind upon a single object) and *dhyāna* (sustained meditation upon that object) is reversed, and (b) the additional limb of *tarka* has been added before samādhi. As the meanings of *dhāraṇā* and *dhyāna* are very close, their reversed order does not cause any serious interpretative problems; and, since *Yoga-Sūtra* 1.17 presents *vitarka*, which means virtually the same thing as *tarka*[57] —i.e. (roughly) 'reflection',[58] 'contemplative inquiry'[59] or 'comprehensive perception'—as the initial level of samādhi, the fact that it represents a distinct limb in the *Maitri-Upaniṣad* does not constitute a major discrepancy. Thus it is reasonable to acknowledge the existence of a mature yoga system—perhaps conveyed along a number of guru-disciple lineages—dating back at least as far as the Upaniṣads of the *Kṛṣṇa-Yajur-Veda*. It is very likely that these Upaniṣads pre-date the development of Buddhism (*ca.* 500 B.C.E.), although the extent of their antiquity is impossible to say.

Another interesting point about the *Maitri-Upaniṣad*—especially for the present study—is the fact that, of all the major Upaniṣads, it is the one which contains the most explicit description of a methodology akin to that presented in later haṭha manuals. Noting the intimate connection between the flow of prāṇa and the instability of mind, it emphasises prāṇāyāma as the foremost means of bringing the mind to a point of stillness (*MU* 6.19), and even mentions the technique of turning the tongue back and inserting it behind the soft palate to prevent the downward flow of bindu, the subtle vital 'nectar' released from the soma-cakra.[60] Attention is paid to the notion of chan-

---

[57] In Sanskrit, the prefix *vi* can be used to denote intensity or severity, thus *vitarka* simply means 'intense tarka'.

[58] Deussen: 388.

[59] Radhakrishnan 1953: 830.

[60] Cf. section on *khecarī-mudrā* in Chapter 8 (pp. 210-11) below.

nelling prāṇa up along suṣumnā-nāḍī, which is said to penetrate through to the soft palate, and focussing upon the potent syllable *om*, thereby enabling the mind to be 'conveyed' towards the goal of Brahman (*MU* 6.21). By immersing oneself in the inner sound—referred to here as *śabda-brahman*—one is held to eventually reach the soundless condition of the 'other' or 'beyond' (*para*), which is the pure Brahman (*MU* 6.22); and this appears to be precisely the method referred to as *nāda-anusandhāna* (contemplation of the inner sound) in the *Haṭha-Yoga-Pradīpikā* (discussed in Chapter 8 below).

'Let the absence of limitation [*mahiman*] contemplate itself'[61] declares the *Maitri*, i.e. let the supreme Self know itself through the medium of the yogin; 'then', the passage continues, the yogin 'moves towards selflessness; and because of this selflessness he experiences neither pleasure (*sukha*) nor pain',[62] the ultimate attainment being a state of 'absolute oneness or wholeness' (*kevalatva*) (*MU* 6.21).

It has, until relatively recently, been all too common within the field of Indology for the early Indian scriptures to be judged according to preconceived ideas about progress. It has been assumed in advance that the Vedic Saṃhitās, simply because they are older than the Upaniṣads and other later texts, must be more 'primitive' in their philosophical and religious outlook. Bearing in mind this prejudice, it is not very surprising that the Vedas have tended to be interpreted as the outpourings of an immature culture, which had yet to develop the systematic modes of self-exploration hinted at in the Upaniṣads and consolidated in later treatises such as the *Yoga-Sūtra*. However, as I have tried to suggest in this chapter, alternative interpretations are possible; careful examination of the available textual and archaeological evidence is leading an increasing number of scholars and yogins alike to recognise the profound psychic and psycho-cosmological insights underlying and infusing the an-

---

[61] Trans. Mitra 1891: 80.
[62] Trans. Zaehner 1966: 233.

cient Vedic hymns, and to revaluate the received version of the history of human civilisation. These alternative interpretations point not so much to a gradual—or even to a punctuated—evolution of the spiritual discipline and life-path of yoga, as to yoga's having already achieved a mature state of development by the time of the most ancient texts known to exist.

Of course, the longevity of an idea or a practice does not necessarily testify to its value, but it is important nevertheless for the rich and ancient heritage of yoga to be appreciated, and yoga's status as the practical foundation of Indian religious wisdom to be acknowledged.

It has been further suggested in this chapter that certain aspects of yoga most strongly associated with the haṭha tradition are evident in the very earliest scriptures—disguised beneath mythic symbolism in the Vedas, but described more explicitly in the Upaniṣads—and that such references support the designation of haṭha-yoga as an integral strand of Vedic Indian soterial philosophy.

2

Yoga and the Indian Darśanas

Having looked in the previous chapter at some points relating to the earliest known textual sources of Indian spiritual philosophy, namely the Vedas and Upaniṣads, it is now pertinent to place yoga within the context of Indian philosophy as it has developed since Vedic times, and to at least mention some of the theoretical themes that underly the practical endeavour of yoga. For this purpose, the present chapter will include a discussion of the principal *darśana*s ('viewpoints' or systems) of Indian philosophy, with particular attention given to the classical Yoga darśana of Patañjali and its relevance to haṭha-yoga.

The six *āstika* darśanas

If we envisage the Indian philosophical tradition as a tree, then the Vedic Saṃhitās may be seen as the roots, and the Brāhmaṇas, Āraṇyakas and Upaniṣads collectively as the trunk. The tree's branches are the multiple philosophical 'schools' which arose during the post-Vedic era, principally due to the attempts of various teachers to interpret the Upaniṣadic doctrines in such a way as to form a consistent and intelligible system of thought. The roots and trunk, then, are constituted by śruti, the 'heard' or 'revealed' wisdom, while the branches are known as *smṛti*, the 'remembered' wisdom; 'remembered' in the sense that, just as a memory is based on a real experience but is not the experience itself, so the post-Vedic texts are said to be based on a revelation of truth but not to be truth's *direct* expression. Thus we find that, while all so-called 'orthodox' (*āstika*) systems of Indian thought share a common faith in the infallibility of śruti, they may not be in total agreement with each other, and may even appear to be at odds with one another over certain nuances of interpretation.

Although the post-Vedic systematisers admit that their authority derives from their allegiance to the Vedic scriptures, and hence is secondary to the Vedas and Upaniṣads themselves, the founding text of each major 'school' is presented not in the form of a long and rigorously argued treatise but as a series of terse statements, known as *sūtra*s, which, like śruti, are believed to be verbal expressions 'of a truth realized by a [*ṛṣi*] in the state of samādhi.'[1] The status of the sūtra texts is, then, slightly ambiguous insofar as they are held to be the products of divine revelation, but not to be of the same order as śruti.

Due to the revelatory nature of the sūtras, the traditions of interpretation which came to be based upon these texts are known as *darśana*s, a term for which Maya Das has offered the following explanation:

> Derived from the root *dṛś*, *darśana* indicates over and above the ordinary perception, a vision of truth, a direct or immediate realization...of truth, a *tattvadarśana*. *Darśana* also denotes a system of philosophy, doctrine, *Śāstra* or *tattvavicāra* in the sense of a treatise on or an enquiry into truth or reality. Aware of the semantic distinctions between *darśana* and *darśanaśāstra*, the Indian philosophers consider philosophy both as *darśana*, the vision of truth, and *darśana-śāstra*, the means to attain it.[2]

There are commonly agreed to be six principal *āstika* or *Vaidika* darśanas, which are distinguished from those darśanas—called *nāstika* ('non-orthodox') or *Vedavāhya* ('outside the Veda')—which do not explicitly align themselves with the

---

[1] Arya 1986: 6.
[2] Das 1990: 93.

belief that the Vedas are infallible revealed documents. The six āstika darśanas are:

1. the Vaiśeṣika darśana, founded upon the *Vaiśeṣika-Sūtra* of Kaṇāda;
2. the Nyāya darśana, founded upon the *Nyāya-Sūtra* of Gautama;[3]
3. the Sāṃkhya darśana, founded upon the *Sāṃkhya-Sūtra* of Kapila;
4. the Yoga darśana, founded upon the *Yoga-Sūtra* of Patañjali;
5. the Pūrva-mīmāṃsā darśana, founded upon the *Mīmāṃsā-Sūtra* of Jaimini;
6. the Uttara-mīmāṃsā or Vedānta darśana, founded upon the *Vedānta-Sūtra* (a.k.a. *Brahma-Sūtra*) of Bādarāyaṇa.

Each of these darśanas is accepted within the broad framework of orthodox Hinduism, which we may refer to as Sanātana-dharma; and from the perspective of Sanātana-dharma (sometimes Anglicised as 'Sanātanism'), the foremost nāstika darśanas—i.e. those which fall outside of its own boundary—are the Cārvāka, Jaina and Bauddha darśanas, founded on the teachings of Cārvāka (who is usually characterised as an exponent of materialism), Mahāvīra of the Jina lineage, and Gautama the Buddha respectively. Certain Śaiva systems are also designated as nāstika by the more strict of Vedic interpreters, but this judgement is based on the false assumption that the primary allegiance of such sects is to the Āgama and Tāntrika texts *over and above* the Vedas, when in fact the Āgamas and Tantras are a continuation of, and cannot be substituted for, the Vedas themselves.[4] With regard to this point, it is important to note that haṭha-yoga—which is for the most part a Śaiva tradi-

[3] Not to be confused with Gautama the Buddha.

[4] The terms *Tantra* and *Tāntrika* have already been explained in Chapter 1 (pp. 16-17). *Āgama* literally means 'coming near', 'approaching' or 'approximating to', and is used, in the Śaiva tradition, to denote a text said to be revealed or dictated by Śiva, which 'brings one near' to the ultimate truth.

tion—views itself as being thoroughly Vaidika, something which is implicit within the general philosophy of the haṭha treatises and explicit within the codes of ethical conduct laid down in these texts.[5] (It should also, in passing, be noted that the status of Sikhism is ambiguous, as its origins are in the Vedic tradition, but it has been influenced by other sources.)

Leaving aside the question of the extent to which the so-called nāstika darśanas diverge from mainstream Vedism, the schema outlined above of the six major āstika darśanas—each being based upon a founding sūtra text—may appear relatively neat; but even here the identity of and boundaries around each 'branch' or 'school' raise complex issues of definition. Many of these difficulties stem from the nature of the sūtra style itself, for, due to the extremely pithy format of the sūtras—whereby the maximum amount of meaning is condensed into the minimum number of words, and each word and phrase is pregnant with a veritable family of possible meanings[6]—the intelligibility of the texts is often largely dependent upon an accompanying commentary. Commentaries on the various sūtras are numerous, and, since they inevitably rely upon the interpretative or hermeneutic abilities of the commentator, they are not always compatible with one another. In fact two commentaries written upon the same original sūtra may be highly antagonistic in their philosophical exposition.

It is not uncommon for the āstika darśanas to be grouped into three pairs; that is, the Vaiśeṣika and Nyāya are paired together, as are the Sāṃkhya and Yoga and the Pūrva- and Uttara-mīmāṃsā. On the one hand, these couplings are useful, for it is certainly the case that the two halves of each pair can complement and shed light upon the philosophy of the other, as long as it is borne in mind that disputes may arise even within the same

---

[5] See *HYP* 1.16, wherein *āstikya* (orthodoxy) and *siddhānta-vakya-śravaṇa* ('study of the siddhānta philosophy', i.e. that of the Upaniṣads) are included among the prerequisites for becoming a yogin.

[6] Feuerstein et al characterise the sūtras as 'telegram-style explanatory treatises' (1995: 17).

darśana. On the other hand, however, the couplings can tend to obscure the fact that all six of the darśanas have a tremendous amount in common, and that they are all directed towards a goal of human liberation or Self-realisation. It would be disingenuous to pretend that intra- and inter-darśana conflicts, especially on the matter of the form that Self-realisation might take, can be simply brushed under the carpet, but it would also, I contend, be detrimental to our understanding of these traditions to get overly caught up in theoretical wrangles and to thereby miss the overriding soteriological thrust of the various darśanas and their similarities in this respect.

One of the key characteristics of Indian philosophy is its non-adherence to the principle of knowledge-for-knowledge's-sake; the philosophical enterprise being seen, rather, as a tool or method for cultivating virtue and self-understanding—just as it originally was in the western world.[7] It is for this reason that, in addition to the term *darśana*, Indian philosophical systems may also be referred to as *mokṣa-śāstra*, *mokṣa* meaning 'deliverance', 'release' or 'liberation' and *śāstra* being the 'teaching' or 'doctrine' for achieving that end.[8]

Without wishing to oversimplify the matter, it is fair to say that all six of the āstika darśanas, plus the traditions of Jainism, Buddhism and Sikhism, subscribe to a philosophical schematic which may be honed down to four basic principles. These were most famously expounded by Gautama the Buddha in his ser-

---

[7] For the ancient Greeks, for example, philosophy (lit. the 'love of wisdom') was a matter of determining how best to *live*, not merely how best to *think*. To be a true philosopher is, as Henry Thoreau has exclaimed, 'not merely to have subtle thoughts, nor even to found a school, but so to love wisdom as to live according to its dictates, a life of simplicity, independence, magnanimity, and trust. It is to solve some of the problems of life, not only theoretically, but practically' (1992: 12). It is predominantly in this spirit that Indian philosophers have traditionally pursued their art, although unfortunately in modern society, and especially in the West, the notion of a philosopher has become increasingly associated with those whose thinking has little direct relevance to life.

[8] Cf. Das 1990: 96.

mon on the Four Noble Truths,[9] but the Buddha did not invent the principles, for they resonate within pre-Buddhist philosophy as much as in that which followed it. The principles are best expressed in terms of a medical analogy, the first—and the starting point of all Indian soteriology—being that human existence is afflicted by an illness. The most common Sanskrit term for this illness is *duḥkha*, which comprises the prefix *dus*, 'implying evil, bad, difficult, hard', etc.[10] plus *kha*, whose meanings include (in *Manu-Smṛti* 9.43) 'the hole made by an arrow,' and (in the *Ṛg-Veda*) 'the hole in the nave of a wheel through which the axis runs'.[11] Hence it is possible to arrive at a literal translation of *duḥkha* as 'difficult (i.e. obstructed or dirty) axle-hole', which metaphorically refers to the inability of the 'wheel of life' (*dharma-cakra*) to run smoothly when under the influence of *avidyā* (perceptual ignorance). *Kha* can also be a synonym of *ākāśa*, which denotes 'space', 'atmosphere', 'sky', or the all-pervasive 'ether' out of which the principal constitutive elements of matter arise; and thus *duḥkha* may alternatively be rendered as 'bad space', 'misty sky', or 'difficult situation'. If, however, a single-word translation is required, then perhaps 'unsatisfactoriness' comes closest, for it connotes a general underlying sense of something's being not quite right—an atmosphere of disturbance, discomfort and at least potential distress which is present even in moments of intense pleasure. As the sage Aniruddha, commenting on *Sāṃkhya-Sūtra* 2.1, states, the physical body is the location of duḥkha, the senses lead to duḥkha, and even pleasure (*sukha*) is duḥkha because it is inevitably followed by distress.[12] The point being made here is not that there are no such things as pleasurable experiences, but that *all* experiences are transitory and are therefore incapable of bringing profound and lasting satisfaction in themselves. This 'unsatisfactoriness', this duḥkha, then,

---

[9] See *Saṃyutta-Nikāya* v. 420, in Thomas 1927: 87-88.

[10] Monier-Williams 1963: 488.

[11] *Ib.*: 334.

[12] Cited in Eliade 1969: 11.

is, according to the Indian darśanas, the illness perpetually suffered by humankind.

The second basic principle agreed upon, either explicitly or implicitly, by the Indian systems concerns the *aetiology* or *cause* of duḥkha, and this is said to consist in a false *relationship* with the phenomenal world. This false relationship is one in which the objects of experience are seen as having meaning and permanence in themselves, rather than as the ephemeral and decaying products of an unmanifest source. Such a relationship—or mode of perception—is said to lead to the belief that enduring happiness and fulfilment can be gained from worldly experiences, and to the notion of those experiences being 'mine'. Thus the relationship is one of *attachment* (*rāga*) to phenomena, the cause being referred to variously as *aviveka* (non-discernment), *avidyā* ('non-seeing', lack of vision),[13] *adhyāsa* (superimposition),[14] etc.

The third principle common to the Indian darśanas consists in an affirmation of the possibility of release from the condition of life known as *saṃsāra* ('wandering'),[15] in which the world is experienced as duḥkha, and this we may call the *prognosis* or predicted eventual outcome (as long as one follows the prescribed method). The state of release invariably involves a transformation of perception, through which one comes to realise the true nature of reality and of one's own identity. It is denoted by myriad terms, including: *mokṣa* (release),[16] *kaiva-*

---

[13] See, e.g. *YS* 2.5: 'Envisioning (*khyātir*) the impermanent, impure, distressing, non-Self as permanent, pure, pleasurable and the Self is *avidyā*.'

[14] See, e.g. *VSB* 1.1.1: 'The mutual superimposition [*adhyāsa*] of the Self and the non-Self...is termed Nescience [*avidyā*]' (trans. Thibaut 1962: 6).

[15] Feuerstein notes (1974b: 50) that *saṃsāra* is 'derived from the verbal root√*sṛ* or "to flow, glide"' and that it denotes 'that which flows on uninterruptedly only to turn back into itself. It stands for the cycle of existence in which man is trapped as in a grinding mill.'

[16] See, e.g.: *Laghu-Yoga-Vāsiṣṭha* 5.9.48: '[*Mokṣa*] is said to be the dissolution of the [individuated] mind upon the obliteration of all aspirations [*āśā*]' (trans. Feuerstein 1990a: 220); *Vaiśeṣika-Sūtra* 5.2.18: '*Mokṣa*...consists in the non-existence of conjunction [i.e. misidentification] with the body' (trans. Sinha in Radhakrishnan and Moore 1957: 394); *VSB* 1.1.4: 'this (moksha) is

lya (absoluteness),[17] *nirvāṇa* (extinction [of attachment and ignorance]),[18] and *turīya* (the 'fourth state', i.e. beyond wakefulness, dreaming and deep-sleep). The English expression that is most convenient and most suggestive of the meaning of such terms is 'Self-realisation' (the capital 'S' indicating that the true spiritual Self or essence of *everything* is implied). (As noted earlier, it should be acknowledged that, while there is agreement between the darśanas on the fact and desirability of Self-realisation, there continues to be argument both within and between darśanas upon the precise nature of such a goal.)

The method of achieving an exulted and emancipated state, however that state is conceived, constitutes the fourth principle in our medical analogy. It may be called the 'medication' or 'remedial process', since the method is designed to 'cure' the 'patient' of duḥkha. Although a precise prescription of technical methods may be absent from the majority of texts associated with the various darśanas, the idea that such methods exist is always implicit within them. The term most commonly used to denote a soterial methodology—i.e. a system of techniques for attaining liberation—is *yoga*, and this term may also refer to the goal or end purpose itself. Thus it should be emphasised that yoga forms, as it were, the 'technical substructure' that provides the experiential core around which the 'ideological superstructures' of the various Indian philosophical systems and religious matrices are constructed.[19]

Bearing in mind, then, that the practise of yoga—that is, of some kind of mind-training designed to bring one to a state of Self-realisation—is fundamental to all the major Indian darśanas, is it not curious that there should be a specific darśana

---

eternal in the true sense' (trans. Thibaut 1962: 28).

[17] See e.g. *YS* 2.25: 'With the absence of that [avidyā], the [perceived] conjunction [of Self and phenomena] is anulled. That [state] is the absoluteness (*kaivalya*) of the Seer (*dṛśeḥ*).'

[18] Although it occurs elsewhere, the term *nirvāṇa* has become most closely associated with Buddhism. See, e.g. *Saṃyutta-Nikāya* 10.261: '*Nirvāṇa* is serenity, peace' (trans. Stcherbatsky in Radhakrishnan and Moore 1957: 345).

[19] Cf. Conze 1962: 19.

called Yoga? In some ways, it *is* curious, but what hasn't yet been mentioned here is that each of the āstika darśanas tends to emphasise a particular aspect of the multifaceted jewel of Indian philosophy, and in the case of the Yoga darśana that aspect is the practical side. Before saying more about Patañjali's system, however, it is worth briefly noting the respective emphases of the other āstika darśanas.

The Vaiśeṣika darśana—which takes its name from the term *viśeṣa*, meaning 'particularity', 'special characteristic' or 'distinguishing feature'—is most notable for its system of ontological classification, wherein the objects of experience are reduced to their fundamental categories.[20]

Nyāya literally means 'that into which a thing goes back' and refers to the project of discovering the root causes underlying things and our knowledge about them. Whilst being extremely broad in its scope and overlapping considerably with the Vaiśeṣika system (which is sometimes regarded merely as a branch of Nyāya), the Nyāya darśana is best known for 'its critical examination of the objects of knowledge by means of the canons of logical proof';[21] or, in short, its *epistemology*.

The Pūrva-mīmāṃsā darśana is chiefly concerned with the investigation or explication (*mīmāṃsā*) of the early or 'former' (*pūrva*) part of the Vedas, i.e. the so-called *karma-kāṇḍa* or 'portion on (correct) action', comprising the Saṃhitās and Brāhmaṇas. Jaimini, the author of the (*Pūrva-*)*Mīmāṃsā-Sūtra*, introduces his project as an enquiry into *dharma* (i.e. true or right conduct); and, in order to establish Vedic injunctions as the proper source of knowledge on this topic, he sets forth a highly sophisticated theory of language in which the relation between the phonetic and the semantic content of a word—i.e. between a word's *sound* (*dhvani*) and its *meaning* (*śabda*)—is held to be 'inseparable' or 'inborn' (*autpattika*). Among many other things, the theory provides a basis from which to argue

---

[20] For a fuller exposition of the Vaiśeṣika and Nyāya darśanas, the reader is referred to Potter (ed.) 1977-96, vols. 2 and 6.

[21] Radhakrishnan and Moore 1957: 356.

for the importance of the accurate pronunciation of mantras in both ritualistic and yogic contexts.

While the Pūrva-mīmāṃsā darśana deals mainly with the ritualistic elements of Vedic doctrine, the Uttara-mīmāṃsā endeavours to provide a comprehensive system of philosophy based on the later (*uttara*) parts of the Vedas, i.e. upon the *jñāna-kāṇḍa* ('knowledge portion'), comprising the Āraṇyakas and, perhaps most importantly, the Upaniṣads. The Upaniṣads are regarded as one of three principal 'pillars' of the Uttara-mīmāṃsā, otherwise known as the Vedānta,[22] darśana; the other two pillars being the *Bhagavad-Gītā* and the *Vedānta-Sūtra* (or *Brahma-Sūtra*) of Bādarāyaṇa. Though all Vedāntins (exponents of Vedānta) agree upon the high authority of these three sources, their expositions and interpretations of them may differ in more or less subtle ways.

The best known sub-schools of Vedānta are: (1) the *Advaita* (non-dual) Vedānta, based primarily upon the work of Śaṅkarācārya (hereafter referred to as Śaṅkara),[23] (2) the *Viśiṣṭa-advaita* (qualified non-dualist) Vedānta of Rāmānuja (11th century C.E.), and (3) the *Dvaita* (dualist) Vedānta of Madhva (1197-1276 C.E.). The first of these three sub-schools, i.e. the Advaita Vedānta of Śaṅkara, has been the most influential, not only of the branches of Vedānta, but of all darśanas in India.

In a philosophical context, the term 'dualism' denotes a system of metaphysics which holds that the smallest number of principles to which reality can be reduced is two, whereas the 'non-dualist' or 'monist' view is that reality ultimately consists in a singular principle. The arguments of and between the various schools of Vedānta are highly refined, and it is inappropriate to launch into them here, although the subject of dualism

---

[22] *Vedānta* means 'end of the Veda', which in one sense simply refers to the later portions of the Vedic canon, but may also be taken to imply the 'pinnacle' or 'supreme synthesis' of that canon.

[23] *Śaṅkara* means 'benevolent', 'auspicious', etc. and is often used as an alternative name for Śiva. *Ācārya* is an appellation meaning 'teacher'. Śaṅkarācārya is reputed to have flourished towards the end of the eighth and beginning of the ninth centuries C.E.

will re-emerge in the following discussion concerning the Sāṃkhya and Yoga darśanas.

Sāṃkhya and Yoga

> That which the practitioners of Yoga perceive is also perceived by the practitioners of Sāṃkhya. Who[ever] looks upon Sāṃkhya and Yoga as one...knows the truth. (Yājñavalkya in *Mahābhārata* 12.304.2)[24]

While it is generally agreed that an extremely intimate relation exists between the Sāṃkhya and Yoga darśanas, the precise nature of that relationship continues to be a matter of controversy for some scholars. 'For all practical purposes,' writes Chandrahar Sharma, 'Sāṅkhya[25] and Yoga may be treated as the theoretical and the practical sides of the same system',[26] whereas Feuerstein, for example, contends that, despite the closeness of their 'pre-Classical' expressions, 'There are numerous philosophical differences between Classical Yoga and Classical Samkhya.'[27] Feuerstein's view stems from his rigorous analysis of the *Yoga-Sūtra* of Patañjali on the one hand, and of the *Sāṃkhya-Kārikā* of Īśvara Kṛṣṇa on the other, the latter text being the most complete extant document of so-called 'Classical Sāṃkhya'. It is my view, however, that Feuerstein imposes upon the *Sāṃkhya-Kārikā* an overly intellectually-oriented interpretation which overlooks its roots in the same processes of meditation described by Patañjali, and thereby draws a false distinction between two entirely complementary darśanas. 'Whereas Classical Samkhya relies primarily on the exercise of discernment (viveka) and renunciation,' writes Feuerstein, 'Classical Yoga stresses the necessity for the cultivation of ecstatic states (samadhi), in which insight can

---

[24] Slightly revised version of Edgerton's trans. (1965: 325).

[25] *Sāṅkhya* is a variant spelling of *Sāṃkhya*. The word literally means 'enumeration'.

[26] Sharma 1960: 169.

[27] Feuerstein 1990b: 177.

penetrate the deeper levels of consciousness and the world.'[28] The problem here lies, firstly, in Feuerstein's interpretation of viveka as an essentially intellectual activity, and, secondly, in his insinuation that viveka is not a vital element within the Yoga system. In fact, however, *viveka*, in Sāṃkhya and in Yoga, denotes the power of discernment arrived at precisely by means of intense meditative discipline, and appears several times in the *Yoga-Sūtra*.[29]

A clear indicator of the mutually supportive nature of the relation between Sāṃkhya and Yoga is the fact that one of the alternative names for Patañjali's darśana is *Sāṃkhya-pravacana*, the latter expression meaning 'enunciation of Sāṃkhya'.[30] While scholars such as J. W. Hauer and Georg Feuerstein have argued that the philosophy of Sāṃkhya was 'foist[ed] on Yoga' by Vyāsa (the author of the *Yoga-Bhāṣya*, the best-known commentary on the *Yoga-Sūtra*),[31] and that, in order to correctly understand the *Yoga-Sūtra*, one must 'combat the over-powering influence exercised by Vyāsa's scholium,'[32] the scholarly yogin Usharbudh Arya has contended that such a view is woefully misguided. Far from distorting the meaning of the *Yoga-Sūtra*, 'Vyāsa, having fully mastered both the Yoga and Sāṅkhya systems, clarifies Patañjali's work with regard to both its Yoga and the relevant parts of its Sāṅkhya contents—but within the context of Yoga.'[33]

If there is a difference between the Sāṃkhya darśana of Īśvara Kṛṣṇa and the Yoga of Patañjali it is, again, primarily one of emphasis, the *Sāṃkhya-Kārikā* being chiefly concerned with listing, classifying and explicating the relations between the various *tattva*s or layers of reality, and the *Yoga-Sūtra* placing greater stress upon the practical methodology for disclosing those tattvas. The terminological differences between

---

[28] *Ib.*

[29] E.g. *YS* 2.26, 2.28, 3.55, 4.26, 4.29.

[30] Cf. Arya 1986: 8, 37.

[31] Hauer, quoted by Feuerstein 1979: 25.

[32] Feuerstein 1980: ix.

[33] Arya 1986: 8.

the *Sāṃkhya-Kārikā* and *Yoga-Sūtra* are trivial, and they do not, contrary to Feuerstein's view, flow from significant conceptual differences. In order to illustrate the conceptual eqivalence of the Sāṃkhya and Yoga metaphysical schematics, the table below is provided, listing the twenty-five Sāṃkhya tattvas, and including the names given in the *Sāṃkhya-Kārikā* and *Yoga-Sūtra* respectively, along with approximate English translations.

Tattva	Term in the *Sāṃkhya-Kārikā*	Term in the *Yoga-Sūtra*
1	*puruṣa* (the Self or true Person)	*puruṣa* or *draṣṭṛ* (the Seer)
2	*prakṛti* ('that which brings forth') or *avyakta* (the 'unmanifest')	*aliṅga* (the 'undifferentiated')
3	*mahat* (the 'great') or *buddhi* (intellect)	*liṅga-mātra* (differentiatedness)
4-9	*ahaṃkāra* ('I-maker', egoity) plus five *tanmātras* (subtle elements)	six *aviśeṣas* (the 'unparticularised'), i.e. *asmitā-mātra* (= ahaṃkāra) plus the five tanmātras[34]
10-25	*manas* (mind or cognitive principle) plus five *buddhīndriyas* (sense capacities), five *karmendriyas* (action capacities), and five *mahābhūtas* (gross elements)	sixteen *viśesas* ('particularised'), as in final sixteen Sāṃkhya tattvas

[34] The tanmātras are not explicitly referred to by Patañjali, but Vyāsa takes them to be included in the *sūkṣma-viṣayatva* (lit. 'state of having subtle objects', i.e. 'subtle realm or sphere') mentioned in *YS* 1.45 (see *YB* 1.45).

The metaphysical categories known as tattvas are held to have been perceived by yogins in deep meditation, and not to be merely the result of ratiocination. As Jajneswar Ghosh points out, the Sāṃkhya method involves giving 'full credit to the sifted testimony of experience instead of explaining away whatever runs counter to a preconceived scheme of simplicity';[35] and so, in Sāṃkhya as in Yoga, experience *precedes* intellectual analysis. The tattvas have then, in turn, been enumerated (the literal meaning of *sāṃkhya* being 'enumeration') to provide an intrapsychic 'map' for the guidance of other meditating yogins. Too often has the Sāṃkhya darśana been evaluated with inadequate attention being paid to its soteriological context, which is profoundly and entirely yogic, and this inadequacy has resulted in the Sāṃkhya tattvas having been assumed to constitute a linear diachronic process of cosmological evolution, when in fact they describe the levels of reality common to both the macrocosm and the human microcosm, and present at all times either in a manifest or potentially-manifest form.

The notion of 'levels of reality' given expression in the Sāṃkhya philosophy is one of two ideas which are crucial to our understanding of the process and goal of yoga; the other is the idea of *misidentification*—i.e. of mistaking the nature of one's own ultimate identity. Both notions are, of course, intrinsically related. The schematic of tattvas may be viewed as a fifth dimensional axis in addition to those of length, breadth, height and duration with which we are ordinarily familiar.[36] It comprises synchronic layers of progressively more subtle substance, which are described as *aspects* or *manifestations* of prakṛti, prakṛti being both the source of universal substance and the power of extension and manifestation. In order to experience these various layers—that is, to penetrate more deeply into the nature of objects—one must cultivate the perceptual faculty through intense meditation.

---

[35] Ghosh 1977: 3.

[36] Cf. Feuerstein 1990b: 256.

The notion of misidentification is connected with that of having a 'false relationship' with the phenomenal world, mentioned earlier with regard to the aetiology of duḥkha. The idea is that we ordinarily identify ourselves with the level of reality corresponding to the grossest outward appearance of things, and fail to perceive the more subtle aspects of reality and hence those of our own beings. As long as we identify ourselves with the body, mind and senses—or, more accurately, the appearances thereof—we will, it is held, continue to experience the world as duḥkha, for these things are forever subject to change, and they give rise to sensations that fluctuate between happiness and pleasure on the one hand, and distress and anxiety on the other. The purpose of yoga is to direct one's attention towards increasingly rarefied tattvas, and to thereby discover and identify with more refined layers of one's own psychophysical complex. This, it is hoped, will lead to the transcendence of psychophysical identification altogether; that is, to the end of *mis*-identification, and to its replacement by the accurate identification of oneself as puruṣa. From the perspective of puruṣa-identity, the body, mind and senses are seen as merely the *vehicles* through which the light of puruṣa may be expressed or 'shine forth' on the material plane.[37]

With regard to Sāṃkhya and Yoga metaphysics, it is important that something be said about the question of dualism, for it is frequently claimed that, in contradistinction to 'non-dualist' traditions such as the Advaita Vedānta of Śaṅkara, Sāṃkhya and Yoga adhere to metaphysical dualism.[38] Feuerstein, for example, has consistently made assertions of this kind, of which the following two quotations provide a taste:

> *ahaṃ brahma-asmi*, 'I am *brahman*'...is the key-note of the whole non-dualistic (*advaita*) branch of Indian soteriology. On the other

---

[37] The concepts of identification and misidentification will be more thoroughly explored in Chapter 5.

[38] For example, Vol. 4 of *The Encyclopedia of Indian Philosophies*, edited by Larson and Bhattacharya, has as its title: *Sāṃkhya: A Dualist Tradition in Indian Philosophy*.

hand, in Classical Yoga which advocates an extreme dualism, the realisation of the Self (*puruṣa*) is experienced as a perfect isolation from the world including its transcendental core.[39]

> [Patañjali] taught a form of radical dualism that remained quite controversial within the fold of Hinduism. According to him, there are two eternal categories of existence—the transcendental Self (*purusha*) and the transcendental world-ground (*prakriti*). The former category comprises countless Selves that are omnipresent, omniscient, and passive spectators of the spectacle of the cosmos. The latter category, the world-ground, comprises all the manifest and unmanifest dimensions and forms of Nature, which are inherently dynamic.[40]

With all due respect to Feuerstein, who has a rightly-deserved reputation as one of the foremost yoga scholars of the 20th century, the characterisation of Pātañjala metaphysics as 'a form of radical dualism' requires considerable qualification. Although Vyāsa refers to the relationship between puruṣa and prakṛti as one of 'beginningless connection (*sambandha*)' (*YB* 1.4), thereby rejecting the notion of one principle's having emerged from the other, this should, I submit, be understood as merely an *approximate* description of a relation which is essentially *ineffable*. Prakṛti cannot be said to dissolve into puruṣa, as to do so would be to attribute to puruṣa the potentiality for transformation or evolution (*pariṇāma*), when in fact this ultimate Self is held to be forever pristine and immutable. Neither can it be claimed that prakṛti is entirely unconnected with puruṣa, for then there would be no way in which experience—which requires the presence of both the subjective and the objective principle—could take place. Thus, even when the primary impulses towards evolution—i.e. the three *guṇa*s or 'strands' of prakṛti—have returned to a state of equilibrium, prakṛti is not, herself, said to dissolve, but to remain in a dormant condition (*SK* 68). The continuance of prakṛti—if only in

---

[39] Feuerstein 1974a: 24.
[40] Feuerstein 1990a: 81.

latent form—'alongside' puruṣa is, of course, suggestive of dualism; but it should be borne in mind that prakṛti's role is always a subordinate one, the process of worldly manifestation for which she is responsible being 'for the purpose of puruṣa' (*YB* 2.18, cf. *SK* 60), i.e. a means to the end of realising our identity *as* puruṣa; and, when this identity is realised, the Seer (*draṣṭṛ*, i.e. puruṣa) is held to abide in its own nature (*svarūpa*) (*YS* 1.3), which is a state of 'absoluteness' (*kaivalya*) (*YS* 4.34). Feuerstein's preferred rendering of *kaivalya* as 'aloneness'[41] is not inaccurate, but I would contend that it is best understood as a unitive state in which the 'all-one-ness' and integrity of reality is realised, rather than the condition of 'isolation from the world' mentioned by Feuerstein above. Whereas 'isolation' connotes a 'closing off' or 'separation' from prakṛti, kaivalya involves an 'opening' and 'expansion' of one's sense of self-identity, to the extent that worldly-identification is transcended. The notion of kaivalya's being a state of supreme non-separateness is equally emphasised in the *Haṭha-Yoga-Pradīpikā* (4.62), which states that, 'upon the dissolution (*vilaya*) of the cognitive mind (*manas*), kaivalya [alone] remains', the phrase 'dissolution of manas' signifying, not the annihilation of the mind, but the cessation of one's identification with it.[42]

When viewed, then, in purely ontological terms—i.e. as a theory of categories of existence—the system presented in the Sāṃkhya and Yoga darśanas may be described as dualistic; however, when the epistemological emphasis of the system is appreciated—that is, when that system is recognised as a model of *perceived* reality which must ultimately be transcended in the final state of yoga—then it may justifiably be called non-dualistic. In short, the philosophy of Sāṃkhya-Yoga begins in dualist analysis and ends in unitive knowledge.[43]

---

[41] See, e.g. Feuerstein 1990a: 164.

[42] This distinction is further discussed in Chapter 5 below.

[43] I use the term 'Sāṃkhya-Yoga' here and hereafter as a convenient abbreviation for 'the Sāṃkhya and Yoga darśanas'.

Continuing on the theme of dualism versus non-dualism, it is worth saying something more about Advaita Vedānta, since, when contrasting its position with that of classical Yoga, Feuerstein and others have tended to imply that the problem of dualistic thinking has been overcome by this branch of Vedānta, when this is far from being the case. In fact, the relation between the absolute principle (Brahman) and the phenomenal world (referred to as *māyā*) has never been adequately defined in Advaita Vedānta, precisely because, on Śaṅkara's own admittance, the relation is *anirvacanīya* ('indefinable').[44] Just as, in Sāṃkhya-Yoga, prakṛti is held to exist 'for the purpose of puruṣa', so, in Advaita Vedānta, the existence of māyā is regarded as necessary in order for us to eventually come to the realisation that she (māyā) is not the ultimate reality (Brahman). The claim is that, just as in the absence of darkness, we could have no conception of light (because there would be nothing with which to contrast it), so, if we forever dwelt in a state of pure knowledge, without anything to *perceive*, then we would remain entirely unaware of our condition. As Radhakrishnan puts it, 'The finiteness is necessary before we can reach the infinite.'[45]

Since the relation between puruṣa and prakṛti, or between Brahman and māyā, is deemed to be beyond simple description, exponents of Sāṃkhya-Yoga and those of Advaita Vedānta both rely upon more or less elaborate analogies to illustrate their respective arguments. These analogies all have their faults and limitations, but it is worth briefly mentioning a few of them here. *Sāṃkhya-Kārikā* 21, for example, refers to the image of a lame but seeing man riding upon a blind man's shoulders, the former standing for the source of consciousness (puruṣa) and the latter for the (unconscious) source of activity (prakṛti). In order for experience to take place—which is itself a prerequisite for Self-realisation—both sentience and movement are nec-

---

[44] Cf. Radhakrishnan 1928: 132.
[45] *Ib.*: 155-56.

essary, and thus 'the halt and the blind' must come together.[46] Another analogy, which appears later in the same text, is that of a dancer (representing prakṛti) performing before an audience (puruṣa), and then desisting from her dance once its purpose has been fulfilled (*SK* 59). A third analogy can be found, among other places, in the *Tattva-Vaiśāradi*, a commentary by Vācaspati Miśra on the *Yoga-Sūtra* and *Yoga-Bhāṣya*. Here, with reference to *Yoga-Sūtra* 4.22, Vācaspati compares puruṣa to the moon, whose reflection appears on the surface of a body of water, the latter representing *buddhi*, the most refined tattva of prakṛti. Puruṣa therefore *appears* to possess movement due to the ripples on the water, but always in fact remains aloof.

An analogy drawn upon in both Sāṃkhya-Yoga and Advaita Vedānta traditions is that of a magnet's effect upon iron filings. In response, for example, to the objection that, if Brahman is both absolute and immutable, there can be no possibility of movement, Śaṅkara notes that 'The magnet is itself devoid of motion, and yet it moves iron;' and adds that 'colours and the other objects of sense, although themselves devoid of motion, produce movements in the eyes and the other organs of sense. So the Lord [Īśvara[47]] also who is all-present, the Self of all, all-knowing and all-powerful may, although himself unmoving, move the universe' (*VSB* 2.2.3).[48] In the Sāṃkhya terminology, the motionless principle would be puruṣa, and that which moves (or evolves), prakṛti, but still the same basic analogy is employed. Such analogies are not, of course, designed to *define* the nature of the relationship between the highest principle of reality and the phenomenal world, only to be suggestive of it.

Now, having spent some time looking at Sāṃkhya and classical Yoga, let us bring the discussion round to the subject of haṭha-yoga.

---

[46] Trans. Jha 1934.

[47] Īśvara, on the Advaita Vedānta view, is *Saguṇa Brahman*, i.e. Brahman represented in terms of having personal characteristics or 'qualities' (*guṇa*).

[48] Trans. Thibaut 1962: 369. It should be noted that Śaṅkara is highly critical of the Sāṃkhya system, despite his usage of similar analogies.

Pātañjala-yoga and haṭha-yoga

Haṭha-yoga neither constitutes a specific darśana in its own right, nor is it perfectly aligned with any of the principal āstika or nāstika darśanas. As noted in Chapter 1, the earliest systemic haṭha treatises form part of the Tāntrika tradition, and their phraseology is commonly, though not exclusively, that of Śaivism. Certain portions of haṭha texts—notably the opening chapter of the *Śiva-Saṃhitā*—are highly reminiscent of Advaita Vedānta with respect to their metaphysical exposition, although it is fair to say that theoretical argument is not the strongest point of these texts, their primary focus being practical instruction.

The nature of the relation between haṭha-yoga and the Yoga darśana of Patañjali is somewhat less than obvious, as there are no explicit references to haṭha in the *Yoga-Sūtra*, nor are there explicit references to Patañjali or his yoga system in the principal haṭha manuals. While the methodology of haṭha has generally been presented in a schema resembling Patañjali's aṣṭāṅga-yoga,[49] there is inadequate detail in Patañjali's technical descriptions for us to determine whether the haṭha manuals provide an authentic elaboration of this system, or merely one of many possible expansive interpretations. In particular, the attention given in the *Yoga-Sūtra* to āsana and prāṇāyāma—two of the most strongly emphasised aspects of haṭha-yoga—is meagre when compared with their treatment in, for example, the *Haṭha-Yoga-Pradīpikā* and *Gheraṇḍa-Samhitā*; and neither the preliminary cleansing practices known as *ṣaṭ-karmāṇi* ('six acts'), nor the important techniques for 'locking' or 'sealing' prāṇa within the body, called *mudrā*s, are explicitly referred to by Patañjali.

Despite these apparent incongruities between haṭha texts and the *Yoga-Sūtra*, the Pātañjala aṣṭāṅga system is compre-

---

[49] The *Gheraṇḍa-Saṃhitā* diverges from this pattern, preferring a 'sevenfold path' (*sapta-sādhana*) (see p. 8 above). Still, however, the basic format is similar to the Pātañjala system.

hensive enough for haṭha-yoga to be encompassed within it, though only if we give a particular interpretation to certain of Patañjali's sūtras. The ṣaṭ-karmāṇi may, for example, be considered to fall under the first of the *niyama*s or 'secondary observances' mentioned in the *Yoga-Sūtra*, namely *śauca*, which translates as 'purification' or 'cleanliness'. As a result of śauca, states Patañjali, one feels 'disgust' (*jugupsā*) towards one's body, and an absence of the desire to associate with others (*YS* 2.40). This may be interpreted as a declaration that, by cleansing the body, one becomes increasingly aware of the extent to which it is polluted, and thus one is spurred on to make the body a worthy temple of the Divine, and to seek only the company of similarly purified individuals. The succeeding sūtra lists the mental consequences of śauca as 'purity of *sattva* [the quality of luminosity and clarity], cheerfulness, one-pointedness, mastery of the senses, and fitness for Self-realisation (*ātma-darśana*)' (*YS* 2.41), all of which are perfectly compatible with the aim of the haṭha cleansing practices, although the more immediate purpose of the latter is to balance the three *doṣa*s (humours) in preparation for prāṇāyāma (*HYP* 2.21).[50]

The absence from the *Yoga-Sūtra* of mudrā—i.e. the technique of contracting certain muscles in order to prolong the retention of prāṇa during advanced breathing exercises—may be accounted for by the relative brevity of attention given therein to prāṇāyāma *per se*. Such brevity should not be taken to indicate that Patañjali attributed little gravity to prāṇāyāma, but is, rather, symptomatic of the sūtra style, in which every statement is honed down to its essential components, and all extraneous detail dispensed with. In fact, prāṇāyāma—the 'control' or 'extended retention' of prāṇa—is a crucial limb of aṣṭāṅga-yoga whose importance should not be underestimated. *Yoga-Sūtra* 2.50 mentions three 'modes' (*vṛtti*) of prāṇa-control, namely (1) *bāhya* (external retention, i.e. retention at the end of

---

[50] The ṣaṭ-karmāṇi are further discussed in Chapter 8 below, as are all of the principal techniques of haṭha-yoga.

an exhalation), (2) *ābhyantara* (internal retention, i.e. retention at the end of an inhalation), and (3) *stambha* ('static' retention). The third of these, according to Vyāsa (*YB* 2.50), involves retaining prāṇa without breathing in or out. The same sūtra adds that the flow of prāṇa is to be regulated with regard to 'space (*deśa*), time (*kāla*) and number (*saṃkhya*),' thus becoming 'long (*dīrgha*) and subtle (*sūkṣma*).' In the next sūtra, the existence of a fourth mode of prāṇāyāma is mentioned, which occurs when 'the spheres of the internal and external are cast off (*kṣepī*)' (*YS* 2.51), that is, again on the authority of Vyāsa's commentary, when inhalation and exhalation have been transcended, and the breath is no longer subject to spacial, temporal or numerical factors. In other words, the retention is complete and of indefinite duration, this being called *kevala-kumbhaka* (absolute retention) in haṭha-yoga.[51] Since the application of 'locks' or 'seals' is intrinsic to the performance of prolonged prāṇa-retention, we may take mudrā to be an implicit component of Pātañjala-yoga, whereas it is made explicit in haṭha texts.

Another notable difference between the *Yoga-Sūtra* and the principal haṭha treatises is the lack of detailed instruction given in the former text relating to āsana (posture). On this subject, Patañjali states simply that

> Āsana [should be] steady (*sthira*) [and] comfortable (*sukha*). (*YS* 2.46)
> [It is achieved] by reducing the restless tendency and by identifying with infinity (*ananta*). (*YS* 2.47)
> Then [one remains] undisturbed by dualities. (*YS* 2.48)

He nowhere so much as hints at the array of diverse postures—sitting and otherwise—promoted in haṭha-yoga, although, again, there is nothing in Patañjali's description which contradicts the haṭha teachings, and we have no reason to assume that a multiplicity of postures was unknown to him. Due, again, to the terse nature of the sūtra style, it is unsurprising

[51] See **Chapter 8** below, esp. pp. 202ff.

that Patañjali refrains from mentioning specific postures. Vyāsa, on the other hand, who is not constrained by such a format, lists thirteen āsanas in his commentary on *Yoga-Sūtra* 2.46, suggesting that, on Vyāsa's interpretation at least, Patañjali's definition may apply to a range of postures. Those mentioned by Vyāsa are: *padmāsana* (lotus posture), *vīrāsana* (heroic posture), *bhadrāsana* (beneficent posture), *svastika* (auspicious [posture]), *daṇḍāsana* (staff posture), *sopāśraya* ('with support'), *paryaṅka* ('around the hip'),[52] *krauñca-niṣadana* ('curlew-sitting'), *hasti-niṣadana* ('elephant-sitting'), *uṣṭra-niṣadana* ('camel-sitting'), *samasaṃsthāna* ('even, steady'), *sthira-sukha* ('steady and comfortable'),[53] and *yathā-sukha* ('at ease' or 'agreeable'). Since all of these appear to be sitting postures, it is impossible to say whether or not Patañjali and Vyāsa were familiar with the other kinds of āsana commonly practised by haṭha-yogins; and, as Vyāsa does not provide any instructive guidance, we cannot be certain how they are to be performed (although the names of some of them are highly suggestive). It is worth noting, however, that postures with the same names as the first four mentioned by Vyāsa appear in several haṭha texts, including the *Haṭha-Yoga-Pradīpikā* (1.21ff.) and *Gheraṇḍa-Saṃhitā* (2.3ff.).

With the helpful assistance, then, of Vyāsa's commentary, and with a sound knowledge of a variety of yoga practices, it is possible to locate haṭha-yoga within the remit of aṣṭāṅga-yoga as presented by Patañjali. As I shall argue in the course of this study, haṭha-yoga should not be viewed as a degenerate or corrupt version of aṣṭāṅga-yoga which devotes disproportionate attention to gross physical aspects of soteriological training; it is, on the contrary, a comprehensive system which includes each of the practical 'limbs' outlined in the *Yoga-Sūtra*, and

---

[52] The name of this posture derives from the fact that a belt or strip of cloth is wound around the legs just below the knees, and around the back just above the hips, in order to hold the body steady.

[53] Although the name of this posture accords with Patañjali's description in *Yoga-Sūtra* 2.46, Vyāsa does not imply that it has any priority over the other āsanas listed.

which is justified in giving special emphasis to postural, breathing and bodily cleansing techniques, as these establish the 'setting' in which progressively refined states of self-identification can occur, leading ultimately to Self-realisation. As Patañjali states, āsana is necessary for prāṇāyāma (*YS* 2.49), and 'by means of that [i.e. prāṇāyāma] the veil over the [inner] light is destroyed, and the mind is made fit for dhāraṇā (concentration)' (*YS* 2.52-53).

3

The Guru-Śiṣya Relationship

> In the midst of the highest heaven there is a shining light; he who has no *Guru* cannot reach the palace; he only will reach it who is under the guidance of a true Guru. (Kabīr, quoted in Brent 1972: 1)

> It is the living guru who leads us inwards.... When...we are able to contact the inner self at will, then we may say that we do not need a guru; but not until then. (Satyasangananda 1984: 6)

Since the chief concern of Part 1 of the present study is to locate yoga, and haṭha-yoga in particular, within its correct philosophical context, it is important that something be understood about the *pedagogical* scenario which has traditionally provided the setting for the transmission of ideas and practical techniques in India. While a close examination of the textual material of haṭha-yoga and of Indian soteriology more generally is invaluable for acquiring a clear comprehension of the doctrinal and technical framework upon which haṭha praxis is based, the texts cannot paint the whole picture. To give an additional dimension to our appreciation of the subject, it is necessary to pay attention to the important relation between teacher and student; between, that is, a *guru* and his or her *śiṣya*s or *cela*s;[1] and this is the purpose of the present short chapter.

The straightforward literal meaning of the word *guru* is 'heavy', which, when applied to a human tutor, may be taken to

[1] The terms *śiṣya* and *cela* both denote a student or disciple, i.e. 'one who is willing to learn'.

imply 'weightiness', profundity and authority.[2] Additionally, within the word are the two syllables *gu* and *ru*; the former, according to the *Advaya-Tāraka-Upaniṣad* (verse 16), signifying 'darkness' and the latter signifying 'the destroyer of that [darkness].'[3] Hence a guru is characterised as being someone (or something) who dispells darkness (spiritual ignorance), replacing it with light (spiritual illumination), or at least *assists* in such a process to a degree which is indispensable to the student.[4] More than this, however, the term denotes Brahman itself; guru is the Self, and it is also someone who has *realised* ('made real') his or her identity as the Self. There is thus a blurring of the distinction between guru as abstract divinity and guru as embodied human teacher. For a devoted disciple, to worship one is to worship the other; the teacher becomes a multifaceted symbol, standing for the disciple's own *guru-tattva* ('guru principle' or spiritual essence) and much else besides. For this reason it is not uncommon to come across in the writings of yogins hyperbolic eulogies such as the following:

> Guru is fire. Guru is Sūrya. Guru is the whole world. All places of pilgrimage in the entire universe reside in the sole[s] of Guru's lotus feet. Brahmā, Viṣṇu, Śiva, Pārvatī, Indra, all Devas and all sacred rivers are eternally seated in the Guru's body. Guru alone is Śiva. [etc.][5]

In such passages it is not explicitly stated whether it is the narrator's human guru or the Absolute (Brahman) who is being lauded; the issue simply does not arise for the dedicated, indeed

---

[2] Muz Murray has proposed that 'In secular Sanskrit, *guru* is considered to derive from the root [*gṝ*] – to praise, invoke or utter, thus being one who invokes the truth in the disciple by his utterance' (1986: 14), but he offers no specific references to support this claim.

[3] Cited in Feuerstein 1990a: 124.

[4] This, like the account of *haṭha* as 'sun and moon' (see p. 3 above), may be regarded as an instance of 'folk etymology', i.e. an account of a word's derivation which bears little or no relation to its actual etymology but which nevertheless serves to explicate its meaning or connotations.

[5] Sastri 1953: 345. (Transliteration of Sanskrit terms has been emended.)

devoted, śiṣya. Mary Scott makes the point that 'Earthly gurus are only surrogates deputising more or less adequately for the guru within[,] to whom, if we are lucky, they may introduce us',[6] but this is not necessarily the view taken by those within Indian spiritual traditions. From the Indian viewpoint, if someone has attained Brahman-realisation, then he or she has *become*—or, rather, has revealed himself to *be*—Brahman. He has established himself as both the goal and the way to the goal.

When engaging in the study of haṭha textual material, it should be borne in mind that the primary function of the early treatises was to codify a mere skeleton of instruction, which was then to be fleshed out by a qualified yogī-guru in face-to-face lessons. Much can be learnt about haṭha-yoga from the available written sources, but the picture will doubtless remain incomplete due to the terseness and density, and occasional downright opacity, of exposition. What is required for a fuller understanding is personal tuition by someone well practised and of high attainment in the discipline.

Amongst the very first instructions laid down in the *HYP* are those relating to the physical environment in which the *sādhaka* (spiritual practitioner) ought to study and practise haṭha-yoga. This is specified as a secluded dwelling known as a *maṭhikā* (1.12-13), and therein the yogin 'should practise only yoga...in the way taught by his guru' (1.14). In his commentary on this passage, Brahmānanda provides quotations from several sources reiterating the invaluable contribution to be made by a guru, including this from a work called *Rāja-Yoga*: 'Kaivalya (absoluteness) is not to be attained by any amount of study of the Vedas, Śāstras and Tantras, without the guidance of a guru' (*J* 1.14). Such emphatic claims are scattered throughout haṭha texts, although, of course, the way in which they are interpreted depends upon whether one sees the guru as a personal teacher, or as some form of divine inspiration from 'within', or both. *HYP* 4.8 states that 'spiritual knowledge (*jñāna*), freedom (*mukti*), stability (*sthiti*) and perfection (*siddhi*) are obtained

---

[6] Scott 1983: 8.

through the teaching of the guru', and that extreme difficulty will be encountered without the guiding compassion (*karuṇā*) of the sadguru (true guru) (*HYP* 4.9, cf. *ŚS* 3.11), a point affirmed in *Śiva-Saṃhitā* 3.14, which reads:

> By the guru's grace (*guru-prasādataḥ*) are all good things concerning oneself achieved; therefore the guru should always be served; otherwise nothing good (*śubha*) will come to be.

So integral is the guru, not only to Indian spiritual practice but to Indian culture in general, that, as Satyasangananda has pointed out, 'In India, almost everyone has a family guru who is regarded as a mentor and guide, who is part of the family.'[7] The guru is someone whose advice will be requested when decisions are to be made, concerning not only explicitly spiritual matters, but apparently mundane issues as well.

Just as a guru is considered to be more than merely a teacher, so his methods of instruction are held to surpass normal methods. The real power of the relationship between guru and śiṣya is said to reside on a more subtle plane than that of ordinary oral or written communication. Merely being in the presence of one's guru, so long as one has faith and an honest intention, is thought to facilitate accelerated spiritual development, and transmission of information is believed to occur telepathically. The Sanskrit term for a gathering of disciples to hear the words of their guru is *satsaṅga*, meaning 'being in the presence of truth', and closely allied to this is the concept of *guru-darśana* ('vision of the guru'), by which it is understood that spiritual upliftment may occur by one's coming under the guru's gaze. It is due to such beliefs that committed disciples are willing to undergo long periods of waiting, and sometimes considerable hardship, simply to be near to their guru.

On the matter of telepathy, Satyasangananda, himself a disciple of Swami Satyananda Saraswati, states that, as long as the initiated śiṣya maintains a high 'level of awareness, ...[t]he guru can communicate with him at any time and at any place, even

---

[7] Satyasangananda 1984: 23.

after he [the guru] has left his mortal body.'[8] Since the shedding of the physical body is not believed to impede guru-śiṣya contact, such a relationship may, in theory, persist over many lifetimes. Indeed, a true relationship of this kind is held to be unbreakable, as is the lineage that stretches back, from one guru to another, into the mists of legendary pre-history. By dedicating oneself to a guru, therefore, one simultaneously makes a connection with one's *parama-guru* (the guru of one's guru), and *that* guru's guru, and so on, back to the primal guru, whose name will vary according to the particular tradition that the guru is part of. In most schools of haṭha-yoga the primal guru is held to be Śiva, also referred to as Ādinātha or Ādīśvara (Primal Lord), and hence, in this tradition, texts will usually open with a dedication to Śiva. As is suggested in the following chapter, what may be understood by the claim that haṭha-yoga originated with Śiva is, first and foremost, that this soteriological discipline is rooted in the knowledge of the supreme reality.

With regard to guru lineages provided in haṭha texts, Mircea Eliade has noted the difficulty of disentangling 'the historical reality that may perhaps lie hidden under these traditions' from the skein of myth.[9] He further comments that the names given in lists denoting the line of didactic transmission 'designate degrees of spirituality rather than flesh-and-blood personages';[10] but this need not be an 'either/or' situation. The names of gurus, siddhas or yogins listed in the haṭha manuals *do* signify levels of spiritual attainment, but, since this is a common feature of most names and titles attributed to Indian gurus, it does not necessarily imply that the lineage lacks any historical basis.

In the matter of 'finding one's guru', and of discriminating between authentic gurus and those that are false, much emphasis is laid on the centrality of 'intuition'. For example, Satyasangananda insists that, 'When the awareness grows and the

---

[8] *Ib.*: 36.
[9] Eliade 1969: 308.
[10] *Ib.*

perception deepens [through satsaṅga and *sādhana* (spiritual practice)], you will spontaneously know the right path and the right guru.'[11] Such a 'spontaneous' recognition, however, must contain a large component of faith; indeed, the intellect is frequently denegrated in discussions of this phenomenon, as evidenced by Satysangananda's comment that 'You are automatically guided to the guru who is meant for you… It is only when we live in the realm of intellect…that we are nagged by questions, doubts and fears.'[12] While the advice to listen more attentively to the intuitive voice of conscience may be appropriate for some, the danger of allowing oneself to be guided by blind faith may prompt other aspirants to look for more objective criteria by which to assess a prospective guru.

B. K. S. Iyengar lists the qualities of a guru as: (a) clarity of perception and knowledge, (b) regularity of spiritual practice (*anuṣṭhāna*), (c) constancy in study (*abhyāsa*), (d) freedom from desire for the fruits of his actions (*karma phala thyāgi* or *vairāgya*), and (e) purity in what he does to guide his pupils in the true essence of knowledge (*paratattva*);[13] but on all of these points, the evaluation must remain subjective. It may be that an 'objective' assessment of spiritual proficiency is a contradiction in terms, but, nevertheless, it seems wise not to throw away intellectual discernment altogether. Swami Akhanananda favours the view that a guru should be rejected if he does not meet the śiṣya's requirements: 'if you come to a Guru in order to ask for things of God, to achieve identity with God, if you fail to do it within a reasonable time in spite of your best efforts, then you have no option but to leave.'[14] Precisely what constitutes 'a reasonable time' in which 'to achieve identity with God' would seem to be a far from straightforward question, but the point being made is that one should retain critical judgement regarding the quality of the guru.

---

[11] Satyasangananda 1984: 13.
[12] *Ib.*: 16.
[13] Iyengar 1981: 40.
[14] Quoted in Brent 1972: 61.

Once convinced that one's guru has been found, then a relationship of the profoundest intensity is expected to develop, and crucial to this relationship is the notion of *ātma-samarpaṇa*, meaning 'self-giving' or 'self-surrender'. On this point, Satyasangananda says that

> total surrender forms the core of the guru[-]disciple relationship. The disciple offers his or her limited self to the guru, completely merging the mind in him, and then receives it back in its fullness. This is the true concept of surrender... The life of every disciple should be dedicated towards the attainment of this goal.[15]

The degree to which the śiṣya is able to surrender his or her life to the guru will depend upon the worldly responsibilities possessed by the śiṣya, and for this reason different levels of initiation are available. Someone who is committed to family life, and perhaps works in some line of business, will tend to be unable to display the same degree of devotion as someone who has taken the vow of a *saṃnyāsin* (renunciant). It is the latter who declares his or her whole life to be dedicated to spiritual attainment and service to the guru. ('If you prostrate at their feet,' Kṛṣṇa tells Arjuna in the *Bhagavad-Gītā* [4.34], 'render them service, and question them with an open and guileless heart, those wise seers of Truth will instruct you in that Knowledge.'[16]) The 'householder' (*gṛhastha*), having obligations outside of his or her relationship with the guru, may become a *karma-saṃnyāsin*, i.e. one who engages in so-called 'worldly' activities though his or her intention is aimed towards a spiritual goal. Rather than serving the guru directly, the karma-saṃnyāsin will tend to donate a proportion of his or her income to the guru, whether in the form of money, food or property, such an offering being termed *dakṣiṇa*.[17] It is largely by means of such gifts that gurus have been able to survive economically.

---

[15] Satyasangananda 1984: 2.
[16] Trans. Goyandka 1943: 47.
[17] Cf. Satyasangananda 1984: 44.

On the question of a śiṣya's vulnerability to exploitation by unscrupulous pseudo-gurus, Satyasangananda remarks that, if a disciple is exploited, the karmic repercussions will be incurred by the guru alone and therefore the śiṣya has nothing to worry about.[18] Such declarations provide little reassurance, however, to would-be disciples, and are a prime example of the doctrine of karma's being used to suppress genuine feelings of injustice. As noted above, it is perhaps wise for śiṣyas to retain some sense of discernment until the ability and appropriateness of the teacher have been gauged.

It is, then, within an intense and intimate pedagogical relationship that Indian spiritual philosophy and practice have traditionally been passed on. The relationship is based on the authority of the guru, this authority deriving more from personal spiritual attainment than from skills in intellectual argument. In India, the most highly respected of philosophers have tended to be gurus, sages and mystics, especially those who have combined profound wisdom with benevolent and virtuous deeds, rather than academics; and it is very firmly within the setting of the guru-śiṣya relationship that haṭha-yoga is rooted.

---

[18] See *ib.*: 78.

4

The Symbology of Śiva

Praise be to him who is the self of Yoga,
  whom the alert, breath-conquered silent yogins,
  who look on everything indifferently,
  behold as light!...

I go for refuge to you, ultimate Lord,
  supreme and ever-blissful soul,
  who rests on nothing but yourself,
  without division,
  supernal Śiva![1]

The soteriological doctrine and praxis of haṭha-yoga has traditionally been set within an elaborate mythological framework, wherein the powerful forces which hatha-yoga is designed to awaken and harness are typically represented as bestial or anthropomorphic deities. To gain anything approaching a clear understanding of the terms of reference in haṭha-yoga, it is important to familiarise oneself with this framework, however complicated and contradictory certain aspects of it may appear to be. In this chapter, I shall focus upon the central figure in haṭha mythology, namely Śiva, and examine some of the imagery, symbolism and philosophical concepts that surround him.

---

[1] From 'To Śiva', *Kūrma Purāṇa* 1.10.43-70, trans. Dimmitt and van Buitenen 1978: 148.

The myth of haṭha-yoga's origin

The principal systematic treatises of haṭha-yoga, such as the *HYP*, *Śiva-Saṃhitā* and *Gheraṇḍa-Saṃhitā*, are presented, not as novel and innovative documents, but as more-or-less precise renderings of a traditional doctrine that stretches far back into the ancient past, perhaps even beyond time itself. The haṭha-vidyā (haṭha vision or knowledge) is held by its early exponents to derive, not from a human source, but from the source of all things—from the great God (*Mahādeva*) or primal Lord (*Ādi-nātha*) Śiva himself. The *Śiva-Saṃhitā* is presented as though spoken by Īśvara (Śiva), the mahāyogin (supreme yogin), and other haṭha manuals invariably begin with a laudatory dedication to this deity, each claiming to offer the authentic teaching of haṭha-yoga as first given to Pārvatī by her divine consort.

The mythic story concerning Pārvatī's initiation by Śiva has several variant forms, but most agree that it took place near to the coast of a remote island many eons ago. A common version has it that Pārvatī fell asleep during the lesson, and that Śiva's words were overheard by a powerful sage named Lokeśvara[2] ('Lord of the world'), who had transformed himself into a fish and was hiding in the sea. Śiva then acknowledged the greatness of Lokeśvara, who subsequently became known as Matsyendra or Matsyendranātha ('Lord of fish'), and granted him the authority to perpetuate the haṭha doctrine.[3] Matsyendra then initiated his disciple Gorakṣa (lit. 'Cow-protector'), who in turn initiated his own disciples, and so the ancient lineage began.[4]

In the haṭha texts, and in related mythological material, the divine origin of the haṭha doctrine is presented as though it were a literal fact—the historically plausible and the grandly mythic merge together as one. It need not be denied, however, that Matsyendra and Gorakṣa, along with the numerous other

---

[2] Known as Avalokiteśvara in Buddhism.

[3] Cf. Eliade 1969: 308-9. Summaries of various legends about Matsyendra can be found in P. C. Bagchi 1986: 9-20.

[4] The precise order of haṭha gurus is a matter of conjecture, but Matsyendra and Gorakṣa are usually given particularly high status.

siddhas ('perfected ones') mentioned in the pedagogical genealogies of haṭha, are likely to be based upon real historical personalities in order to construct a symbolic reading of haṭha-yoga's origin. Śiva may be understood to represent the transcendent Self (*paramātman*), who, according to yoga philosophy, is every individual's ultimate identity. Pārvatī stands for (a) the 'power' (*śakti*) of the Self to instigate the manifestation of the perceptible world, (b) the potentiality for 'extension' (*pradhāna*) *as* this world, and (c) the perceptible world or universe itself (*actualised* pradhāna or prakṛti). Since the human personality—comprising a mental-physical matrix—is an aspect of the perceptible universe, Pārvatī also symbolises the *jīvātman*—the ostensibly individuated, 'living self'. It being the goal and destiny of each individual, according to yoga philosophy, to realise his or her true identity as the transcendent Self, the practitioner of haṭha-yoga regards himself as *wedded to* that Self until the point is reached when he knows himself to *be* the Self. Hence we are all, from the perspective of the egoic personality, Pārvatī, and, from the absolute perspective, Śiva. Śiva and Śakti (Pārvatī)—immutable source and dynamic power respectively—are a unity perceived from two different perspectives. If we take Pārvatī to stand for each individual self (jīvātman), then the fact that she falls asleep in the story of haṭha-yoga's origin suggests that, ordinarily, we are not 'awake' enough to hear or comprehend the voice of our true Self, and that it is therefore necessary to look for a guru to guide us.

Symbolism in yoga

> *parokṣapriyā iva hi devāḥ pratyakṣa-dviṣaḥ.*
> ('The gods are fond of the cryptic, as it were, and dislike the evident.') (*Bṛhadāraṇyaka-Upaniṣad*)[5]

Before looking in detail at the symbology surrounding Śiva, it is worth pondering for a moment the extent of, and possible

[5] Quoted by Swami Adidevananda in his Foreword to Harshananda 1981: xii.

reasons for, the use of symbolism in yoga texts generally. The first thing to note is that the ancient Indian culture that gave birth to haṭha-yoga was infused with symbolic ritual at every level, much of which survives to this day. A prime example is the practice of bathing at the place where two or three rivers meet: in addition to the act of washing's being a metaphor for inner (psychospiritual) purification, the conjunction of rivers represents the convergence of *iḍā* and *piṅgalā* nāḍīs at the *ājñā-cakra* in the human subtle body.[6]

Yogic symbolism is the well-spring, too, of much Indian epic poetry. The *Bhagavad-Gītā*, which constitutes sections 13-40 of the sixth book of the grand epic *Mahābhārata* ('Great [epic of the war of the] Bhāratas'[7]), is well known for its psychological symbolism. The very battlefield of Kurukṣetra may be taken to signify the human mind or heart, whereupon, as M. K. Gandhi observed, 'Some battle or another is fought...from day to day.'[8] Inbetween the forces of *dharma* ('righteousness' or 'order') and *adharma* ('unrighteousness' or 'disorder'), stand Kṛṣṇa and Arjuna, representing the paramātman and jīvātman respectively, the latter aspiring to become one with the former but uncertain of which course of action to take.

An analysis of India's other great epic, the *Rāmāyaṇa* ('Life of Rāma'), also reveals an elaborate fabric of yoga imagery. The principal characters, Rāma and Sītā, are again symbolic of the paramātman and the jīvātman respectively. Sītā is kidnapped by the demon Rāvaṇa, who stands for egoism, vice, desire, attachment and sensuality, his ten heads representing the five sense capacities plus the five action capacities of the human body.[9] She is carried off to the 'underworld' called Laṅkā

---

[6] Cf. *HYP* 3.109-110, wherein iḍā is represented as the river Gaṅgā and piṅgalā as Yamunā. Nāḍīs, and related subtle physiological notions, are further discussed in Chapter 7 below.

[7] *Bhārata*: 'descendants (of Bharata)'; cf. Feuerstein 1974a: 47. Bhārata is also the name for the country of India.

[8] Gandhi 1960: 8.

[9] The five sense capacities (*buddhīndriyas*) are: *śrotra* (hearing), *tvac* (touch), *cakṣus* (sight), *rasana* (taste), and *ghrāṇa* (smell); the five action capacities

and kept prisoner within Aśokavana, the garden which represents the world of sensual experience. There she dreams of being reunited with Rāma, and devotedly concentrates her mind upon him. Eventually, Rāma is able to rescue his consort from this state of captivity and to bring her back to her true home, so that she may realise her true identity; and this he does with the aid of Hanumān, the Lord of monkeys, who represents prāṇa, the 'vital force'. Thus the union of the one who has gone 'wandering'—or, in this case, been captured by the ego—and the paramātman is established, which is, of course, the goal of yoga.[10]

Extricating the historical from the mythical content of tales such as those of the *Mahābhārata* and *Rāmāyaṇa*, or of the fabled initiation of Pārvatī by Śiva, is a task fraught with difficulties. It would seem that, in the minds of the authors of these narratives, no contradiction existed between symbolic and literal events. Both history and mythology are used as tools for the enunciation of a deeper and longer-lasting truth—that of the identity of jīvātman and paramātman. Hence, when Śiva is invoked in the opening śloka of a haṭha text, it is as the highest Self of the writer and reader *and, at the same time*, as the greatest of yogins, who sits with matted locks cascading over his ashen shoulders on the remote and snowy edifice of Mount Kailāsa. The eternal paradox of the power of the transcendent Absolute 'manifesting' as the phenomenal universe is everywhere echoed in Indian soteriological literature.

The blurring of the figurative and the literal extends into the most technical passages of the haṭha-yoga texts, thereby making a sprightly sense of discernment a necessity on the part of the reader. In his commentary on the *HYP*, Vishnudevananda cautions the reader to 'never take anything literally in Yoga',[11]

(*karmendriyas*) are: *vāc* (speech), *pāṇī* (manipulation), *pāda* (locomotion), *pāyu* (excretion), and *upastha* (procreation). Cf. Larson and Bhattacharya 1987: 49.

[10] Cf. Iyengar 1981: 41.

[11] Vishnudevananda 1997: 57.

thereby implying that there is *always* a symbolic meaning to be found. Such advice can, no doubt, be taken too far, as there are certainly statements that can best be understood in a literal manner; but the touch of hyperbole in the warning is justified if it encourages greater awareness of the multivalent nature of yoga treatises.

An example of what can happen if religious instructions or myths are taken literally rather than figuratively, as intended, is the past history and present continuance of animal sacrifice in some Hindu rituals (albeit a small minority). As V.-L. Mitra has pointed out, the notion of *puruṣa medha* in the Veda has been misunderstood to refer to 'the offering of a *male being*, a man, a horse, a bull or a he-goat or male of any animal,' when it in fact denotes *self*-sacrifice, the giving up of personal attachments, which is requisite for (though its ultimate fulfilment is attendant upon) the realisation of one's true identity.[12]

So, if the danger exists that great harm may be caused by taking a symbolic description too literally, what justification can there be for such a style of expression? There are, I think, four chief answers to this question: First, if one accepts the claims of illustrious yogins to have achieved a state of supra-phenomenal knowledge to be genuine, then it may also be presumed that, from such an 'absolute' perspective—i.e. a 'perspective' that encompasses and transcends *all* (conditional) perspectives—any distinction between the 'literal' and the 'figurative' is bound to break down. Such distinctions may be meaningful from a mundane and relative point of view, but, from a viewpoint which sees only *one* literal truth—that being the supreme Reality (Brahman)—it may be supposed that *all* phenomena will take on a merely symbolic appearance; and for this reason, it may be assumed, the utterances and writings of renowned yogins are devoid of clear boundaries between the 'actual' and the 'metaphoric' when discussing the phenomenal world. As Mircea Eliade puts it, with regard to haṭha treatises 'it is a delicate problem to distinguish between the "concrete"

[12] Mitra 1891: 33.

and the "symbolic," tantric *sādhana*[13] having as its goal precisely the transubstantiation of every "concrete" experience, the transformation of physiology into liturgy.'[14] As this statement suggests, the goal, at least as expressed in haṭha- or Tantric yoga, is to *sacralise* the body and to *ritualise* every action it performs.

A second reason for the extensive use of symbolic description in yoga texts is its *heuristic efficacy*. Since the aim of yoga is to go beyond the understanding of reality afforded by ratiocination, the human faculties of reason and language are viewed by the authors or compilers of yoga material primarily in terms of their instrumental value in unlocking the door to Self-realisation. When the criterion governing which terms to employ shifts from that of 'correspondence to some (supposedly) actual object, situation or event' to 'potency for engendering spiritual awakening', then the likelihood of finding symbolic terms more suitable to the purpose increases; for it is through symbol and metaphor that multidimensional meanings can be revealed, some of which may bypass the censoring mechanism of the rational mind.

Third is the fact that much of the subject matter of yoga texts is of a nature more 'subtle' than gross physical matter, and hence 'gross physical' descriptions are impossible. The constituent aspects of the subtle human anatomy outlined in the yoga treatises—the nāḍīs (channels) and cakras (wheels) and the various *kośa*s (sheaths)[15] —along with the modes of 'force' or 'energy' that pervade it—the *prāṇa*s (vital airs) and the *Kuṇḍalinī-śakti* (coiled power)—are simply not susceptible to ordinary description, and a more innovative use of terminology is required.

The fourth main reason derives from the esoteric nature of much yoga material. That is, many of the doctrines and tech-

---

[13] That is, sādhana (spiritual practice) based on the teachings contained in the Tantras.

[14] Eliade 1969: 252.

[15] See Chapters 6 and 7 below.

niques expounded therein have tended to be regarded as 'secret' or 'occult', and hence suitable to be known only by the fully initiated. Injudicious propagation of such ideas opens the door to their corruption and dilution, and allows powerful techniques to be practised by those to whom they may prove harmful due to ill-preparedness. In order, then, to keep the uninitiated largely in the dark concerning the intricacies of yoga, the textual material is frequently concise to the point of inscrutability and/or veiled in opaque terminology; or, alternatively, it is so deeply embedded in an elaborate narrative—as in the great Indian epics mentioned above—that only an initiate could scrape away the exoteric flesh to reach the bony esoteric core of the story.

The practice of imploring the receiver of certain information to pass it on only to close relations or initiated disciples extends back to the Upaniṣads[16] and is certainly prevalent within the haṭha tradition. *Śiva-Saṃhitā* 1.19, for example, cautions that

> This *yoga-śāstra* (doctrine of yoga), here being taught, is to be kept secret; and must be revealed only to those great selves (*mahātman*) [who are] sincere devotees.

Similarly, *HYP* 1.11 states that yogins who wish to attain *siddhi* (perfection) should refrain from broadcasting their knowledge of haṭha, 'for it is potent when concealed (*gupta*) [though] impotent when [indiscriminately] revealed.' If we apply this proclamation to the *HYP* itself, it would seem that the credited author/compiler, Svātmārāma, by revealing the haṭha-vidyā, has broken his own code. What is more likely, however, is that the *HYP*, and similar treatises, were originally intended only as aids to the instruction of yogī-śiṣya by yogī-guru, and not to be made available to the wider, uninitiated, population.

---

[16] See, e.g.: *Chāndogya-Upaniṣad* 3.11.5; *Śvetāśvatara-Upaniṣad* 6.22: 'This highest mystery of the Veda's end [*Vedānta*]/ Was propounded in an earlier age;/ Let it not be told to an unquiet man,/ Or to one who is neither son nor pupil' (trans. Zaehner 1966: 217). Cf. Deussen 1906: 10-15.

The exponents of haṭha-yoga are keen to emphasise the importance of going *beyond* the written or spoken text by putting its teaching into practice. '*Yoga-siddhi* (perfection in yoga) is not acquired', states the *HYP*, 'by merely reading the *śāstras*...; practice (*kriyā*) alone is the cause of perfection' (*HYP* 1.65-66). *Gheraṇḍa-Saṃhitā* 3.65 compares the religious scriptures, such as the Vedas and Purāṇas, to 'public women', in contradistinction to Śāṃbhavī (a name of the Goddess) who is known directly by means of yoga, and particularly, in this instance, by means of *Śāṃbhavī-mudrā*, which involves focusing one's (inner) gaze upon the space between the eyebrows, i.e. in *ājñā-cakra* (*GS* 3.64).[17] Śāṃbhavī, Gheraṇḍa continues, 'should be guarded as though she were a lady of a respectable family' (a comment which reveals as much about traditional Indian social attitudes as it does about yoga).

The meanings of *Śiva*

Now that the general notion of symbolism in yoga has been introduced, a more detailed exploration of some of the mythological and philosophical ideas associated with Śiva can be carried out. Few of these ideas are expounded at length in the haṭha manuals themselves, but it is nevertheless the case that they form the substratum of belief, or the ideological framework, which permeates the language of haṭha and provides the setting for its soteriological practices.

The term *śiva* itself may be said to mean 'the one in whom all things lie'.[18] It appears in several Vedic passages as an epithet of the god Rudra,[19] and in that context it may be rendered simply as 'auspicious' or 'beneficent'. Similarly, *rudra*, which can mean 'howler' or 'roarer' as well as 'red, shining, glittering',[20] is one of the many epithets possessed by the god Śiva in

---

[17] According to Brahmānanda (*J* 4.37), the attention should be directed towards *anāhata-cakra* in the region of the heart (cf. pp. 215-16 below).
[18] Cf. Monier-Williams 1963: 1074.
[19] E.g. *ṚV* 2.33.1-7.
[20] Monier-Williams 1963: 883.

later mythological material such as the Purāṇas. It has been commonly assumed, therefore, that, even if Rudra and Śiva are not identical, there is at least a strong continuity between them. The nature of both of these deities is ambivalent, each being associated with storms, violence and destruction on the one hand, and with mercy and benevolence on the other.

In the highly sophisticated soterial-philosophical tradition known as Kashmiri Śaivism,[21] the term *Śiva* may be understood in both an abstract and a personalised sense. Abstractly, it stands for Brahman, the 'Absolute', and may, in this sense, be prefixed by *Parama*, *Parama-Śiva* meaning the 'highest' or 'supreme' Śiva. This is the transcendental (*viśvottīrṇa*) and characterless (*nirguṇa*) aspect of Śiva (although still commonly referred to by the personal pronoun 'He'). The immanent aspect, on the other hand, is termed *Śiva-tattva* (the 'existent principle of Śiva'), which is the *prathama spanda* or 'initial vibratory impulse (towards emanation)' of Parama-Śiva. The 'power' or 'energy' of Śiva is characterised as a feminine consort, Śakti. Although Śiva and Śakti are often represented as distinct deities, they may best be understood as the static and dynamic poles of the creative, or emanative, process. As Jaideva Singh remarks in his Introduction to the *Śiva-Sūtra*, 'Śakti...is nothing separate from Śiva... She is His *ahaṁvimarśa* (I-consciousness), His *unmukhatā* or intentness to create.'[22] The symbolic representations of both Śiva and Śakti throughout the various Śaiva traditions are immensely fascinating and colourful, and it is to some of these that our attention now turns.

Iconism and aniconism in Śaiva symbology

Śiva is symbolised and worshipped in many forms. Representations of him, or of the divine principle for which he stands, fall

---

[21] The soteriological view that sees Śiva as the highest principle may be generally referred to by the Anglicised term *Śaivism.* Although there are several varieties, or sects, of Śaivism, the purpose here is not to provide a comprehensive survey.

[22] Singh 1979: xxii. The *Śiva-Sūtra* is attributed to Vasugupta and dates from the early 9th century C.E.

into two main categories: firstly, there are those which are *iconic* or anthropomorphic, displaying the god in human form; and, secondly, there are *aniconic* images or sculptures, in which Śiva is represented by (or *as*) a smooth, dark egg-shaped stone or dome-topped pillar known as a *Śiva-liṅga* or simply *liṅga*. The first kind of representation is termed, in Sanskrit, *sakala*, meaning 'with (*sa-*) parts (*kala*)' or 'with attributes'; the second kind, the liṅga, is termed *niṣkala*, 'without parts'.[23]

The basic meaning of *liṅga* is 'sign' or 'emblem'; it is a thing that stands for something else or which marks its presence, and thus may be defined as the principle of representation, signification and differentiation. Stella Kramrisch posits *layana* or *laya* (absorption, dissolution) as a possible etymological origin of the word, since, in certain metaphysical systems, liṅga is that into which everything is absorbed (and from which everything emerges and unfolds).[24] As was noted in the table on p. 52 above, in the *Yoga-Sūtra* of Patañjali (*YS* 2.19), the term *liṅga-mātra* is used as a synonym of the primary manifestation of prakṛti, that manifestation being referred to as *mahat* or *buddhi* in the Sāṃkhya texts. In this context, *mātra* implies 'wholeness' or the 'totality' of a thing, and hence *liṅga-mātra* may be rendered as 'differentiatedness-as-such'. Prakṛti herself is held to remain *aliṅga*, i.e. unmanifest or 'undifferentiated', although it is in her that the threefold potentiality for manifestation known as *triguṇa* is harboured. The use of the terms *liṅga* and *aliṅga* differs slightly in most explicitly Śaiva systems from that of the classical Sāṃkhya and Yoga darśanas. For the Śaivas, it is Śiva-tattva himself who is the liṅga, while Parama-Śiva—the aspect of Śiva that is beyond all representation—is aliṅga. This latter principle may also be called the *liṅgin*, meaning the one who 'possesses' the emblem of the liṅga, who 'wears' it as a garment; he is Parameśvara, the 'Supreme Lord', of whom the perceptible universe is a mere shadow or symbol. On this view, Prakṛti is the 'subtle body'

---

[23] *Śiva Purāṇa* 1.5.8-11, cited in Kramrisch 1981: 172.
[24] Kramrisch 1981: 173.

(*sūkṣma-śarīra*) or 'form' of Śiva, just as Śakti is his 'power' or 'creative pulsation',[25] this subtle body also being known as the *liṅga-śarīra*, the intangible matrix which gives rise to the tangible world. On the microcosmic level, the liṅga-śarīra is the human subtle body, composed of five 'subtle elements' (*tanmātra*s) which give rise to the 'gross elements' (*mahābhūta*s) that make up the *sthūla-śarīra* or 'gross physical body'. In haṭha-yoga, it may be noted here, it is principally upon the liṅga- or sūkṣma-śarīra that the techniques are designed to work.

The aniconic stone liṅgas mentioned above, which act as media of worship and take pride of place in Śaiva shrines, are really only symbols of symbols, i.e. symbols of the cosmic liṅga which is itself a symbol of Śiva. These liṅgas may be situated on their own or, more frequently, in conjunction with a *yoni* (vulva, womb), the *liṅga-yoni* standing for the 'masculine' and 'feminine' poles of the process of cosmic creation or transformation from one state to another (see Appendix A, p. 245). Such symbolism has spurred some interpreters to characterise ceremonies involving the liṅga-yoni as phallic worship or mere lauding of the human sexual act. It is true that sexual intercourse, in the microcosmic sphere of human relations, shares a correspondence with the macrocosmic (or 'macranthropic') 'union' of Śiva and Śakti, but the two activities are by no means equivalent. The metaphysical concepts behind the Śiva-liṅga symbology are far more subtle and sophisticated than a straightforward phallus-liṅga identity allows (unless *phallus* is understood in a broad sense as the initiator or generator of manifestation rather than simply as a penis). This being said, however, the fact that the liṅga can take the form of an erect phallus ought not to be shied away from; indeed ithyphallicism[26] is a key aspect of Śaiva symbology. When Śiva is represented by an erect phallus—or is portrayed in human form with an upright penis—then the image can no longer be termed ani-

---

[25] Cf. J. Singh 1979: 258.

[26] *Ithyphallic*: 'with erect phallus'.

conic, although neither should it be construed entirely literally as simply a sexually excited man. As Wendy O'Flaherty points out in her detailed study of Śaiva mythology,[27] the image of Śiva as 'the ithyphallic yogi' is deeply ambiguous,[28] the erect phallus being both 'a sign of priapism' and 'a symbol of chastity' in Indian culture.[29] Alain Daniélou comments that the phallus of Śiva 'is swollen with all the potentialities of future creations';[30] and these potentialities may indeed 'burst forth', as it were, at some point, but there is nothing uncontrolled about such a process. The upright phallus symbolises chastity because it suggests Śiva's ability to retain his creative essence. A reference to Śiva in the *Mahābhārata* reads: 'He is called *ūrdhvaliṅga* ["upright phallus"] because the lowered *liṅga* sheds its seed, but not the raised *liṅga*.'[31] Developing this capacity to retain sexual potency, and to channel the subtle essence of sexual fluid (*bindu*) upwards rather than downwards and out through the genitals, is an important aspect of haṭha-yoga, as the relationship between bindu, prāṇa and citta is held to be an extremely intimate one.

Trimūrti

In modern-day India, Śiva is only the second most popularly worshipped form of the Divine, the most popular being the god Viṣṇu, who, like Śiva, is represented in many ways. Viṣṇu and Śiva, together with Brahmā, constitute the *trimūrti* ('three faces') of Brahman, in which context Brahmā stands for the expansive or emanative potency of the Absolute, Viṣṇu for the power of existence and preservation, and Śiva for that of contraction, dissolution and absorption. 'Dissolution' or 'absorption' (*pralaya*) should be understood here, not in a negative sense as a withdrawal into nothingness, but as a positive process of (re-)integration—a returning to the source in preparation

---

[27] O'Flaherty 1973.
[28] *Ib.*: 11.
[29] *Ib.*: 9.
[30] Quoted in O'Flaherty *ib.*: 10.
[31] *Ib.*: 9.

for renewed evolution. On the human level, this is the very purpose of yoga—the translocation of one's sense of identity from the world of gross phenomena, via the myriad 'layers' of reality, to the fundamental essence. In the Purāṇic myths, Brahmā, Viṣṇu and Śiva all, at different times, play the role of supreme Deity, with the other two aspects taking on subsidiary positions; and, in the haṭha tradition, it is Śiva who is generally taken to represent all three aspects.[32]

The three members of the trimūrti correspond to the three 'strands' of the *triguṇa*,[33] which constitutes the nature of prakṛti, perhaps most notably described in the scriptures of the Sāṃkhya darśana.[34] The three guṇas are *sattva*, *tamas* and *rajas*, these terms' respective meanings depending largely upon the context in which they are examined. Each guṇa may be regarded as a kind of 'root tendency' out of which grow a number of 'sub-tendencies'. Broadly speaking, sattva (lit. 'truth-ness' or 'real-ness') is the impulse towards, or potentiality for, illumination and lucidity; tamas (lit. 'darkness') is the impulse towards closure, obscuration and inertia; and rajas is the energetic impulsion required for sattva and tamas to become actualised. On the surface, sattva and tamas may appear to be antagonistic tendencies, but they are only so in the way that inhalation and exhalation are antagonistic; both are essential to the dynamic process of evolution, as is the expansive energy of rajas. In the trimūrti, Brahmā corresponds to rajas, Viṣṇu to sattva, and Śiva to tamas. This may seem to be contradicted by the fact that Śiva is commonly pictured as white, while Viṣṇu is characterised as dark,[35] but, as Swami Harshananda remarks, 'There is nothing strange in this since the opposing guṇas are inseparable. Hence Śiva is white outside and dark inside

---

[32] In *Śiva-Saṃhitā* 1.34, for example, Śiva is made to say that 'This entire universe...derives from me; all things are sustained by me; all are absorbed into me.'

[33] *Tri*: 'three'; *guṇa*: 'strand', 'aspect', 'tendency', 'characteristic'.

[34] See, especially, *SK* 11-16.

[35] *Kṛṣṇa*, the name of the eighth avatāra ('descension, incarnation') of Viṣṇu, literally means 'the dark one'.

whereas Viṣṇu is the reverse.'[36] As mentioned above, context is all-important to the meaning of the guṇas, and thus the correspondence between triguṇa and trimūrti is only helpful for describing certain processes, such as, for example, the cyclical expansion, sustenance and contraction of the universe. In yoga, however, the intention is to reduce the influence of tamas and rajas within the mind (*citta*, *buddhi*), and to thereby enable the mind to settle into its true nature as predominantly *sāttvika* (constituted by sattva), and this has nothing to do with cultivating the dominance of Viṣṇu over Brahmā and Śiva. It should be borne in mind that the triguṇa theory is a *model* of how disparate but complementary tendencies interact to engender formation and transformation in the universe. The guṇas are principles derived from logical deduction which stand for the irreducible qualities of perceptible, or potentially perceptible, reality, and any search for an atom or molecule of sattva, or of tamas or rajas, is highly unlikely to bear fruit.

Naṭarāja

One of the most popular iconographic representations of Śiva, in which he takes on the roles of all three facets of trimūrti, is that of the *Naṭarāja*, the 'Lord of the dance' or 'Dancing king'. As such, he is shown posing in mid-dance with a ring of fire encircling his elegant, and decidedly androgynous, form. His left foot is raised, and his right foot stands upon a demon named Apasmāra-puruṣa, an embodiment of avidyā (nescience).[37] Śiva's matted locks of hair fan out like wings from behind his head, and each of his four arms is deliberately positioned to signify a controlled and benevolent attitude (see

---

[36] Harshananda 1981: 62.

[37] *Apasmāra*, 'convulsiveness, unsteadiness' + *puruṣa*, 'person' = 'the one who is unbalanced and falls down'. The contrast with Śiva is stark, the latter being in perfect equilibrium. It should be remembered, however, that the demon is, in a sense, supporting Śiva, thereby connoting the positive value of avidyā; for, were it not for avidyā's initial influence, we would be unable to arrive at a full realisation of the infinite (cf. discussion of māyā and prakṛti, p. 57 above).

Appendix A, p. 247). In this form, Śiva is the dancer and the universe is his dance (*tāṇḍava*). He spins the web of existence through the rhythm of his movements and the oscillating beat of the small drum (*ḍamaru*) held in his uppermost right hand, yet only those who have attained yogic insight can know the dancer himself.[38] 'I am the originator, the god of abiding bliss', Śiva announces in the *Kūrma Purāṇa* (2.4:33), 'I, the yogi, dance eternally'.[39] The dance is both creative and destructive; it brings the universe into existence, maintains that existence, and then, as one evolutionary cycle comes to a close, the dance becomes frenzied, thereby providing the mechanism of dissolution. As Kramrisch vividly describes:

> The stamping of his foot, the gyrations of his body, his flailing arms toss the mountains into the air; the ocean rises, the stars are lashed and scattered by Śiva's matted hair.[40]

Within this devastating display, however, lie the seeds of renewal, as the mirthful and revelling deity liberally disperses potent ash from his body. '[F]rom his flowing hair', continues Kramrisch, 'the rivers will flow again into existence...and the rays of sun and moon will be seen again for what they are, the hair of Śiva'.[41]

The use of dance as a metaphor for the perpetual unfolding and crumpling up of the cosmic fabric is a uniquely evocative one. Dance is organised movement—rhythmic, pulsating, passionate—and the universe and everything in it is pictured as an expression of that movement, a sequence of infinite complexity derived from a single source. At the close of each dancing cycle, Śiva is said to retire to his quiet home, symbolised in the mountains of the Himālaya, but, even in the stillness of the great god's deep self-contemplation, the impulse towards activity is harboured.

---

[38] Cf. Kramrisch 1981: 439.
[39] Trans. Kramrisch *ib.*
[40] *Ib.*
[41] *Ib.*

Bhairava

Another of the many forms in which Śiva appears in the rich fabric of myth woven in the Purāṇas is that of Bhairava—an emaciated and malodorous mendicant—whose name means 'fierce', 'ferocious', or 'frightful'. In one tale associated with Bhairava, Rudra is the son of Brahmā, and, while perched upon his father's shoulder, he cuts off Brahmā's head (or the uppermost of Brahmā's five heads), and the skull sticks to Rudra's left hand. Rudra is then obliged to take the *kāpālika* vow, the penance for murdering a brāhmaṇa, *kāpālika* meaning 'bearer of skulls'. He subsequently wanders through the cosmos as Kapālin ('Skull-bearer'), also named Bhikṣāṭana ('Supreme beggar'), using Brahmā's skull as a begging bowl. During this ceaseless pilgrimage he enters the forest of Deodar, wherein he happens upon a group of ṛṣis engaged in the performance of austerities and ritual fire worship. The ṛṣis have become so enrapt in the external accoutrements of spiritual discipline, however, that they fail to recognise the Lord, Śiva, in his form as a bedraggled vagrant.[42] This can be read as a warning not only about the dangers of over-ritualisation, but also against seeking the spirit in beautiful things alone, all things, no matter how ostensibly ugly, being considered to have their origin in the Divine.

Bhairava is also portrayed as a dancer, frolicking in the macabre environment of the crematory. Wearing a garland of skulls, and scattering the bones and ashes of burnt corpses, he embodies the paradox of joy in the midst of gloom and decay. His revelling displays a transcendence of mortality and worldly fears. 'To him who had overcome death,' comments Kramrisch, 'its shapes—the skulls and bones—were but ornaments swaying with his dancing body.'[43]

As though to inject an extra layer of complexity into the form of Bhairava, in other Purāṇic myths, the same name is attached to one of two sons (the other being Vetāla) who were

---

[42] Cf. Kramrisch 1981: 286-87.
[43] *Ib.*: 296.

born to Tārāvatī (an incarnation of Pārvatī) after her being ravished by Śiva;[44] or, according to another version, the sons emerge from drops of Śiva's seed, spilt when his and Pārvatī's love-making is interrupted by 'the gods'.[45]

Other forms and epithets of Śiva and Śakti

Other forms in which Śiva is represented include Dakṣiṇāmūrti, Haryardhamūrti, and Ardhanārīśvara (see Appendix A, pp. 248-50). The name of the first of these, Dakṣiṇāmūrti, literally translates as 'south-facing', and derives from the fact that, in this form, Śiva is portrayed as a 'universal teacher...[who] was seated facing south...when he taught the sages in a secluded spot on the Himālayas'.[46] He symbolises the perfect guru, epitomising the qualities of poise, strength, self-control, wisdom, and benevolence.

Haryardhamūrti means 'half Hari face', *Hari* being a common name for Viṣṇu. In this form, which is also known as Harihara or Śaṅkaranārāyaṇa, the divine principle is depicted as Śiva and Viṣṇu merged together, the right side of the body being adorned with Śaiva symbols, the left with those of Viṣṇu. It is a clear attempt to present potentially rival deities as merely two aspects of the same principle, emphasising that personalised gods are ways of envisioning the Divine and should not be interpreted too rigidly or dogmatically.

Ardhanārīśvara ('half woman, half Lord') is another image of the human form composed of two distinct halves, Śiva again being the right side, but this time Pārvatī is the left. Here the ultimate identity of the static 'masculine' pole and the dynamic 'feminine' pole, described in Śaiva philosophy, is emphasised.

In addition to the several forms of Śiva outlined above, he is also known by innumerable names and epithets, which refer to aspects of his nature or appearance. Such epithets include: Bhola ('Fool'), Mahādeva ('Great deity'), Mahākāla ('Mighty

---

44 Cf. O'Flaherty 1973: 69.
45 *Ib.*: 308-9.
46 Harshananda 1981: 71.

time'), Mahāyogin ('Great yogin'), Śaṃbhu ('Beneficent'), Śaṅkara ('Auspicious'), Sthāṇu ('Standing firmly, motionless'), Tryambaka or Trilocana ('Three-eyed'),[47] and so on. As Mahāyogin, he has also been called Paśupati, 'Lord of animals', which term denotes control over the so-called 'animal passions', it being the aim of the yogin to master his instincts, feelings, senses and emotions, as opposed to remaining their slave.

Finally, it is important to mention that Śiva's partner, wife or consort is also represented in a variety of forms, and is referred to by many names and epithets. In her placid and beneficent aspect, she is known as Pārvatī ('[Daughter] of the mountains' or 'Mountain stream'), or as Umā ('Child'), Gaurī ('Golden, shining one'), or Satī ('True', 'Faithful'). As the last of these, she is sometimes characterised as being a faithful wife to the point of burning herself on her husband's funeral pyre, an act which has, unfortunately, been interpreted in a literal fashion by a small minority of families in India, who exert a subtle (or, on rare occasions, not so subtle) pressure upon widows to follow Satī's example. Satī's sacrifice is, however, symbolic; she, as the personification of the manifest universe, is 'burnt up' in the process of yoga, as she unites with Śiva and is reabsorbed into her source.

In her other aspects, the Goddess (Devī) can be more active, and even fearsome and violent. In relation to Śiva in his aspect as passive consciousness, Devī is Śakti, the personification of power, energy, activity. As potential force, she is the 'coiled one' or serpent known as Kuṇḍalinī-śakti. She is also represented as Durgā, whose name literally means 'difficult', 'inaccessible' or 'hard to reach'. Under this title, she is usually depicted as a slayer of demons (i.e. the dark or detrimental aspects of human nature), riding a tiger or lion and wielding various weapons with her eight arms. Another of her fearsome aspects—and most monstrous of all—is Kālī, the epitome of

---

[47] 'The three eyes of Śiva represent the sun, the moon and the fire, the three sources of light, life and heat' (Harshananda 1981: 62).

destructiveness, with her drooling blood-red tongue, necklace of skulls, belt of severed arms, three glaring eyes and multiple weapons. The name *Kālī* may mean 'black' or 'the black one', but it can also mean 'time' (*kālī* being the feminine form of *kāla*), which, as Harshananda observes, 'is all-destroying, all-devouring.'[48] She tramples upon the corpse of Śiva, but Śiva is also her foundation, and Kālī is nothing apart from him.

Although an exhaustive exposition of the numerous depictions of Śiva, and of related features of yoga mythology, is beyond the scope of the present study, I trust that this chapter has helped to emphasise not only the tremendous richness and diversity of texture in this field, but also its vast complexity and frequent contradictoriness.[49] In haṭha-yoga, Śiva is both the origin of the teaching—the supreme guru—and the ultimate goal of the practice, the aim being to realise the state enjoyed by the 'breath-conquered yogins' mentioned in the Purāṇic hymn quoted at the beginning of this chapter—to realise, that is, one's true identity as 'the self of Yoga,/ ...without division,/ supernal Śiva!'

---

[48] Harshananda 1981: 114.

[49] Readers interested in Śaiva mythology in particular are referred to the excellent works by O'Flaherty (1973) and Kramrisch (1981) cited in several passages above.

Part Two

THEORETICAL ASPECTS OF HAṬHA-YOGA

5

Haṭha-Yoga and Rāja-Yoga

Praise be to Śrī Ādinātha ('Revered Primal Lord', Śiva) who has taught the haṭha-yoga-vidyā, which is a ladder for those whose will is to ascend to the heights of rāja-yoga. (*HYP* 1.1)

The *HYP* opens with the above śloka, wherein haṭha-yoga is declared to be a means to a higher end, namely rāja-yoga. In this chapter I shall take a close look at the notions of haṭha- and rāja-yoga and show how they relate to one another, as well as to several other 'varieties' of yoga which are commonly mentioned in literature on this subject. In examining yoga's final goal, detailed consideration will be given to Patañjali's definition of yoga as *citta-vṛtti-nirodha* (*YS* 1.2) and to the multiple 'levels' of *samādhi*; such close attention being crucial for an understanding of the purpose of yoga in all its forms.

The various yogas

When encountering the literature of yoga, it is easy to become bewildered by the apparently vast array of different varieties of this soterial discipline. Among the varieties mentioned in the *Bhagavad-Gītā*, for example, are: *jñāna-yoga* (yoga of wisdom, knowledge, true perception), *bhakti-yoga* (yoga of devotion), *karma-yoga* (yoga of action), *dhyāna-yoga* (yoga of meditation), and *sāṃkhya-yoga* (yoga of enumeration [of metaphysical principles]). Those mentioned elsewhere include: *mantra-yoga* (yoga of sound vibration), *laya-yoga* (yoga of dissolution), *kuṇḍalinī-yoga* (yoga of [elivating] Kuṇḍalinī-śakti), *rāja-yoga* (royal or kingly yoga), and the main subject of the present study—haṭha-yoga. Even within haṭha-yoga itself there are multifarious 'schools', 'styles' or 'traditions', often bound up with a particular teacher and usually claiming to be more or less 'authentic'. In the modern era, there exist, for example, schools devoted to: *Aṣṭāṅga Viṅyāsa Yoga* ('eight-limbed moving/flowing yoga'),[1] revived in the present century by Śrīmān T. Krishnamāchārya (1888-1989) of Mysore, South India, and promoted by one of his disciples, K. P. Jois (b. 1915); *Viniyoga*,[2] centred upon the teachings of Krishnamāchārya's son, T. K. V. Desikachar; and *Iyengar Yoga*, propounded by another of Krishnamāchārya's students, B. K. S. Iyengar (b. 1918). To these styles may be added that of the many Sivananda Yoga Vedanta centres around the world, based on the teachings of Swami Sivananda Saraswati of Rishikesh and his foremost disciple, Swami Vishnudevananda; and that of the Bihar School of Yoga, founded by Swami Satyananda Saraswati, as well as several other internationally known schools and lineages. There are also, of course, innumerable lesser-known haṭha teachers diligently handing on their wisdom from one generation to another without desire for worldly fame. All of these, in whole or in part, may be said to promote a form of haṭha-yoga.

In establishing the relationship between the various types of yoga, it is important to reaffirm what the term *yoga* itself means. Its significance is, essentially, twofold: on the one hand it refers to the *goal* of spiritual practice,[3] and, on the other, to

---

[1] *Nyāsa* means 'placing', and the prefix *vi* means 'special' or 'particular'; and thus *viṅyāsa* refers to a series of postures performed in a particular way.

[2] *Viniyoga*, which literally means 'apportionment, distribution, division' (Monier-Williams 1963: 970), is used by Desikachar to denote a form of yoga 'adapted to the needs of the individual' (Desikachar 1995: back cover).

[3] Whenever terms such as 'spiritual practice' and 'spiritual discipline' are used in the present work, they should be understood as short-hand expressions for what is, in actual fact, a system of *mental and physical training* designed to facilitate an improved clarity of perception and awareness of one's true identity. According to yoga philosophy, there can, in a strict sense, be no such thing as 'spiritual practice'; the spirit—i.e. the 'essence' or true Self (puruṣa, ātman)—is in no need of practice, since it is eternally pure and per-

the *path* or technical system for achieving that goal. Now, although the *path* of the various yogas may differ to a greater or lesser degree, the goal invariably consists in some form of liberated state, commonly expressed (at least within Hindu traditions) as the 'union'—or, more accurately, the *identification*—of the personal self (jīvātman) and the supreme Self (paramātman).[4] It is likely that many of the disputes that have arisen between supposedly rival schools of yoga owe more to the semantic difficulties involved in describing unitive mystical states than to actual differences of destination. Furthermore, it is frequently the case that the name of what might appear to be a discrete yoga 'path' refers only to an *aspect* of yoga practice more generally; and thus, accounts of two 'types' of yoga may in fact be describing the same mode of practice, only viewed from a different angle and with the emphasis differently placed. Unnecessary confusion has been caused in the past by commentators who are largely unfamiliar with yoga as a practical discipline having identified 'this' and 'that' kind of yoga as distinct, and perhaps even as antagonistic, when they are, in fact, simply neighbouring facets of a single, though complex, enterprise. Sampurnanand makes this point well when he says that 'Certain aspects of the practice of Yoga have been needlessly apotheosized and elevated to the false dignity of separate sciences, without paying heed to their interrelations.'[5] When, for example, in the *Bhagavad-Gītā* Lord Kṛṣṇa speaks of jñāna-, bhakti- and karma-yoga, he is not talking about three entirely separate ways of carrying out one's spiritual practice,

---

fect. It is, rather, the mind and body that require purification and training, in order that the Self (or spirit) may be *realised*.

[4] The term *yoga* is also used in non-Hindu traditions such as Jainism and Buddhism, but a full examination of such uses is beyond the remit of the present work. It should be noted that, for Buddhists, the notion of an ultimate Self is highly problematic due to the Buddha's apparent repudiation of the idea that any positive statement can be made about the ātman, though there is still a very real sense in which the goal of Buddhist yoga is to reveal the truth about human identity.

[5] Foreword to Banerjea 1962: xxi.

but, rather, about three aspects of the ideal life. The choice to be made by Arjuna, the warrior on the battlefield of Kurukṣetra, which is, by implication, the choice to be made by us all, is not between acting, on the one hand, and being devoted to Brahman on the other, or between acting and seeking revelatory knowledge (jñāna); the choice is between acting out of wisdom or acting out of ignorance. What is required, ultimately, is action (karma) that accords with one's own true nature (*svadharma*), performed with insight (jñāna) and an attitude of worshipful devotion (bhakti) to Brahman; in other words, a combination of all three 'yogas'.

Similarly, haṭha-yoga is not altogether isolated from mantra-, laya-, kuṇḍalinī-[6] and rāja-yoga, for, in a certain sense, each of them interweaves with and penetrates the others. In the somewhat disjointed fifth chapter of the *Śiva-Saṃhitā*, it is stated that each of the four principal varieties of yoga—namely mantra, laya, haṭha and rāja—befits a different grade of *sādhaka* (aspirant); mantra-yoga being suitable for the *mṛdu* (soft, weak or gentle) aspirant, laya for the *madhya* (middling, average) aspirant, haṭha for the *adhimātra* (lit. 'above measure', i.e. above average), and rāja for the *adhimātratama* ('best of the above average', excellent). The very best (*śreṣṭa*), it is said, are able to 'transcend the world [of phenomenal existence] (*laṃghana-kṣama*)' (*ŚS* 5.10). But, although extensive lists of the qualities that characterise each of these grades of aspirant are provided, not enough is said about the four types of yoga to accurately assess the distinctions between them. This lack of clear distinctions implies again that what is being enunciated is a greater emphasis upon an aspect of the yoga process, rather than an individuated form.

Arthur Avalon contends that a difference exists between haṭha-yoga, on the one hand, and mantra-, laya- and rāja-yoga on the other, regarding their respective approaches to prāṇā-

[6] *Kuṇḍalinī-yoga* may be regarded as a direct synonym of *haṭha-yoga*, since the explicit purpose of haṭha is to awaken the Kuṇḍalinī-śakti and facilitate her unimpeded ascension through suṣumnā-nāḍī (cf. pp. 172ff. below).

yāma. 'Prāṇāyāma', he writes, 'is recognized as one of the "limbs" of all the (Aṣṭāṅga) forms of Yoga. But whereas it is used in Mantra-, Laya- and Rāja-Yoga as an auxiliary, the Haṭha-yogī as such regards this regulation and Yoga of breath as the chief means productive of that result (Mokṣa), which is the common end of all schools of Yoga.'[7] It is true that prāṇāyāma is the central practical component of haṭha-yoga, but it is also the case that mantra—understood in the sense of 'sound vibration' rather than simply the audible chanting of sacred phrases—is intrinsic to haṭha, as certain mantras are linked with, and held to emanate from, particular centres of vital force within the subtle body (see Chapter 7, esp. pp. 159ff.), and the 'inner sound' (nāda) becomes the focus of concentration in the practice of nāda-anusandhāna (discussed in Chapter 8, pp. 216-18). Similarly, laya—meaning 'dissolution' or 'absorption'—is precisely what is said to take place in the advanced stages of haṭha-yoga, as the mind becomes increasingly 'absorbed' in the nāda, which is itself the auditory manifestation of Śakti (*HYP* 4.29ff.). Rāja-yoga, too, need not be seen as an alternative system to that of haṭha, for it is, rather, the very culmination of haṭha practice, an idea which will shortly receive further attention. Thus, since mantra and laya may rightly be viewed as continuous with haṭha, and rāja-yoga is the pinnacle of all three, it makes little sense to draw a distinction between them on the basis of some hypothesised difference of approach to prāṇāyāma. Indeed, it is a view common to all traditions of yoga that the connection between breath, prāṇa and mental activity is extremely intimate, and therefore, if the 'common end' of *mokṣa* (liberation) is to be realised, prāṇāyāma—in the sense of control and retention of vital force—is fundamental.

Before moving on to a more detailed discussion of rāja-yoga, it is worth saying a little more about mantra and laya. The word *mantra* has the same verbal root as *manas*, which

---

[7] Avalon 1974: 199.

denotes 'mind' or, more specifically, the faculty of the mind that organises sensory data and internally generated thoughts into intelligible units of perception. The common root is *man*, 'to think', and, as the suffix *tra* implies instrumentality, *mantra* may be translated as 'thought-power', with any *particular* mantra being a 'vehicle' that carries one's mental focus towards subtler levels of self-identity.[8] Since all thoughts are held to constitute 'ripples' within the 'mind-field' (*citta*), and to 'vibrate' at a certain rate, mantras are viewed as embodiments of specific vibrations, which are experienced as more or less subtle sounds. At the grossest level of manifestation, a mantra may take the form of an audible syllable, word or phrase, whose recitation accompanied by intense concentration—a practice known as *mantra-japa*—encourages the mind to conform to the mantra's vibratory rate. 'Beneath' or 'within' such a 'gross' mantra are its more refined aspects, which are inaudible to the ordinary faculty of hearing, but may, through the cultivation of intrapsychic awareness, be perceived as an 'internal sound' (*antar-nāda*). From the time of the Vedas and Upaniṣads onwards, the most potent of all mantras has been considered to be the syllable *om*.[9] Often referred to as *praṇava* (roughly 'word of praise', from the root *nu*, 'to laud'), *om* represents the primal emanation of Brahman, and is the auditory embodiment of Īśvara ('the Lord'), who is *saguṇa-Brahman* ('Brahman with attributes'). In *Yoga-Sūtra* 1.27, for example, it is said that 'expressive of [Īśvara] is praṇava', and its repetition is cited as an aid to meditation (*YS* 1.28).

The power of *om* is noted in the *Manu-Smṛti* (commonly known as *The Laws of Manu*)—an ancient text on Vedic rites and customs—which states that the praṇava should always be uttered at the beginning and end of a lesson in the Veda, for

---

[8] Feuerstein neatly defines *mantra* as 'thought or intention expressed as sound' (1990a: 211).

[9] For a full discussion of the symbolism surrounding this mantra, see, e.g., V.-L. Mitra's essay 'Om Tat Sat', one of the introductory chapters to his translation of the *Yoga-Vāsiṣṭha* (1891: 34-89).

'unless the syllable *Om* precede[s it,] (the lesson) will slip away [from the student], and unless it follow[s it,] it will fade away.'[10] In the *Maitri-Upaniṣad*, meanwhile, *om* is declared to be the arrow, whose tip is the mind, which is fired by the 'bow' of the aspirant's body towards a target, dark and unknown:

> Pierce the darkness, and thou wilt come to That which is not shrouded in darkness... —Brahman... And seeing Him, thou wilt draw nigh to immortality.[11]

In addition to contemplating the nāda, which resonates spontaneously within the yogin's subtle body as a consequence of Kuṇḍalinī's ascension, several haṭha texts also emphasise japa of the *oṃ* mantra as a means of purifying and focussing the mind. The *Gorakṣa-Śataka* (88-89), for example, states that:

> That wonderful *bīja* (seed)—that supreme light *om*—should be constantly recited, worshipped with the body, and reflected upon by the mind.
> Just as the lotus leaf [is not wet] by water, so, by constantly reciting the praṇava, the pure and the impure alike remain untainted by sin (*pāpa*).

Again, then, it should be stressed that mantra-yoga and haṭha-yoga are thoroughly intertwined. Mantra provides the internal focus for the haṭha-yogin, while the haṭha techniques for ridding the body of impurities are essential if the more advanced stages of mantra-yoga are to be attained. The mere repetition of praṇava does not constitute mantra-yoga—the whole of one's body and mind must become assimilated into the sound.

So what of laya-yoga? According to ancient Indian cosmology, on the macrocosmic level, every 'inhalation' or 'night' of Brahmā engenders an involutionary process culminating in laya (or *pralaya*)—a cosmic hiatus wherein all manifest phenomena are dissolved. The state of pralaya is, however, pregnant with the potential for a new evolution, which occurs upon an

---

[10] *MS* 2.74, trans. Bühler 1886: 44.
[11] *MU* 24, trans. Zaehner 1966: 234.

'exhalation', or the dawning of a new 'day', of Brahmā, these 'days' and 'nights' of Brahmā (the productive or emanative aspect of Brahman) being held to last for thousands of millions of years respectively, and to be part of a spiralling process that extends backwards and forwards in time to infinity (cf. Appendix D). These cosmic evolutions and involutions are held to be echoed in the 'descension into gross matter' of human self-identity, and the subsequent 'returning to the source' thereof. This return to, or identification as, the source of all things is considered to be inevitable, though it may take innumerable lifetimes to be realised in any particular human being. *Laya-yoga* denotes the acceleration of this process by means of various yoga techniques, and no single system of yoga has a monopoly over the term. As noted already, in haṭha-yoga manuals such as the *HYP*, *laya* is the term used to describe the mind's 'absorption' into the nāda, and is also one of several synonyms of the supreme state of Brahman-identity (*HYP* 4.3-4), of which *rāja-yoga* is another (see below). Thus, at least from the haṭha viewpoint, laya-yoga is an integral aspect of haṭha-yoga.

Rāja-yoga

Rāja derives from *rāj*, meaning both 'to shine' and 'to govern', and hence *rāja-yoga* may be variously translated as 'kingly', 'ruling', 'regal' or 'radiant' yoga. Although the term does not in fact appear in the *Yoga-Sūtra*, it has been commonly used by later exponents of yoga to denote either (a) the whole system of aṣṭāṅga-yoga outlined by Patañjali, or (b) the final three 'limbs' of that system, the combined performance of which is also known as *saṃyama* (roughly 'restraining' or 'holding together', fixing one's attention upon a single object). The three component aspects of saṃyama—namely dhāraṇā (concentration), dhyāna (meditation) and samādhi (identification)—are termed the *antaraṅga* ('inner limbs') as opposed to the so-called 'outer limbs' (*bahiraṅga*) of yama through to pratyāhāra,[12] as saṃyama is more explicitly concerned with mental training. Sometimes this distinction is employed to distinguish haṭha- from rāja-yoga, the claim being that haṭha is concerned only with 'external' aspects, while rāja constitutes 'the real practice of Yoga—namely, the understanding and complete mastery over the mind.'[13] In the haṭha texts themselves, haṭha-yoga is indeed viewed as a necessary precursor to rāja-yoga, but it should be emphasised that the latter term is used principally as a synonym for the highest state of samādhi—the pinnacle or 'crowning glory' of yoga—and *not* to denote any process extrinsic to haṭha itself. Haṭha is held to be a complete system, and to constitute the means by which the end known as rāja is achieved. Thus we find, in the *HYP* for example, pronouncements such as the following:

> haṭha-yoga-vidyā...is, as it were, a ladder to climb to the lofty heights of rāja-yoga. (1.1)
>
> By mastery of *kevala-kumbhaka* (absolute retention), *vāyu* (vital breath) is held still, and also, without doubt, the state of rāja-yoga [is attained]. (2.74-75)
>
> At the culmination of prāṇa-retention, the mind (citta) should be without any perceptual object; verily, by practise of [this] yoga is the state of rāja-yoga arrived at. (2.77)
>
> Practitioners without complete knowledge of rāja-yoga are ostensibly performers of haṭha, but lack the fruit of their efforts. (4.79)
>
> All the practices of haṭha and laya are for the attainment of rāja-yoga; one who ascends the peak of rāja-yoga avoids *kāla* (lit. 'time', i.e. death). (4.103)

---

12 All eight limbs have already been listed on pages 10 and 35 above.

13 Editor of Satchidananda's translation of the *YS* (1990: xi). In his *Encyclopedic Dictionary of Yoga*, Feuerstein notes that 'It [rāja-yoga] is often contrasted with *hatha-yoga*, in which case *rāja-yoga* stands for the higher spiritual practices, whereas *hatha-yoga* is seen as a preparatory discipline' (1990a: 285).

In *HYP* 2.76, it is stated that there can be 'no success in rāja-yoga without haṭha, nor in haṭha without rāja-yoga; therefore the practise of both brings completion (*niṣpatti*).' This should, I contend, be taken to mean, not that there are two modes of procedure—one called haṭha and the other rāja—which are mutually reflexive; but, rather, that the *goal* known as rāja-yoga cannot be achieved without the *practice* of haṭha, and the practice of haṭha remains incomplete until rāja-yoga is attained. The first line of the same śloka appears in the *Śiva-Saṃhitā* (5.181), with the second line reading: 'therefore the yogī should follow the instructions in haṭha received from a true guru (*sadguru*)', thereby emphasising that it is *haṭha* which leads to rāja-yoga, and not vice versa or that the one assists the other. It is thus somewhat perverse to present haṭha as 'inferior' to rāja-yoga, as though the two represented a 'lesser' and a 'greater' form of yoga respectively; or, even worse, to view haṭha as 'decadent'[14] in contradistinction to some imaginary 'pure' alternative.

Some gurus may lay greater stress upon mental concentration, and others upon the cleansing of the gross and subtle bodies—and the former may tend to label their system *rāja-yoga*, and the latter refer to their's as *haṭha-yoga*—but, in the final analysis, bodily purity *and* mental acuity are required, and in the haṭha texts we find both receiving attention. A skilled teacher would, of course, emphasise what is most important for each particular student according to the latter's present condition.

Commenting upon the spiritual methodology of Gorakṣa, one of the legendary founders of haṭha-yoga, Sampurnanand makes some pertinent remarks regarding the reasons for haṭha's bodily emphasis:

> It was not that he [Gorakṣa] believed that the practice of bodily contortions or the control of bodily functions was the final goal of Yoga, nor was he under the delusion that such control of the body

---

[14] As does, for example, J. H. Woods 1966, cited in Feuerstein 1990a: 131-32.

would, in and by itself, produce *Samādhi* and self-realisation. What he did, and quite rightly, was to emphasise the irrevocable necessity of going through the lower stages, which are apt to be neglected and ignored because they seem so difficult and, by a process of wishful thinking, so unnecessary.[15]

It is, perhaps, inevitable that theoreticians who are unfamiliar with yoga praxis will seek to find neat pigeonholes for the various aspects of yoga; and the fact that haṭha manuals *include* information about advanced postural and breathing techniques has led some commentators to assume that this is *all* haṭha consists of. It is high time, however, that the holistic nature of haṭha, as a discipline intent upon the very summit of rāja-yoga, were acknowledged.

The goal of yoga

[T]o find ourselves is to know our source. (Plotinus)[16]

HYP 2.78 lists the indicators of success in haṭha-yoga as follows: 'beauty (*vapus*) and slimness (*kṛśatva*) of physique, radiant complexion (*vadane prasannatā*), the "bursting forth" (*sphuṭa*) of the "inner sound" (nāda), clear eyes, freedom from illness, control over [subtle] seminal fluid (bindu), intensification of the "inner fire" (agni), and purity of the nāḍīs.' Such signs do not constitute the final goal of haṭha, but are, rather, conditional aims of the discipline, useful insofar as they assist in the attainment of—and indicate progress towards—samādhi or rāja-yoga, the latter being more fully discussed in the *HYP*'s fourth chapter.

In order to establish a clearer idea of what is meant by the term *rāja-yoga*, it may be helpful to begin by listing its synonyms given in *HYP* 4.3-4. These are:

samādhi—union, integration;
unmanī—negation of the (cognitive) mind;

---

[15] Foreword to Banerjea 1962: xxii.
[16] *Enneads* 6.9.7, quoted in Murphy 1992: 192.

manonmanī—fixedness of mind;[17]
amaratva—immortality (lit. 'non-death-ness');
laya—absorption, dissolution;
tattva—'that-ness', truth, realness;
śūnyāśūnya—void yet not void, voidless void;
paramapada—supreme state;
amanaska—beyond (cognitive) mind;
advaita—non-duality;
nirālamba—without support (i.e. self-sufficient);
nirañjana—without stain, pure;
jīvanmukti—living liberation;
sahaja—ownmost or natural state;
turya—fourth state, i.e. the state beyond wakefulness (*jāgrat*), dream-sleep (*svapna*) and deep sleep (*nidrā*).

It is a state-of-being characterised by Svātmārāma as perfect equilibrium, in which nothing is lacking; the union, or identification, of jīvātman and paramātman (*HYP* 4.7); the dissolution of the distinction between manas (cognitive mind) and ātman (Self), just as salt dissolves into water (*ib.* 4.5). The mind's absorption in the Self coincides with, or is attendant upon, the cessation of the movement of prāṇa, which 'dissolves into the void (*śūnya*)' (*ib.* 4.10).

Although a term such as *unmanī* suggests that, in the highest state, the mind is somehow negated, confused or perplexed,[18] this should be understood as a *transcendence* of ordinary modes of perception—a 'shaking off' of the conceptual categories through which we ordinarily view reality—and the attainment of unimpeded awareness which, from the standpoint of the everyday mind, is unintelligible. The state involves a complete mergence of 'knowing' and 'being': it is not so much that one *perceives* the eternal essence of reality, as that one knows oneself to *be* that essence. Reality, no longer divided into 'self' and 'other', is realised to be All One.

---

[17] Vasu 1976: 114.
[18] Cf. Monier-Williams 1963: 194.

At this juncture it is worth turning our attention to the definition of yoga provided in the second sūtra of Patañjali's *Yoga-Sūtra*,[19] for it is by unravelling this terse statement that one may approach an understanding of the goal of all yoga systems. The sūtra comprises just four words: *Yogaś citta-vṛtti-nirodhaḥ*; but within those four words lies the central doctrine of yoga. The first word, *yogaś*, is *yoga* in the nominative case,[20] and the sūtra equates this with 'citta-vṛtti-nirodha'. Although an apparently straightforward definition is being offered, the complexity of these Sanskrit terms allows for a wide range of alternative translations. Below is a relatively small selection of the numerous existent renderings of the sūtra:

> Yoga is the annihilation of the modifications of the mind. (Sivananda 1955b: 62)
>
> [Yoga is] the neutralization of the alternating waves in consciousness. (Yogananda 1981: 224)
>
> Yoga is the control of the modifications of the mind-field. (Arya 1986: 93)
>
> Yoga is the dissolution of vṛttis into their origin in the mind-field. (*Ib.*: 95)
>
> The restraint of the modifications of the mind-stuff is Yoga. (Satchidananda 1990: 3)
>
> Yoga is the cessation of the turnings of thought. (B. S. Miller 1996: 29)

In the above examples, *citta* is variously rendered as 'mind', 'consciousness', 'mind-field', 'mind-stuff' and 'thought'. None of these terms entirely captures its meaning, although

---

[19] *YS* 1.2 is known as a *lakṣana-* (indicative) or *nirdeśa-* (descriptive, definitive) sūtra, as it defines the subject matter of the treatise.

[20] It would normally be *yogaḥ*, but, for reasons of euphony—or, as it is called in Sanskrit grammar, *sandhi* (juncture)—the final 'ḥ' becomes 'ś' when it is followed by the 'c' of *citta*.

only the last is unhelpful and misleading. *Citta* may be regarded as a kind of short-hand for *antaḥkaraṇa*—the 'inner cause' or 'inner instrument'—which, according to the Sāṃkhya darśana, comprises the three aspects of buddhi, ahaṃkāra and manas.[21] Buddhi is the most refined aspect of the three and is, as Paul Schweizer remarks, 'responsible for the higher level intellectual functions, which require intuition, insight and reflection.'[22] In Patañjali's definition of yoga as *citta-vṛtti-nirodha*, it is the buddhi aspect of citta which is most strongly implied, since it is buddhi which has the potential to 'reflect' the pure light of puruṣa. *Ahaṃkāra* literally means 'I-maker', and denotes the faculty or tendency for producing a sense of egoity and for attaching the notion of 'mineness' to the activities of buddhi and manas. Manas (from the root *man*, 'to think') has two functions, one of which is to organise the raw data obtained via the senses into a usable picture of reality; the other being to 'take care of' experiences (composed of various arrangements of sense-data) in the form of 'subliminal impressions (*saṃskāra*) and memory traces (*vāsanā*).'[23] Comprising all three aspects, then, *citta* stands for the mind in its entirety, but perhaps with a more dynamic emphasis than is afforded by the term *antaḥkaraṇa*. Since mind, in the Indian context at least, is more a conglomeration of faculties and phenomena than a single entity, it is easy to see why some translators have opted for terms such as 'mind-field' (in the case of Arya) and 'mind-stuff' (Swami Satchidananda) in an attempt to approximate the concept of citta. Barbara Miller's rendering of *citta* as 'thought' is misleading due to its narrowness. Thoughts may arise within the 'sphere' of citta, but citta is not coextensive with them.

Vṛtti refers to a 'turning', 'rolling' or 'whirling' motion, such as in the spinning of a wheel. It suggests movement, momentum, habituation, and may also signify a 'whirl', 'wave', 'ripple' or other distorting influence upon a pool of otherwise

---

21 *Sāṃkhya-Kārikā* 32.
22 Schweizer 1993: 848.
23 B. S. Miller 1996: 15.

calm water. In yoga psychology, the term denotes distortions or modifications in the perceptual capacity of citta. Thus, if *citta* is defined as 'mind', *citta-vṛtti* are the 'modifications of the mind' which prevent the light of puruṣa—whose nature is held to be pure consciousness—from being clearly reflected, and which therefore prevent us from identifying ourselves as, and abiding in, the true Seer or Self (*YS* 1.3-4). The analogy of the moon and its reflection is relevant here. In Vācaspati Miśra's *ṭīkā* (commentary) on the *Yoga-Sūtra* and *Yoga-Bhāṣya*, for example, he writes that,

> Just as the full moon, although stationary and round, appears to be moving and ruffled without any activity on its part, due to its reflection in the clear moving water, so *puruṣa* without any activity or attachment on its part, appears to possess activity or attachment on account of its reflection in the mind [buddhi].[24]

The vṛttis (movements, ripples), then, must be pacified before the Self can be realised in its fullness, and this process involves a systematic transformation of citta. Since many of the vṛttis—or, rather, many of the tendencies towards the emergence of vṛttis—are so firmly ingrained within the mind, far more than a mere 'ironing out' of mental crinkles is required; the process of yoga must be one involving deep penetration and the uprooting of habituated psychic modes. Any vṛtti (mental state or process) has the power of reinforcing itself each time it occurs, leaving behind 'subliminal impressions' in the mind known as *saṃskāras*. Saṃskāras are (analogically) like grooves or ruts that provoke automatic or inhibited responses to situations, and for this reason Feuerstein has referred to them as 'subliminal activators'.[25]

---

[24] *Tattva-Vaiśāradi* 4.22, trans. Whicher 1992: 159-60.

[25] Feuerstein 1990b: 179. Svoboda (1998: 40) has remarked that *saṃskāra* derives from *sama* ('same') plus *kāra* (from *kṛ*, 'to do'), and thus 'means the doing of something in a consistent, reproducible, digestible way.' In another context, *saṃskāra* denotes a Hindu rite or ceremony, but we are not concerned with that context here.

Yoga psychology has it that citta—and even its most transparent or *sāttvika* aspect, buddhi,—is not the ultimate experiencer or perceiver. It is, rather, a phenomenon, i.e. an item of perceived, or potentially perceivable, reality (as distinguished from reality as it is in itself); and the presence of any phenomenon necessarily *implies* the co-presence of a perceiver that, or who, is distinct from it. The view held by the Sāṃkhya and Yoga darśanas is that this 'implied perceiver' is *absolutely non-phenomenal*; that is, it can never become an object of consciousness, since its nature is, in a sense, consciousness itself. This Perceiver, Seer or Self whose nature is consciousness is termed *puruṣa*, and it is puruṣa that is held to 'shine through', 'illuminate' and 'be reflected in' citta, the latter principle being essentially insentient in conformity with all aspects of the manifest universe. When Paramahansa Yogananda, then, speaks of citta as 'consciousness' (quoted above), it should be understood as *transitive* consciousness only, i.e. one's consciousness *of* an object, which takes place in the sphere of citta but only occurs at all due to the 'presence' of puruṣa. Citta may be regarded as a *vehicle* for consciousness, providing a mechanism by which puruṣa can perceive and enjoy its own nature; and, for this enjoyment to be realised to the fullest possible extent, citta must be made 'pure'; in other words, its sāttvika (translucent, lucid) component must be maximised. Characterising citta as a mirror, we might say that all smudges and stains must be removed from its surface; or, using the already mentioned analogy of an expanse of water, citta must be made free of disturbing currents, waves and ripples. It is the 'dissolution' of these distorting factors that constitutes nirodha.

Monier-Williams defines *nirodha*[26] as 'restraint, check, control, suppression, destruction,'[27] while Feuerstein opts for 'restriction'.[28] Of all these terms, however, Pandit Usharbudh

---

[26] The spelling of *nirodha* with a final 'ḥ' occurs in the original sūtra because the word is in the nominative case.
[27] Monier-Williams 1963: 554.
[28] Feuerstein 1990a: 239.

Arya agrees only with 'control', stating, with regard to 'suppression' and 'restriction', that 'Nothing can be further from the intent of Patañjali and Vyāsa. *Nirodha* is neither suppression nor restriction, nor even absence.'[29] Arya himself presents two possible translations of Patañjali's second sūtra, both of which have been quoted above (p. 107). In the first, *nirodha* is rendered as 'control', and, in the second, as 'dissolution'. On this view, a fine distinction is drawn between the notion of vṛttis 'dissolving' or 'merging' into citta, on the one hand, and that of 'rendering the vṛttis non-existent' on the other.[30] Yoga, says Arya, consists in the former, but not in the latter. The vṛttis are not destroyed or 'annihilated' (to use Sivananda's term), for they are not separate from citta. As Bhojarāja, writing in the 11th century C.E., comments, 'The vṛttis are the parts (*aṅga*) of the whole (*aṅgin*), which is [citta]';[31] hence to annihilate the vṛttis would be to annihilate the mind; and, although certain passages in yoga texts do imply that a 'deadening' of the mind is desirable, it should be remembered that the mind only 'dies' in the sense that it becomes such a pure reflector of puruṣa as to appear indistinguishable from it. A common error made by those who comment upon yoga theory without being fully conversant with its practice is to assume that nirodha means 'dulling' and ultimately 'killing' the mind, and thereby eradicating any possibility of continuing to function as a human personality. Upon such an assumption, the goal of yoga is viewed as an ontological severance between puruṣa (the source of consciousness) and prakṛti (the source of phenomena, including citta) in which the mind is expunged. In the words of Lionel Barnett, for example, puruṣa, in the final stage of yoga, 'casts off the broken fetter of *Buddhi*, and dwells for evermore in solitude (*kaivalya*).'[32] 'Solitude', like 'isolation', presents a

---

[29] Arya 1986: 95.

[30] *Ib.*: 97.

[31] Quoted in Arya *ib.*: 96.

[32] Barnett 1905: 34. Such an interpretation has also been propounded by Koelman (1970: 249-50) and Zaehner (1969: 31), to name but two.

potentially misleading impression of the yogic notion of *kaivalya*, for this state should not be viewed as one in which puruṣa is isolated *from* anything but, rather, as the realisation of puruṣa's 'absoluteness'.

Ian Whicher has tried to avoid the pitfalls of an ontologically-biased reading of the goal of yoga by reinterpreting *citta-vṛtti-nirodha* as 'the cessation of [*the misidentification with*] the modifications (*vṛtti*) of the mind (*citta*)',[33] and this has given a much needed emphasis to the epistemological connotations of yoga. 'It is my contention', writes Whicher, 'that *nirodha* denotes an epistemological emphasis and refers to the transformation of self-understanding, not the ontological cessation of *prakṛti* (i.e. the mind and *vṛttis*).'[34] Whicher's refreshing interpretation allows for the temporary dissolution of all mental content into the ground of citta during supra-cognitive states of puruṣa-identification while, at the same time, stressing the possibility and desirability of an ongoing condition of *embodied freedom* (*jīvanmukti*). The latter condition may be envisaged as one in which the yogin's capacity to operate in the world as an intelligent and moral actor is maximised, not diminished, by the translocation of his or her sense of self-identity that puruṣa-realisation involves. The yogin is no longer 'attached to', or 'misidentified with', the mind and its modifications, and is therefore able to express himself or herself *through* or *by means of* those mental processes without being enslaved by them; without, that is, relinquishing the heightened and expanded sense of Selfhood intimated by the term *kaivalya*.[35]

In the context of haṭha-yoga, the term *nirodha* relates not only to the dissolution and control of mental vṛttis but also to the intended effect of yoga practice upon the 'vital force' or

---

[33] Whicher 1995: 47. The brackets are Whicher's but the emphasis has been added.

[34] *Ib.*: 49.

[35] The fullest and most recent presentation of Whicher's thesis can be found in his book *The Integrity of the Yoga Darśana: A Reconsideration of Classical Yoga* (1998).

'life principle' known variously as *prāṇa*, *vāta* or *vāyu*. The relationship between citta and prāṇa is held to be extremely intimate, any change in the condition of one having a corresponding effect upon that of the other. *HYP* 2.2 states, for example, that,

> when *vāta* is disturbed, then citta is disturbed; when [vāta is] undisturbed, [then citta is] undisturbed; thus the yogī attains steadiness (*sthaṇutva*) [by means of] *vāyuṃ nirodhayet*.

In the phrase *vāyuṃ nirodhayet* ('the nirodha of prāṇa'), it is inappropriate to translate *nirodha* as 'dissolution', for the yogin's aim is to *retain* the vital principle within the body, not to dissolve it. Here, then, nirodha may be understood as a 'suspension (of flow)' or the 'harnessing' of prāṇa, this latter notion being supported by the bestial metaphor used in *HYP* 2.15:

> Just as a lion, elephant or tiger becomes tame very gradually, so vāyu should be treated with [equal] care, lest it kill the practitioner (*sādhaka*).

Prāṇa (the vital force) and prāṇāyāma (the method of harnessing it) will receive fuller attention in Chapters 7 and 8 respectively. Let us now turn to the important notion of *samādhi*.

Degrees of samādhi

Among the terms used in yogic literature to refer to the highest state(s) of self-identification, *samādhi* is one of the most common. It appears as a synonym of *rāja-yoga* in the *HYP*, and also occurs in other haṭha manuals such as the *Gheraṇḍa-Saṃhitā*, the seventh chapter of which is devoted to a discussion of 'samādhi-yoga'. Furthermore, in his commentary on the opening sūtra of the *Yoga-Sūtra*, Vyāsa states that 'yoga is samādhi' (*YB* 1.1), thereby drawing attention to the crucial position of samādhi within yoga praxis. The respective meanings of *yoga* and *samādhi* are, indeed, very close: just as the former can denote the 'joining' or 'yoking' of two things, so *samādhi* can mean 'putting together', 'integration', or 'completion'. In the context of spiritual discipline—or the training of the mind to *reflect* one's spiritual nature—both terms signify more than a mere 'joining together', referring, rather, to the *identification* of the apprehender (*grahītṛ*), the apprehended (*grāhya*) and the activity of apprehension (*grahaṇa*) (*YS* 1.41) that occurs as a result of intense meditation (saṃyama) upon an object.

Objects employed for the purpose of meditation are various. Much of the third chapter of the *Yoga-Sūtra*, known as the 'Vibhūti-pāda' (*vibhūti* meaning 'gift', 'manifestation', 'offering'), comprises a list of numerous possible objects upon which saṃyama may be performed, along with the special powers thereby accrued. Among the objects mentioned are: sounds or words (*śabda*); qualities such as 'friendliness' (*maitrī*) and the 'strength of elephants'; the 'inner light' (*pravṛttyāloka*, lit. the 'coming forth of light'); the sun (sūrya) and moon (candra); the 'circle of the navel' (*nābhi-cakra*) and other centres in the 'subtle body' (*YS* 3.17ff.). In the *Gheraṇḍa-Saṃhitā* (6.1-22) three modes of meditation (dhyāna) are outlined, namely *sthūla-* (gross), *jyotir-* (light) and *sūkṣma-* (subtle) dhyāna. The first involves using creative visualisation to place before one's mind's eye the image of one's guru, a deity, or some other object such as a 'lotus centre' (*padma*) in the subtle body. The object in this case is only 'gross' (*sthūla*) in the sense that it is perceived *as though* it were solid and distinct. Jyotir- (or *tejo-*) dhyāna is meditation upon, or exclusive contemplation of, the 'inner light' of the 'living self' (jīvātman). This light or 'flame' may be contemplated in the *mūlādhāra-cakra* (corresponding to the perineum), or as the luminous expression of praṇava (the syllable *oṃ*) in the 'brow centre' (*ājñā-cakra*). Sūkṣma-dhyāna, according to Gheraṇḍa, is the contemplation of the awakened Kuṇḍalinī force as she ascends along the 'royal path' (*rāja-mārga*) and 'unites with' the ātman, or 'true Self' (*GS* 6.18-19). 'The yogin', it is declared, 'achieves success (siddhi) in this [sūkṣma-] dhyāna-yoga by *śāṃbhavī-mudrā*' (*GS* 6.20), śāṃbhavī-mudrā being described earlier in the text (*GS* 3.64) as fixing one's attention in the 'inner eye' (*netrāntara*) and 'beholding the Self' (cf. pp. 215-16 below).

The three types of dhyāna specified in the *Gheraṇḍa-Saṃhitā* may be seen as progressively more subtle grades of meditation, requiring increased concentration, and furnishing more potent results with regard to the status of one's self-identity and perception of reality. First an image with a clear form is meditated upon; then the object is simply light, without any perceptible boundaries; and finally one becomes absorbed in the true formless nature of the Self. The notion of successive 'levels' of intense meditation to the point of identification with the object meditated upon is presented more clearly in several other yoga treatises. An example is the process of *nādānu-sandhāna* (meditation upon the inner sound) described in the fourth chapter of the *HYP*, and this will be discussed later (pp. 216-18 below); here, however, it will be useful to provide at least a brief explanation of the several stages of samādhi as presented in the *Yoga-Sūtra*, for this schematic goes some way to assisting our understanding of the whole purpose behind yoga practice.

The first distinction to be made concerning the different degrees of samādhi is that between *saṃprajñāta-samādhi* on the one hand, and *asaṃprajñāta-samādhi* on the other. This distinction is first made by Vyāsa in his commentary on *Yoga-Sūtra* 1.1 and refers to the difference between 'cognitive' and 'supracognitive' states of self-identity. *Saṃprajñāta* means 'integrative knowledge'—i.e. cognising an object, 'knowing' that object, and thus, in an epistemological sense, *becoming one with* that object—whereas *asaṃprajñāta* refers to a state in which all objective cognition has been transcended and one has 'become', or *identified oneself as*, puruṣa, the ultimate *subject*. Before saying more about this highest state of samādhi, let us first attempt to be clear about the lower stages.

Saṃprajñāta-samādhi

In this stage of samādhi—which, in addition to 'samādhi of integrative knowledge', may be termed 'cognitive samādhi' or 'samādhi with cognitive support'—the mind is so intently focussed upon a single object that all extraneous vṛttis are dissolved. Citta takes the form of its object, and thus the meditator identifies with that object. Since all perceptible objects are held to be manifestations of prakṛti—the foundational source of extension and perceptibility—any object is a potential 'gateway' to that source; and, since the mind, too, is an object, and thus has its basis in prakṛti, such 'gateways' open into deeper layers of one's own nature. The crucial point is that, according to the metaphysics of Sāṃkhya-Yoga, when prakṛti 'gives rise to' increasingly dense and perceptible 'layers of substance' (*tattva*) she does not, as it were, 'become' or 'transform into' those layers. Rather, she remains as the undifferentiated substratum of a multidimensional universe of apparently individuated items. How, or in what form, any particular item is perceived—whether as 'gross' physical matter, or as 'subtle' matter, or as the essence or ground of all matter—depends not upon the item itself, but upon the *depth of perception* on the part of the perceiver; and it is this 'perceptive depth' that the mind-training of yoga is intended to achieve.

No matter what object the yogin meditates upon—whether it be the image of a deity, a cosmological symbol (*yantra*), a sacred phrase or 'word-of-power' (mantra), or any of innumerable other possible objects—the results obtained in saṃprajñāta-samādhi may be more-or-less roughly divided into the following four 'stages' or 'levels', which are listed by Vyāsa in *Yoga-Bhāṣya* 1.1 and by Patañjali in *Yoga-Sūtra* 1.17, and are discussed in various commentaries thereon.[36]

---

[36] Over the centuries, various commentators have proposed competing schematics for the different stages of samādhi, these arguments chiefly concerning which of the more refined tattvas is identified with in *ānanda-* and *asmitā-*samāpatti. The schematic presented here is based on Vyāsa's commentary (*YB* 1.17), and is in basic agreement with that elaborated by Arya (1986: 219-47).

1. *Vitarka-samāpatti*[37]

Vitarka generally means 'thinking about' or 'contemplation', and in yoga it has the technical meaning of cognising, to the point of identifying with, a sthūla (gross) object, including anything partaking of one or more of the sixteen *viśeṣa*s (particularised tattvas) (cf. table of tattvas, p. 52 above). In practical terms, it refers to the 'internalisation' of an apprehendable object (*grāhya*) such as, for example, the sun or moon, a star or image of a deity, etc. through the process of intense meditation. The practice is subdivided into *savitarka-* and *nirvitarka*-samāpatti, the former term denoting the identification with a grāhya accompanied by an associated word and concept, and the latter denoting the 'direct', unaccompanied identification with that grāhya (*YS* 1.42-43).

2. *Vicāra-samāpatti*

Deeper than the level of contemplation signified by *vitarka* is that of *vicāra*-samāpatti, in which the vṛtti of the 'gross form' of an object of meditation 'dissolves' into that of its 'subtle aspect', the subtle aspect partaking of the so-called *aviśeṣa*s (unparticularised tattvas), comprising the five *tanmātra*s (subtle principles)[38] plus ahaṃkāra. Arya notes that, 'As the immediate cause of the *tan-mātrās*, ahaṁkāra begins to be brought under control in this samādhi, but primarily it is the object of concentration in the next samādhi [i.e. *ānanda-samāpatti*, see below].'[39] One way of describing what takes place in vicāra-samāpatti is to say that, as *vairāgya* (non-attachment) is cultivated towards the

---

[37] *Samāpatti* may be defined as 'concordance' or 'synchronicity' and, in the context of yoga, it means 'identification in samādhi' (Whicher 1992: 260). The four versions of samāpatti outlined in this section are therefore merely variant modes of (saṃprajñāta-) samādhi.

[38] A more literal translation of *tanmātra* would be 'extension-as-such' or 'measure of extension', but 'subtle principle' or 'subtle element' is perhaps more helpful.

[39] Arya 1986: 230.

gross aspect of an object, identification with the *abstract ground* of any particular sense-datum begins to occur. This 'abstract ground' consists in the 'soundness' or 'audibility' of a sound, the 'tangibility' of a touch-sensation, the qualities of 'colour-as-such' and 'formness' in a visual object, and so on. Like vitarka-samāpatti, the practice is subdivided into *savicāra* and *nirvicāra* varieties, the nuance between them being, according to Vyāsa, that in savicāra-samāpatti the subtle object is experienced as though conditioned by relations of space, time and causation, whereas in nirvicāra-samāpatti the same object 'is not delimited by [such factors], nor limited to those attributes which are apparent only in its present time. All of its possibilities and potentials are realized as being one with an undivided and unitary intelligence (buddhi).'[40]

3. *Ānanda-samāpatti*

Although, in Vedānta theology, *ānanda* denotes the supreme and unbroken 'bliss' of absolute awareness, and thus appears in the threefold characterisation of Brahman as *saccidānanda*,[41] in the context of samprajñāta-samādhi it refers to the *conditional* state of 'rapture' or 'intense happiness' resulting from the transcendence of identification with the tanmātras. In ānanda-samāpatti, the yogin identifies with ahaṃkāra, the faculty of citta responsible for identification itself; in other words, self-identity has become centred in the *instrument* of apprehension, and the vṛttis of identification with gross and subtle elements have been dissolved therein.[42]

---

[40] *Ib.*: 402-403. Cf. *YB* 1.44.

[41] *Sac* (*sat*: truth, being) + *cid* (*cit*: consciousness) + *ānanda* (bliss).

[42] Cf. Baba 1976: 9 (n.2). Vācaspati Miśra suggests (*Tattva-Vaiśāradi* 1.46) that, as with vitarka- and vicāra-, ānanda- and asmitā-samāpatti should be divided into *sa-* and *nir-* varieties. Such a model assumes, however, that the conceptual attributes of space, time and causation, that were presumably transcended in the nirvicāra stage, have been re-attributed to the more refined tattvas of ahaṃkāra (in the case of ānanda-) and buddhi (in the case of asmitā-

4. *Asmitā-samāpatti*
Asmitā-samāpatti is the final stage of saṃprajñāta-samādhi and consists in identifying oneself with the source of 'I-am-ness'—i.e. the highest, most sāttvika, psychic faculty, namely buddhi or mahat. The use of the term *asmitā* is slightly confusing, given that it may ordinarily denote the sense of egoity generated by ahaṃkāra; in the present context, however, Ian Whicher suggests that it be understood to mean 'the pure "am-ness" that is still first personal but not egoistic.'[43] Invoking the water analogy that we have already drawn attention to, Vyāsa describes the mind (citta) that has achieved the state asmitā-samāpatti as 'pacific and infinite like a great ocean without any waves'.[44]

Thus we see that, according to the doctrine codified in the classical yoga texts, the discipline of samādhi engenders the systematic dissolution of gross into increasingly subtle vṛttis. With each progressive stage of samprajñāta-samādhi comes the nirodha of vṛttis associated with previous stages. In other words, a honing takes place of the practitioner's perception and sense of identity, enabling him or her to move on to more refined 'targets'. In his commentary on *Yoga-Sūtra* 1.17, Vācaspati Miśra draws an analogy between samādhi and archery, stating that,

> Just as the novice archer first hits only a 'gross' target, and then, later, a more 'subtle' one, so the yogin begins by contemplating objects constituted by the gross elements (mahābhūtas)...before aiming at more refined objects. In this way, increasingly subtle levels of experience are uncovered. The object-supported mental contemplation (*cittasya-ālambane*) is directed [in progressive

samāpatti), and hence it does not conform to the notion of a graded progression of mental states, from savitarka- up to asmitā-samāpatti (cf. Whicher 1992: 278).

[43] Whicher 1998: 245.

[44] *YB* 1.36, trans. Arya 1986: 355.

stages] towards the gross phenomena, the tanmātras and the unmanifest ground that underlies them.[45]

Saṃprajñāta-samādhi is designed to take the yogin to the point at which his or her apperceptive faculty is acute enough to distinguish between 'the three essential...categories postulated by Sāṃkhya', namely (a) the phenomenal manifestations of prakṛti (*vyakta*), (b) prakṛti herself (*avyakta*), and (c) puruṣa.[46] The ability to (epistemically) 'hold apart' these categories is called *vijñāna* (special or discriminative knowledge) in the *Sāṃkhya-Kārikā* (verse 2) and *viveka-khyāti* (discerning vision) in the *Yoga-Sūtra* (2.26-28, 4.29; cf. 3.55, 4.26, *YB* 1.2), the attainment of such precise and penetrating discernment involving the eradication of avidyā—the root of all 'afflicted vṛttis' (*kliṣṭa-vṛtti*)—and the discontinuance of *saṃyoga* (conjunction), the latter term denoting what is merely a *perceived* or *apparent* fusion of puruṣa and prakṛti (*YS* 2.24-25). In other words, the existence of the Self must be seen to be unconditional and independent of the phenomenal world.

Although viveka-khyāti is a prerequisite for the supreme goal of yoga, it is not the goal itself. It can be viewed as a highly refined mode of perception, or 'intellective revelation' as Bangali Baba has termed it[47]—the purest, least afflicted or distorted vṛtti, whose constant presence is described as *dharma-megha samādhi* (*YS* 4.29)[48]—but, *as* vṛtti, it is still a manifestation of prakṛti, and must therefore itself be disidentified with, or detached from, in order for the yogin to attain the highest state of yoga.

---

[45] Extending Vācaspati's metaphor, we might say that the ultimate goal of yoga is to locate one's identity, not in any of the archery targets, no matter how 'minute' or 'subtle', but in the archer himself (or herself)—i.e. in puruṣa.

[46] Feuerstein 1980: 114; cf. *Sāṃkhya-Kārikā* 3.

[47] Baba 1976: 2, 52.

[48] *Dharma*: 'natural law', 'natural order', i.e. the way things ought to be; *megha*: 'raincloud'; hence dharma-megha samādhi may be regarded as a state of being in which the yogin is a 'cloud of dharma'—attuned to the universal order and showering everyone with virtue.

Asaṃprajñāta-samādhi

The several-tiered discipline of cognitive, or saṃprajñāta-, samādhi is intended to clear the way for, or remove the barriers to, the realisation of one's identity, not as any stratum of prakṛti, but as absolute subjectivity—the true Self and source of consciousness, often referred to as *ātman* or, more commonly in the literature of Sāṃkhya-Yoga (including the *Yoga-Sūtra*), *puruṣa*. The state in which this realisation is made may be referred to as *asaṃprajñāta-samādhi* (e.g. *YB* 1.18)—which, as noted earlier, roughly translates as 'supracognitive samādhi'—or as *nirbīja-samādhi* (e.g. *YS* 1.51, 3.8), which term will be explained below. When compared with this state, proclaims Patañjali, even saṃyama appears as an 'external limb' (*bahir-aṅga*) (*YS* 3.8).

Bīja means 'seed' or 'germ', and thus, in a metaphorical sense, the 'source' or 'origin' of something. It may occasionally be used as a synonym of *bindu* (point, dot), which denotes the essence of masculine sexual energy, manifesting on the gross physical plane as semen. In Chapter 7 the notion of *bīja-mantra*—roughly 'seed sound'—will be introduced in relation to the cakras or 'centres of vital force'; but in the present context we are concerned with the notion of *bīja* as a synonym of *saṃskāra*—i.e. the 'seed of vṛttis'. Saṃskāras, being the psychic 'ruts' that incline the mind to perceive the world in certain habitual ways, naturally predispose us towards identification with manifestations of prakṛti—the 'grossest' being the external physical form of one's body, and the most refined being the highest aspect of intellection, namely buddhi. All such modes of identification may be characterised as vṛttis which prevent the true Self from being pristinely reflected in the mind. Progression through the stages of saṃprajñāta-samādhi has the effect of systematically sublating afflicted vṛttis by those which are less subject to the distorting influence of avidyā (nescience). Vyāsa notes (*YB* 1.46) that each of the modes of samāpatti is 'seeded' or 'with seed' (*sabīja*), and this is because they each depend on a particular 'object of support' (*ālambana*), whether that be a gross or subtle object, or the faculties of egoity and perception themselves. Identification with an object, no matter how subtle or refined, is, according to yoga philosophy, still a *mis*identification, and thus even the heights of asmitā-samāpatti harbour the seed of continued ignorance of one's true nature. If the yogin's true identity as puruṣa is to be realised, and this realisation is to be sustained, then the exultant state of nirbīja-samādhi ('samādhi without seed') must be attained repeatedly by means of intense meditation and, according to most traditional accounts of the topic, by the 'grace' (*anugraha*) of the Self (or guru) personified as Īśvara.[49] As Whicher asserts, 'The yogin is not satisfied with generating "better" *saṃskāras*...the yogin wants to generate none at all' and to dissolve or 'burn' those that already exist.[50] The repeated attainment of asaṃprajñāta- or nirbīja-samādhi establishes saṃskāras of nirodha which both replace the previous saṃskāras of misidentification and *dissolve themselves* at the same time (since they leave only a trace of an *absence* of identification). As Bhojarāja puts it, 'the saṃskāras born of nirodha burn the saṃskāras born from *ekāgratā* [single-pointed attention] and also burn themselves.'[51] It is because the ordinary mental patterns, including subconscious motivating forces, are dissolved in this state that it is referred to in the haṭha literature by such terms as *unmanī* and *amanaska* (cf. pp. 105-6 above), these expressions being suggestive of a condition that is somehow 'other than' or 'outside' the mind. With regard to the effect of yoga practice on mental activity, the term 'dissolution' is, of course, far preferable to alternatives such as 'destruction', 'eradication', 'termination', etc., since vṛttis and their saṃskāric causes are the constructive components of the personality-matrix, and are therefore essential if one is to function on the

---

[49] See, e.g., *YB* 1.25: 'Even though He [Īśvara] has no reason to benefit (*anugraha*) Himself, His purpose is to confer grace (*anu-graha*) to the beings...' (trans. Arya 1986: 295).

[50] Whicher 1992: 298.

[51] *Rāja-Mārttaṇḍa* 1.18.

psychophysical plane. Far from being literally 'killed' in the supreme state of yoga, the mind and personality are *purified* of all *dogmatic*, *habitual* and *automatic* modes of response, and the path is cleared for purposeful self-creation and willful control over vṛttis. By means of assiduous practice, and repeated arrival at asaṃprajñāta-samādhi—which is what *rāja-yoga* may be taken to denote in the chief haṭha texts—this 'supra-cognitive state' eventually unfolds into the permanence of kaivalya (cf. *YS* 4.34).

Stages of *saṃprajñāta-* (or *sabīja-*) samādhi:

- *Savitarka-samāpatti*: identification with a 'gross' object accompanied by conceptual and linguistic attributes.
- *Nirvitarka-samāpatti*: identification with a 'gross' object unaccompanied by conceptual or linguistic attributes.
- *Savicāra-samāpatti*: identification with a 'subtle' object accompanied by notions of time, space and causation.
- *Nirvicāra-samāpatti*: identification with the pure form of a 'subtle' object.
- *Ānanda-samāpatti*: identification with ahaṃkāra, the faculty of egoity, resulting in conditional 'bliss'.
- *Asmitā-samāpatti*: identification with buddhi, the most refined aspect of intellection, resulting in an unalloyed sense of 'am-ness'.
- *Viveka-khyāti*: discernment between buddhi, prakṛti and puruṣa
- *Dharmamegha-samādhi*: a state in which viveka-khyāti is constant.

Asaṃprajñāta- (or *nirbīja-*) samādhi: identification as puruṣa.

Kaivalya: a permanent state of asaṃprajñāta-samādhi—'absoluteness!'

Summarised in the table on the previous page are the various states of samādhi as presented in the *Yoga-Sūtra* and *Yoga-Bhāṣya*. Although this schematic, or any near equivalent, is absent from those treatises most immediately connected with haṭha-yoga, it is my contention that it constitutes merely a more elaborate account of the highest stages of yoga *per se*, and not one that competes with any haṭha conception.

In this chapter, then, I have begun the process of showing why the idea that haṭha-yoga incorporates only the 'lower' or 'physical' elements of yoga is mistaken. Haṭha is a distinct tradition within the broader field of Indian soteriology that places a strong emphasis upon the integrity of physical, subtle-physical and mental discipline for the attainment of the very highest goal. This goal is referred to as, amongst other things, *rāja-yoga*, and, I have contended, corresponds to the kaivalya of the *Yoga-Sūtra*. In the next chapter, haṭha-yoga's view of the body will be used as a springboard from which to launch into a further exploration of its theoretical underpinnings.

6

The 'Body' in Haṭha-Yoga

> The greatest conquest in the world is self-conquest, and for an average person that begins with conquest of the body. (P. U. Arya 1985: 24)

> Hatha Yoga in its various aspects is a means to reach a new understanding of the body and how to use it as the most wonderful tool humans have. (Swami Radha 1993: 18)

> The body is not to the Hathayogin a mere mass of living matter, but a mystic bridge between the spiritual and the physical being. (Aurobindo 1970: 507)

Haṭha-yoga is often regarded as physical or bodily yoga. Such a view is mistaken and over-simplistic if that is *all* haṭha is considered to be; but it is certainly the case that haṭha-yoga works very much *with* and *through* the body, and that its conceptualisation of the body is crucial to haṭha's theory and practice. This conceptualisation—which involves a whole 'subtle' physiological dimension—forms the main subject of discussion in the present chapter, although first it is necessary to tackle a very real, if ill-informed, attitude taken by some towards haṭha-yoga.

Unwarranted prejudice against haṭha-yoga

Occasionally in Indian religious thought an ill-considered snobbishness is expressed towards those spiritual disciplines that work explicitly with the physical body. Behind this view lurks the unhelpful idea that, because human identity is not limited to, and is in fact greater than, the physical body, the body itself must be 'bad' in some way, and therefore by giving attention to it one is engaging in 'impure' activity. Support for this contempt of the body can be found, as Feuerstein has noted,[1] in many traditional texts dating back to the Upaniṣads. To illustrate this point, Feuerstein quotes the following passages from the *Maitrāyaṇīya-* (or *Maitri-*) *Upaniṣad* and *Agni-Purāṇa* respectively:

> Venerable, in this ill-smelling, unsubstantial body [which is nothing but] a conglomerate of bone, skin, sinew, muscle, marrow, flesh, semen, blood, mucus, tears, rheum, feces, urine, wind, bile, and phlegm, what is the good of enjoyment of desires? In this body, which is afflicted with desire, anger, greed, delusion, fear, despondency, envy, separation from the desirable, union with the undesirable, hunger, thirst, senility, death, disease, sorrow, and the like—what is the good of enjoyment of desires? (*MU* 1.3)

> An ascetic (*yati*) regards his body at best as an inflated bladder of skin, surrounded by muscles, sinew and flesh, filled with ill-smelling urine, feces and dirt, a dwelling place of illness and suffering and an easy victim of old age, sorrow and death, more transient than a dew drop on a blade of grass, nothing more or less than the product of the five elements. (*Agni-Purāṇa* 51.15-16)

The highly respected Indian svāmin, Ramakrishna (1836-1886), adopted a similar attitude towards the body as that expressed in the above passages. Although he was well-known for his numerous mystical visions, and was reputed to have great healing powers, when dying from cancer at the age of fifty he refused to use those powers on his own body, referring to it, according to Nikhilananda, as a 'worthless cage of flesh.'[2] Other yogins, however, have taken the view that, although the body may become unclean if it is improperly cared for, it has the potential to be a perfect spiritual vehicle. Indeed, declara-

---

[1] Feuerstein 1974b: 186.
[2] Nikhilananda 1969: 69, quoted in Murphy 1992: 476.

tions made in texts such as those quoted above, to the effect that the body is a decadent and transient dwelling place, may be interpreted as hyperboles designed to counteract the tendency to become overly attached to the physical aspect of one's being; and the stream of soteriology that views the body as a potential source of splendour, and ultimately a manifestation of the divine essence, runs equally deeply back into Indian history.

In the *Yoga-Vāsiṣṭha*, an extensive tract of more than twenty-four thousand stanzas attributed to Vālmīki, the legendary author of the *Rāmāyaṇa*, an important point is made concerning the way in which the body is perceived: 'For the ignorant person,' it states, 'this body is the source of endless suffering; but to the wise person, this body is the source of infinite delight.'[3] The claim is, therefore, that one's view of the body has an affinity with the degree of one's (spiritual) awareness. Though one whose perception of reality is tainted by self-misidentification experiences enslavement to the body, with the flowering of wisdom comes body-mastery and the fruitful harnessing of its potential.

It is in the Tāntrika tradition—within which haṭha-yoga is embedded—that we find the most explicit pronouncements of a body-positive spiritual philosophy, and this Tāntrika view is powerfully encapsulated in the following extract from Arthur Avalon's *Serpent Power*:

> He [i.e. the Tāntrika-yogin] realises in the pulsing beat of his heart the rhythm which throbs through, and is the sign of, the universal life. To neglect or to deny the needs of the body, to think of it as something not divine, is to neglect and deny that greater life of which it is a part, and to falsify the great doctrine of the unity of all and of the ultimate identity of Matter and Spirit. Governed by such a concept, even the lowliest physical needs take on a cosmic significance... The whole body and all its functions are [Śakti's] manifestation. To fully realize Her as such is to perfect this particular manifestation of Hers which is himself.[4]

---

[3] *YV* 4.23.18, trans. Feuerstein 1997: 8.

[4] Avalon 1919: 269.

A prejudicial attitude regarding the bodily dimension of haṭha-yoga can sometimes become entrenched—and diverge wildly from the truth—when the propounder fails to distinguish between those physical disciplines that are designed to *purify* the body as a vehicle of subtle energy on the one hand, and those that are practised as austerities, and which may harm the body while bringing greater strength to the will, on the other. Vihari-Lala Mitra makes this unfortunate confusion when he describes haṭha-yoga as consisting 'of the forced contortions of the body in order to subdue the hardy boors to quiescence' and as 'rather a training of the bodys [*sic*] than a mental or spiritual discipline of a moral and intelligent being for the benefit of the rational soul.' Spitting further venom—and managing to insult not only sincere haṭha-yogins but also the general population of India—Mitra adds that 'The votaries of this system are mostly of a vagrant and mendicant order, and subject to the slander of foreigners, though they command veneration over the ignorant multitude [*sic*].'[5] Such wayward opinions would not be worth quoting were it not for the fact that Mitra was responsible for a monumental feat of yoga scholarship, namely the first translation from Sanskrit into English of the *Yoga-Vāsiṣṭha* mentioned above. Despite this immense achievement, however, Mitra fully exposes his distorted conception of yoga when he writes towards the end of his introductory essay entitled 'The Yoga Philosophy' that yoga 'has nothing to do with the body which is of this earth, and which we have to leave here behind us.'[6] Such an attitude is, I submit, based on a gross misreading of yoga theory, and, I can only presume, a lack of familiarity with yoga practice. It is true that, in most traditions of yoga, the physical body, along with the *sūkṣma-śarīra* (subtle body) and *kāraṇa-śarīra* (causal body), is regarded merely as a 'vessel' or 'covering' (*upādhi*) in, or through, which the true identity of a human being 'shines' to a lesser or greater extent according to one's level of spiritual development, but this hardly means that

[5] Mitra 1891: 17.
[6] *Ib.*: 32.

yoga 'has nothing to do with the body'. On the contrary, the body is held to be *essential* for significant spiritual progress to take place. If it were spiritually advantageous to be without a physical body then the first instruction for yogins would be to commit suicide, but this is patently not the case. As Eliade notes, 'it is only through *experiences* that freedom is gained. Hence the gods (*videha*, "the dis-incarnate")—who have no experience because they have no body—are in a condition of existence inferior to the human condition and cannot attain to complete liberation.'[7] It is, admittedly, repeatedly emphasised in the yoga literature that one ought to cultivate an attitude of *non-attachment* (*vairāgya*) to the physical body; *Gheraṇḍa-Saṃhitā* 7.3, for example, states that *mukti* (release) is achieved by separating the mind from *ghaṭa* (lit. 'the pot', i.e. the body) and uniting it with paramātman (the supreme Self); but this detachment or 'separating' does not entail an ontological discontinuation, only a translocation of self-identity.

In her otherwise interesting and innovative study entitled *Kundalini in the Physical World*, Mary Scott, like V.-L. Mitra, displays a profound misunderstanding of haṭha-yoga. She makes two important false assumptions, the first being that haṭha 'is a discipline of the body alone,' and the second being that bodily achievement has little or nothing to do with success in yoga.[8]

> Theoretically [writes Scott], if one carried out Asanas and Pranayamas in a context of devotion and participated in all the prescribed rituals, it could lead one to bliss and the experience of expanded consciousness associated with Samadhi. This, however, could only be done by so much hard work over so long a period that one might well die before reaching one's goal. It would, moreover, be an *exclusively bodily achievement* and, as Sri Aurobindo points out, physically acquired skills die with one—a

[7] Eliade 1969: 40.
[8] See Scott 1983: 11-12.

> powerful argument against using Hatha yoga alone in a country where the belief in reincarnation is general.[9]

From the viewpoint of haṭha-yoga itself, the idea that progress in it represents 'an exclusively bodily achievement' is absurd, since at the very heart of its philosophy is the principle that hygiene of the physical body affects the flow of prāṇa through the subtle channels, and that the flow of prāṇa in turn affects the relative turbulence or tranquility of the mind. No hard-and-fast distinction is made between 'bodily achievement' and some other kind of success, for physical and mental purification are two components of the same continuum. Scott herself points out in a later passage that 'The dichotomy between soul and body, between mind and matter, so characteristic of Western thought is quite absent from Indian philosophy',[10] by which I take her to mean that, on the Indian Tāntrika model, a continuity exists between the mutually natural processes of minds and bodies. This is indeed the case, and exposes the notion of 'physically acquired skills' as a misnomer. The body may be an instrument *through which* skills are acquired, but it is not the sole carrier or possessor of those attainments. The haṭha-yogin who has yet to arrive at absolute perfection and immortality knows that his physical body will be shed at death, but there is no reason for him to believe that the effort he has put into perfecting the body will be wasted. According to the principle of *karma*, the kind of physical body into which one reincarnates is no mere accident, but will be influenced by one's state of spiritual evolution, and any effort directed towards purifying the bodily vessel in the present life will bear fruit in a future one.[11]

---

[9] *Ib.* (emphasis added).

[10] *Ib.*: 28.

[11] Cf. *ŚS* 1.89: 'Due to [the effects of] previous actions (*pūrva-karmaṇaḥ*), the "sheath" (*kośa*) made of food is obtained. That body is agreeable (*sundara*) or afflicted by distress (*vidur-duḥkha*) [according to] self-enjoyments.'

To reiterate, then: The kind of relationship that is considered desirable for the haṭha-yogin to have with his or her own bodily vehicle(s) is one, not of detestation and disgust, but of non-attachment. As Balasubramanian has pointed out, 'It is not the continuation of the body that is bondage, but only a false identification with it (*dehābhimāna*)';[12] hence there is no necessity to shed the body in order to achieve Brahman-identity.

Kāya-sādhana

> [*H*]*aṭha-yoga* does not seek mere transcendental experiences. Its objective is to transform the human body to make it a worthy vehicle for Self-realization. (Feuerstein 1990a: 133)

From the yogic viewpoint, the body, mind and senses constitute instruments or tools for the respective processes of (a) experiencing the world and (b) coming to realise our true nature. If these instruments are to work efficiently then it is vital that the yogin maintains them in the best possible condition, and, furthermore, endeavours to strengthen and purify them to the utmost.

The Sanskrit term for the development or cultivation of the body for a spiritual purpose is *kāya-sādhana*, *kāya* meaning 'body' and *sādhana* meaning 'spiritual practice' (or, more literally, 'that which leads to the fulfilment of the goal'). The related terms *kāya-siddhi* and *kāya-saṃpat* refer to the state of 'bodily perfection' acquired through such practice. (Sometimes in the above expressions the word *kāya* may be replaced by its synonyms *piṇḍa* or *deha*.)

According to *Yoga-Sūtra* 3.47, kāya-saṃpat consists in 'beauty (*rūpa*), gracefulness (*lāvaṇya*), strength (*bala*), and "adamantine robustness" (*vajra-saṃhananatva*)'; and such a condition is said to proceed from saṃyama upon the 'gross' (sthūla) and 'subtle' (sūkṣma) elements (*YS* 3.45-46). This implies that bodily perfection is viewed as a consequence of, as opposed to a prerequisite for, meditative discipline, although

---

[12] Balasubramanian 1990: 21.

the relation between the two should perhaps be better understood as one of mutual enhancement; in other words, the body must be purified for yoga to occur, yet yoga is itself the purifying process.

While techniques designed to hone the body so that it may provide better access to higher states of being receive more explicit attention in the treatises of haṭha-yoga than in those of other yoga traditions, the notion of the body's being a 'vessel' or 'pot' (ghaṭa) (to use Gheraṇḍa's terminology) which must, in some sense, be made worthy of the spirit is one that extends back as far as the *Ṛg-Veda*, and persists throughout the post-Vedic era. In a hymn to Soma, for example, the following verse appears:

> Ready is thy filter (*pavitra*) Lord of prayer; supreme, thou pervadest each and every limb. The cold, unripened vessel cannot receive that; only vessels made ready receive that.[13]

The translator of this verse, Jeanine Miller, notes that the necessary purification is portrayed as a 'burning action', represented by the fire-deity Agni;[14] and this idea of 'heating' is echoed in the later haṭha manuals, where the bodily vessel is said to resemble 'an unbaked urn left in water [which] inevitably decays' unless 'purification by baking well in the fire of yoga (*yoga-anala*) is performed' (*GS* 1.8). 'Burning' or 'heating' is the literal meaning of *tapas*, which is listed among the niyamas (observances) in the *Yoga-Sūtra* (2.32) and *HYP* (1.16), and which, according to *Yoga-Sūtra* 2.43, establishes 'bodily perfection by destroying impurities of the senses'. *Tapas* is frequently translated as 'austerity', but it is better understood as the 'spiritual flame', zeal or urge which is fanned through yogic disciplines, not merely by extreme asceticism, hardship or bodily deprivation.

In order to comprehend the nature of the haṭha-yogin's relation to his or her own body, some clarification is needed of

---

13 *ṚV* 9.83.1, trans. J. Miller in Feuerstein and Miller 1971: 149.

14 Miller *ib.*

what is meant by the body's being described as a 'vessel', and this requires a little excursion into Vedānta metaphysics. Underlying the practices of haṭha-yoga is the Vedāntic view that the true identity of every human being—and of all apparently discrete entities—is ultimately a single divine Reality. In the Upaniṣads, this singularity is referred to, or at least hinted at, by various terms, including *Tat*,[15] *Brahman*, *puruṣa*, *paramātman*, and so on; and it is this 'Self' which has been, is, and forever shall be who we really are. Its true state is held to be one of eternal and changeless perfection. Gauḍapāda, the guru of Śaṅkarācārya's guru (Govinda), puts it thus: '[puruṣa] can be neither born nor destroyed, is neither bound nor active [i.e. actively seeking deliverance], neither thirsts for freedom nor is liberated.'[16] Theologically speaking, the view expressed in the Vedānta of Gauḍapāda, and that of Śaṅkara,—and which reverberates through the philosophy of haṭha-yoga—may be termed *panentheism*. Simply put, panentheism states that divinity—or the divine principle—is both immanent *and* transcendent; that everything in some sense 'derives from' that divine source, and yet the source itself remains 'beyond' and greater than the manifest universe. The universe, and everything of which it is composed, is held to be 'an effect of Brahman and non-different [*ananyatva*] from it',[17] and yet Brahman is not exhausted by the universe.[18] What changes when the universe comes into existence and begins to unfold is not, then, Brahman itself, but the *form* through which that one reality is 'per-

---

15 Lit. 'That', perhaps most famously used in the expression *tat-tvam-asi*, 'That thou art' (*Chāndogya-Upaniṣad* 6.9.4).

16 Gauḍapāda, *Māṇḍūkya-Kārikā* 2.32, quoted in Eliade 1969: 31. The statement bears a marked similarity to *Sāṃkhya-Kārikā* 62, which reads: 'It is certain that puruṣa is neither bound nor liberated, nor does he undergo change; it is prakṛti who, through taking on many forms, is bound, is liberated, and undergoes change.'

17 *VSB* 2.1.20, trans. Thibaut 1962: 342-43.

18 Cf. Murphy 1992: 193. Panentheism should not be confused with *pantheism*, proponents of which hold that the universe and God (or the Divine) are coterminous.

ceived'; and the Sanskrit term for this form is *upādhi*. *Upādhi* translates roughly as 'limitation',[19] 'restriction' or 'false relation', but may be understood as the 'vehicle' or 'vessel' through which the light of divinity is 'filtered'. Upādhis are the limiting conditions under which we perceive and experience the Infinite and Eternal as innumerable finite objects which come to be, have existence, and then decay into imperceptibility. As Śaṅkara puts it:

> by this limiting finite connection...the Self assumes [as it were] those particular names and forms (*nāma-rūpa*) [of deities, humans, animals, and so on]. The difference between these things...is due to the difference of the limiting conditions [upādhi] and to nothing else. For all the [Upaniṣads] conclude that there is 'One only, without a second'.[20]

The implication of the theory expressed here is that to talk of the human psychophysical complex—comprising body, mind and senses—as a 'vessel' or 'container' in which the spirit or Self dwells is only to use an analogical method of describing the actual situation. In truth, the psychophysical complex is held to be a *disguised form* (upādhi) of the Self; and thus what is required is not that we obliterate the form, but that we alter our perception of it in such a way as to perceive its true nature. As well as being a limiting condition, upādhi should be equally understood as a *power* or *force* emanating from the Absolute in order that experience can take place; and thus these substitutes-for-reality—i.e. all apparently individuated entities, including our own minds and bodies—are both the walls of our perceptual prison *and* the gateways to our liberation. To repeat Vālmīki's proclamation: 'For the ignorant person, this body is the source of endless suffering; but to the wise person, this body is the source of infinite delight.'[21]

---

[19] Lott 1980: 43-44.

[20] *Bṛhadāraṇyaka-Upaniṣad-Bhāṣya* 3.8.12, quoted in Lott 1980: 44.

[21] *YV* 4.23.18, trans. Feuerstein 1997: 8.

From the traditional Indian perspective, the whole process of cosmic evolution consists in an irresistable unfoldment that is working towards the end of universal Brahman-realisation, the task of the yogin being, as Gopi Krishna puts it, 'to accelerate the operation of the mighty law of human evolution, in order to achieve the consummation of the process in one life-time'—'to create a gifted human being blessed with a trans-human state of consciousness.'[22] For the haṭha-yogin, this task involves actively transforming the 'vessel' through a combination of physical, subtle-physical and intrapsychic techniques, so that the psychophysical complex is not merely maintained, but is positively 'refined' and 'etherealised'.

The notion of *jīvanmukti*

> He who never has the thought of 'I' with regard to the body and the senses and the thought of 'this' in respect of something different to the *tat* [the Absolute], is regarded as a *jīvan-mukta.* (Śaṅkara, *Viveka-Cūḍāmaṇi* 438)[23]

We have already noted two senses in which the body may be regarded as an 'instrument'; that is, firstly, for the purpose of gaining life experiences, and secondly, for gaining access to more refined modes of self-identity. Both of these senses, however, relate to the pre-enlightened yogin, thus leaving the question of what happens *next*. What, one might reasonably ask, is the role of the body, and of the whole personality-matrix, once Self-realisation has been achieved?

In most Indian soteriological traditions, spiritual advancement is regarded as going hand-in-hand with ethical development, and thus the perfected yogin is held to become a source of virtue for the betterment of all. Having aligned his or her perceptive faculties with truth, the yogin is then able to manifest dharma—the divine 'law' or correct 'order' of things—upon the material plane. As the *Bhagavad-Gītā* states, for exam-

---

[22] Krishna 1993: 5.
[23] Trans. Feuerstein, in Feuerstein and Miller 1971: 164.

ple, the Self-realised person does not cease to perform actions, but performs them 'without attachment (i.e. without self-interest), *desiring*-to-effect (*cikīrṣu*) (instead) the world's cohesion [*saṅgraha*].'[24] Of the one who abides in Brahman, Lord Kṛṣṇa gives to Arjuna the following descriptions:

> identifying himself with the selves of all creatures... (*BG* 5.7)

> without hatred of any creature, friendly and compassionate, without possessiveness and self-pride, equable in happiness and unhappiness, forbearing, contented,...mastering himself, resolute in decisions,...who is free from jubliation, impatience, fear and vexation,...independent,...skilfull..., impartial, unruffled,...neither hates nor rejoices, does not mourn nor hanker,...remains the same towards friend or foe, in honour or dishonour,...devoid of all self-interest (*saṅga-vivarjitaḥ*),...equable when praised or blamed,... firm of mind—such a man is dear to me. (*BG* 12.13-19)[25]

One who has achieved this condition of 'embodied liberation' is known as a *jīvanmukta*, and the condition itself as *jīvanmukti*, this being one of the synonyms for the highest state listed in *HYP* 4.3-4 (see p. 106 above). In haṭha-yoga, once practitioners have reached this pinnacle of attainment, they will often serve humanity by becoming teachers themselves, and in this way the guru-śiṣya tradition is perpetuated.

In discussing the philosophy of Gorakṣa, A. K. Banerjea implies that the supreme state cannot be maintained simultaneously with empirical existence, and so the yogin—if he is to continue living in the world—must allow his sense of identity to be drawn back, as it were, from the heights of *nirutthāna-daśā*,[26] which Banerjea refers to as 'Absolute consciousness', to the 'lower planes' of *vyutthāna-daśā* (lit. 'rising-up' or 'awakening' state).[27] On this view, then, the state of supra-

---

[24] *BG* 12.13, trans. Gelblum 1992: 121.

[25] Trans. Gelblum *ib.*

[26] Lit. 'without-arising' or 'without-giving-rise-to' state, i.e. the state in which no further saṃskāras of worldly identification are generated.

[27] Banerjea 1962: 53.

cognitive-/asaṃprajñāta-samādhi, which may be equated with nirutthāna-daśā, can only be a state of temporary blissful suspension, unless the yogin is to cease activity altogether. It should not be assumed, however, that the yogin's achieving the highest state of samādhi has no or little effect upon his everyday mode of perception, for, according to Banerjea, when such a yogin 'returns' to the phenomenal world and engages in activity,

> the light of the Samādhi-Experience is clouded, but not lost. The empirical consciousness, while descending to the plane of relativity, carries with it some sweet and blissful memory of the Absolute Experience and the spiritual enlightenment attained therein. As a consequence the enlightened Yogi's outlook on the world of objective experiences is thoroughly transformed. He looks upon everything, within and without, from the standpoint of the Truth of the Absolute Experience.[28]

In another passage, Banerjea expresses the same idea more figuratively, stating that the fulfilled yogin is able to 'bring down the light of...transcendent experience to the intellectual and mental and vital planes.'[29]

Paramahansa Yogananda's report of the highest stages of yoga differs from that of Banerjea insofar as Yogananda declares full Self-realisation to be entirely compatible with mundane existence. On this view, it is saṃprajñāta-samādhi—referred to by Yogananda as *sabikalpa-samādhi* ('samādhi-with-difference')—that involves a 'bodily condition of suspended animation', whereas in *nirbikalpa-samādhi* ('samādhi-without-difference')—i.e. asaṃprajñāta-samādhi—the yogin 'realizes fully his identity as Spirit', 'without bodily fixation; and in his ordinary waking consciousness, even in the midst of exacting worldly duties.'[30] Thus, for Yogananda, the realised

---

[28] *Ib.*: 53-54.
[29] *Ib.*: 32.
[30] Yogananda 1981: 238. *Sabikalpa* and *nirbikalpa* are Bangāli variants of the Sanskrit terms *savikalpa* and *nirvikalpa* respectively.

yogin does not need to 'descend...to the plane of relativity' in order to carry out activities involving the mind, body and senses, but is able to live, as it were, on two 'levels'—or in two 'worlds', the absolute and the conditional—simultaneously.

The accounts of the ultimate state which appear in the haṭha literature tend to concur more with Banerjea than with Yogananda, with the body being described as inert and the mind and senses passive. In the final chapter of the *HYP*, for example, we read that:

> There is no doubt that the yogin who has transcended all states and all cognitive operations, and who *appears as though dead*, is liberated. (*HYP* 4.107; emphasis added)

> The yogin who is firmly absorbed in samādhi has no sense of self or other; nor does he smell, taste, touch or hear. (*HYP* 4.109)

Brahmānanda comments that 'in samādhi there is no experience of sense-objects' (*J* 4.110), and likens this state to one of suspended animation or complete motionlessness, in which the yogin appears to be asleep (*supta*), yet remains fully awake (*J* 4.112). With the flow of breath having ceased, the yogin's body resembles a corpse, but due to the complete retention of prāṇa, the yogin could be said to be more alive than at any other time. Nowhere do the main haṭha manuals themselves touch upon what occurs, or ought to occur, *after* this blissful catatonia has been arrived at (presumably, to anyone who gets there, the answer will be obvious).

In his study of the Tamil siddha tradition of southern India, followers of which are noted for their employment of haṭha techniques, Kamil Zvelebil uses the terminology of alchemy to describe the practice of these yogins. It involves, reports Zvelebil, the 'transmutation' or 'transubstantiation' 'of the corruptible into the incorruptible body',[31] the aim being 'to kill death' and to bind body (kāya) and consciousness (cit) to-

---

[31] Zvelebil 1996: 23.

gether.[32] From this point of view, the intention is not so much to transcend the physical body as to reach a state where the *distinction* between consciousness (or the true Self) and substance is transcended. To this account we might add the claim of M. G. Kaviraj that, for the followers of Gorakṣa, jīvanmukti does not constitute the final attainment, but is, rather, a prerequisite for a higher state of liberation. 'The Nātha[33] ideal', writes Kaviraj, 'is first to realise *Jivanmukti* through *piṇḍa-siddhi* [= kāya-siddhi] which secures an Immaculate Body of Light free from the influence of Time, i.e. a deathless undecaying spiritual body[;] and then to realise *Parā-Mukti* or Highest Perfection through the process of mutual integration (*samarasī-karaṇa*).'[34]

The human being as 'multilayered'

It will already have become clear from the above discussion that underlying the practice of haṭha-yoga is a conception of the human body that is both highly complex and considerably at odds with the standard western materialist model. Central to the yogic conception is the notion of the human being's comprising a series of 'layers' of substance, from the 'gross' and 'external' through to the 'subtle' and 'internal'. In addition to the schematic of tattvas presented in the Sāṃkhya darśana and discussed in Chapters 2 and 5 above, the personality matrix is also described in terms of progressively rarefied 'bodies' (*śarīra*) or 'sheaths' (*kośa*), a brief account of which is given below.

The notion of three bodily levels, known as the *sthūla-śarīra* ('gross' body), *sūkṣma-śarīra* ('subtle' body), and *kāraṇa-śarīra* ('causal' body), is common to both Vedānta and Sāṃkhya-Yoga metaphysics. According to Feuerstein, the verbal

---

[32] *Ib.*: 22.

[33] *Nātha*, meaning 'lord' or 'master', is an honorific title given to a *mahā-siddha* (great adept), and also denotes a particular Śaiva sect which traces its lineage back to the legendary haṭha-yogins, Matsyendra and Gorakṣa.

[34] Kaviraj, Prefatory Note to Banerjea 1962: xvii.

root of *śarīra* is *śrī*, 'meaning "to fall apart",'[35] while Monier-Williams mentions *śri*, 'support or supporter', as another possible source.[36] Both roots are suggestive of secondariness or conditionality, which quality certainly applies to the śarīras. Each śarīra is held to constitute a covering or form—in other words, an upādhi—that masks the true nature of the Self (ātman), and must therefore be successively disidentified with. The sthūla-śarīra is the gross external form, corresponding roughly to the physical body known to materialist science. This is shed at the point of physical death, although the personality continues to exist, operating through the sūkṣma-śarīra.

As described in the Sāṃkhya darśana (e.g. *SK* 32ff.), the sūkṣma- (or liṅga-) śarīra comprises an 'inner' and an 'outer' instrument. The former is the antaḥkaraṇa (outlined on p. 108 above), while the 'outer instrument' (*bāhyakaraṇa*) is the collective term for the five 'sense capacities' (*buddhīndriya*) plus five 'action capacities' (*karmendriya*) (listed on pp. 75-76, fn.9). Although, it is held, this 'subtle body' is capable of migrating from one sthūla-śarīra to another, thus engendering the process of reincarnation, the world can only be experienced when both sthūla- and sūkṣma-śarīra are present (*SK* 40).

The kāraṇa-śarīra or 'causal body' is so-called because of its status as 'the original embryo or source of the body'.[37] It does not stand for anything recognisably 'body-like', but may, rather, be equated with prakṛti or māyā as the unmanifest *potential* for embodiment, or, according to some accounts, with mahat or buddhi, the initial evolute of this unmanifest potentiality.[38]

---

[35] Feuerstein 1990a: 329. The verbal root *śrī* should not be confused with the term of veneration, also spelt *śrī*, which denotes glory, splendour, radiance, etc.

[36] Monier-Williams 1963: 1057.

[37] *Ib.*: 274.

[38] See, e.g. Arya 1986: 246. Arya in fact distinguishes between 'higher buddhi' (= mahat) and 'lower buddhi', the former being related to the kāraṇa-śarīra and the latter to the sūkṣma-śarīra. The justification for such a distinction is, however, unclear. It should also be noted that Arya (*ib.*) considers

The second model of the multilayered human being to be discussed in this section, and which is also shared by Sāṃkhya-Yoga and Vedānta, is known as *pañca-kośa* due to its distinguishing five (*pañca*) 'sheaths' or 'coverings' (*kośa*, alternatively spelt *koṣa*), which are said to overlay the ātman like a sheath encases a sword.[39] Probably the earliest extant source of this doctrine is the *Taittirīya-Upaniṣad* (esp. 2.2-5), wherein the human being is described as a conglomeration of five 'selves', each composed of a particular substance, principle or faculty. Each of these selves is characterised as an *ātman*, although they should not be conflated with the supreme (parama-) ātman, of which they are merely veils. In later texts the 'lesser' or 'conditional' modes of self became known as kośas and are referred to respectively as: (1) *annamaya-kośa*, (2) *prāṇamaya-kośa*, (3) *manomaya-kośa*, (4) *vijñānamaya-kośa*, and (5) *ānandamaya-kośa*.

Anna literally means 'food', but may be taken to refer to all the substances ingested for the maintenance and sustenance of the physical body, including the physical gas particles of the air. *Maya* means simply 'made of' or 'constituted by'; so the annamaya-kośa is 'the sheath constituted by food', i.e. the 'gross' physical body corresponding to the sthūla-śarīra.[40]

The prāṇamaya-kośa is 'the sheath constituted by prāṇa'. According to *Taittirīya-Upaniṣad* 2.3, the anna- and prāṇamaya-kośas should be thought of as occupying the same bodily space and form, only the latter is of a more subtle nature. Prāṇa, about which more will be said in the following chapter, is the 'vitality' or 'life-force' that infuses the body, giving it life and maintaining its organic structure. This sheath, in combination with the following two, corresponds to the sūkṣma-śarīra.[41]

---

liṅga-śarīra to be a synonym of *kāraṇa-* as opposed to *sūkṣma-śarīra*, which again seems spurious.

[39] Cf. Śaṅkara, *Māndūkyopaniṣad-Bhāṣya* 3.11, in Nikhilānanda 1944: 175.

[40] Sometimes this sheath is referred to as *annarasamaya-* (food and liquid) *kośa* (see, e.g. Śaṅkara *ib.*).

[41] Cf. Swāmī Mādhavānanda's note to *VC* 125 in Śaṅkarācārya 1992: 46.

The manomaya-kośa is the 'manas-constituted sheath', manas being the 'lower mind', the organiser of sense-data and 'caretaker' of memories. Manas forms a 'sheath' around the Self in the sense that, by attributing mental activity to the Self, one obscures its true nature and becomes falsely identified as a 'thinking thing', when in fact the Self is transcendent of all mental states and processes.

Vijñāna denotes the higher operations of intellection, and has been variously translated as 'wisdom', 'understanding', 'ideation', 'awareness',[42] etc. *Taittirīya-Upaniṣad* 2.4 states that vijñāna is 'interior to', and imbues the functions of, manas, and thus the vijñānamaya-kośa may be regarded as *prior to* the manomaya-kośa insofar as it is 'closer' to the Self. *Vijñāna* is a synonym of *viveka*, the power of buddhi to 'reflect' the pure light of puruṣa and to discriminate or 'sift' the subjective from the objective reality; yet, since vijñāna is not itself puruṣa, it remains a mistaken locus of self-identity which must be sublated.

Of the ānandamaya-kośa, it is said in the *Taittirīya-Upaniṣad* (2.5) that it is contained 'within' the vijñānamaya-kośa, and that it has 'joy as the head,/ Contentment as right arm, and delight the left./ Bliss is the heart, and Brahman the foundation.'[43] As was noted in connection with ānanda-samāpatti (p. 118 above), while the term *ānanda* often refers to the state of absolute bliss which stands outside of conditional emotions, it may also signify a lesser mode of enjoyment. On this point, Usharbudh Arya remarks that, when self-identity is placed in the ānandamaya-kośa, 'the self, by nature devoid of the dichotomy of pain and pleasure, is mistaken to be happy or unhappy, suffering pain or enjoying pleasure.'[44] Thus, on this view, the ānanda sheath veils the true nature of the Self—which is entirely self-sufficient—with the appearance of a limited

---

[42] By, respectively: Easwaran 1988: 143; Zaehner 1966: 139; Arya 1986: 488; and Feuerstein 1990a: 182.
[43] Trans. Easwaran 1988: 143.
[44] Arya 1986: 245.

ecstasy, existing only as the opposite pole of unhappiness. As the *Taittirīya-Upaniṣad* suggests, however, 'Brahman [is] the foundation' of ānanda, just as it is the ultimate foundation of each of the kośas; and thus, beneath these coverings lies the source of all.

As has been suggested in the above discussion, the principal purpose behind the bodily schematics of śarīras and kośas is to specify various 'spheres' or 'loci' of misidentification. In other words, rather than being pictured literally as so many kinds of 'body' or 'sheath', they are best regarded as qualities or faculties that are ordinarily falsely attributed to the Self, and which therefore tend to obscure the Self's true nature. On this interpretation, the annamaya-kośa represents our wrongly identifying the immortal Self with the mortal human body; the prāṇamaya-kośa stands for our attribution to the Self of life activities; manomaya-kośa, the attribution of mental processes; vijñānamaya-kośa, the attribution of transitive consciousness; and ānandamaya-kośa, the attribution of joy and its opposite emotional state. The process of yoga—and especially the systematic refining of one's sense of self-identity that occurs through the successive 'stages' of samādhi (see pp. 113ff. above)—is intended to relieve the assiduous practitioner of all false conceptions of the Self, and thus, metaphorically speaking, to 'peel away' the sheaths that cover the Self like the layers of an onion: to allow the śarīras to 'fall away' or 'disintegrate', leaving only the true Self remaining in its absoluteness (kaivalya).

Microcosm and macrocosm

> Man know thyself and thou shalt know the universe. (Temple of Delphi)

Before moving on to a more detailed examination of the subtle physiology of yoga in the following chapter, it is important to say something about the intimate relation that is held to obtain between the human and the cosmic spheres. Just as, in various yoga traditions extending back to the Vedic period, the boundary between the symbolic and the actual—between the figurative and the literal—is blurred, so is that between physiology and cosmology. Consequently, in such traditions, and not least in that of haṭha-yoga, it is common for human attributes to be spoken of in cosmological terms and, correspondingly, for cosmic phenomena to be discussed using anthropomorphic language.

The *Ṛg-Veda* famously includes the story of the sacrifice of 'primal man'—the cosmic puruṣa—which tells of the creation of the universe, with the agency of certain *deva*s ('gods' or 'shining ones'), from an ostensibly enormous human body:

> From his mind the moon was born,
> And from his eye the sun,
> From his mouth Indra and the fire,
> From his breath the wind was born.
>
> From his navel arose the atmosphere,
> From his head the sky evolved,
> From his feet the earth, and from his ear
> The cardinal points of the compass:
> So did they [the gods] fashion forth these worlds.[45]

Similarly, in later literature, the human being is regarded as a microcosm and, as such, he is the locus of all levels of existence and an embodied stairway to the transcendent reality. He is, in short, *kṣudra-brahmāṇḍa*, 'little cosmos', or simply *brahmāṇḍa*.[46] In the *Viśvasāra-Tantra*, for example, it is stated that 'what is here is elsewhere; what is not here is nowhere',[47] which expression has at least a double meaning, this being (a) that the Tantra itself is the epitome of all knowledge, and (b) that what is here *in the human being* includes the whole of existence. Any Tantra, or any other work of Indian soteriology,

---

45 *RV* 10.90.13-14, trans. Zaehner 1966:10.

46 See, e.g. *ŚS* 2.6: 'In this body, known as brahmāṇḍa...'.

47 *yad ihāsti tad anyatra yannehāsti na tat kvacit* (quoted in Avalon 1974: 22-23).

is of course only ever a key for unlocking the door to the mysteries that lie hidden within the human psychophysical complex. It is, according to yoga philosophy, the intrapsychic journey, and not the reading of texts alone, that will bring about the disclosure of the Self.

The 'inner quest' or 'journey' is often represented as a kind of pilgrimage, and the image of the human being as an entire landscape containing numerous holy sites appears in both Hindu and Buddhist Tāntrika traditions. The Buddhist sage, Saraha, pronounces, for example, that

> Here (within this body) is the [Gaṅgā] and the Jumnā...here are Prayāga and Benares—here the sun and the moon. Here are the sacred places, here the *pīṭhas* and *upa-pīṭhas*[48] —I have not seen a place of pilgrimage and an abode of bliss like my body[49]

while in the *Śiva-Saṃhitā* (2.1-5) we find the following elaborate description:

> In this body is Mount Meru, surrounded by seven islands;
> here, too, are rivers, seas, mountains, fields, and guardians of the fields.
> Herein are sages, all the stars and planets,
> sacred pilgrimages, temples (*pīṭhāni*) and presiding deities of the temples.
> Agents of emanation and contraction, sun and moon;
> here indeed are mist (*nabhas*, i.e. ākāśa), air, fire, water and earth.
> All objects of the three worlds (*trailoka*) [are in] the body,
> performing their various functions around Meru.
> The yogī alone knows all this, there is no doubt.

Mount Meru signifies the central axis or suṣumnā-nāḍī, corresponding to (but not identical to) the spinal cord. The *saptadvīpa*—'seven islands' or 'seven lands'—that 'surround' or 'are possessed by' Meru represent the seven 'planes' associated

---

[48] *Pīṭha*: 'temple', 'resting place', 'sitting place; the prefix *upa* (lit. 'next to', 'alongside') can denote 'secondary' or 'minor'.

[49] Quoted in Eliade 1969: 227-28.

with the cakras, each 'plane' being the vista that opens for the yogin after each progressive penetration into the depths of reality. And the other astronomical and geographical referents, too, symbolise aspects of this 'inner world' of subtle bodily forces and phenomena.

The use of such imagery is rooted in yoga's transpersonal, and *transhuman*, conception of the source of human identity, which conception itself emerges from the mystical insights of yogins. One of the paradoxes of yoga meditation is that, through going 'inwards'—i.e. through peeling away the layers of one's own inner make-up—one moves towards an expanded and more widely encompassing sense of selfhood. If, as the advaita- (nondualistically-) oriented philosophy of haṭha-yoga has it, the Self of every apparently individuated human being is equally the transcendent origin of the whole cosmos, then, as one comes closer to that innate Self, the distinction between one's own body and the universe as a whole inevitably collapses. Though the body remains as a useful vehicle of action, the yogin's identification with it has been sublated.

7

The Subtle Bodily Matrix

Of the ideas discussed in Chapter 6, perhaps the two most important are: (a) that of the body as the site of soterially-oriented discipline; and (b) that of the human being as a multilayered organism; that is, a psychophysical complex which can be schematised as a series of graded 'levels' from the grossest physical elements to the most refined aspects of mind. Beyond the immediate grasp of the ordinary physical senses, the 'subtle' bodily aspect of the human being is held to comprise a matrix of thread-like 'channels' (nāḍīs) which are the conduits for the 'vital force' referred to variously as *prāṇa*, *svara*, *vāta*, *vāyu*, etc. The haṭha-yogin is expected to acquire a detailed knowledge of his subtle physiology—to become sensitive to the movements of prāṇa by refining his awareness beyond the scope of the physical senses—for, on the hatha view, it is by controlling and redirecting these forces that greater mental clarity will be gained. Hence we read in the *Gorakṣa-Śataka* (13-14):

> The yogin must know [i.e. be familiar with] the six cakras, sixteen *ādhārā*s (supports),[1] 300,000 [nāḍīs], [and] five *vyoman*s[2] in his own body in order that perfection (siddhi) [in yoga be achieved].

---

[1] According to *J* 3.73, the sixteen vital centres known as ādhārās are located at the big toes (*aṅguṣṭha*), ankles (*gulpha*), knees (*jānu*), thighs (*ūru*), scrotal seam or perineum (*sīvanī*), penis (*liṅga*), navel (*nābhi*), heart (*hṛd*), nape of the neck (*grīvā*), throat region (*kaṇṭha-deśa*), soft palate or uvula (*lambhikā*), nose (*nāsikā*), middle of the brow (*bhra-madhya*), forehead (*lalāṭa*), top of the head (*mūrdhā*), and the 'hollow of Brahman' (*brahma-randhra*) at the top

> The yogin must know his own body as a temple (*gṛha*) [supported by] a single column, [with] nine doors [and] five presiding deities, in order that perfection [in yoga be achieved].

And, in the *Śiva-Saṃhitā* (3.9), it is stated that

> He who knows the microcosm of the body (*brahmāḍa*) in this way [i.e. in terms of its subtle components and forces], [and who is] free from all bad deeds, achieves the highest state.

To attain anything approaching a full comprehension of the phenomena associated with the subtle bodily matrix described in the haṭha literature would be a sisyphean task, and not one which the present chapter sets itself. Rather, the purpose here is simply to examine some of the central concepts in a way that sheds some light upon the practical discipline of haṭha. Since such terms as *prāṇa*, *nāḍī*, *cakra*, etc. are so integral to the anatomical and practical terminology of haṭha, they have inevitably come up fairly frequently in this study already, but it is hoped that the fuller treatment given here will help to elucidate their usage elsewhere.

Prāṇa

There is no easy way of defining *prāṇa* in terms compatible with modern physics, physiology and biochemistry. It is the Sanskrit term for life, vigour, vitality, and may denote the physical 'air' or 'breath' inhaled and exhaled by the lungs, but also the more subtle and all-pervading 'breath of life'—the source of, and sustaining force behind, the whole evolving universe. Sarasvati Buhrman has referred to prāṇa as 'nourishment', adding that it is received not only through the breath but also 'from the sun and the stars, from the earth, and through our

---

of suṣumnā-nāḍī.

[2] *Vyoman*, like *kha*, is a synonym of *ākāśa*, meaning 'space', 'ether', 'atmosphere', 'air' or 'sky'; hence the five vyomans may be regarded as five 'spaces' which are disclosed to the yogin through introspection. Briggs (1973: 287) identifies the five vyomans with the five 'sheaths'.

food.' As *ojas* (vitality), continues Buhrman, prāṇa forms 'the reservoir of vital energy in our body'.[3]

The concept of prāṇa is often signified by the term *vāyu*—which, again, has the meanings of 'air', 'breath', or 'wind'—or by *prāṇa-vāyu*. Less frequently, the term *sūkṣma-prāṇa-vāyu* may be used[4] (*sūkṣma* meaning 'subtle'), making explicit the fact that something even less tangible than air is being referred to. Feuerstein identifies prāṇa as '*spanda-śakti*[—]the subtle "vibratory power" penetrating the whole cosmos', and notes that, in the *Yoga-Vāsiṣṭha* (3.13.31), 'the word *vāyu*...is defined as "that which vibrates" (*spandate yat sa tad*).'[5] In certain Vedic texts prāṇa-vāyu, in its five principal aspects, is equated with the 'cosmic winds' which 'weave' both humankind and the universe as a whole.[6] Hence prāṇa may be regarded as a formative force or impulse as well as a penetrative one. It is both constitutive and operative; that is, it is out of prāṇa that the universe is said to be made, and it is by means of prāṇa's continual 'flow' that the universe is sustained. If Śakti is the 'power' of the emanative impulse (Śiva-tattva), which itself derives from the Absolute (Parama-Śiva, Brahman), then prāṇa is that power manifested as a force which has governance over various particular operations, in both the universal and the human sphere. At a fundamental level, the universe itself may be characterised as vibration, and it is this primordial 'energy' or 'movement-as-such' for which *prāṇa* stands.

Mary Scott speculates that prāṇa may best be regarded as a 'patterning' force in nature, which provides the organised matrix into which otherwise inorganic molecules grow to become living forms.[7] Contending that current western scientific models fail to successfully account for the origin and continuing replication of life-forms, Scott suggests that the 'strait-jacket'

---

3 Buhrman 1998: 33.

4 See, e.g. Avalon 1974: 6.

5 Feuerstein 1971: 26.

6 See, e.g. *AV* 10.2.13, 11.4.15; *Bṛhadāraṇyaka-Upaniṣad* 3.7.2; cf. Eliade 1969: 235.

7 See Scott 1983: 48.

of material reductionism should be removed from our thinking about the natural world, and that the notion of non-physical 'field-forces' be at least 'toy[ed] with'.[8] A variant of such a proposition would be to suggest that the notion of 'physicality' be extended to include substances and forces presently inaccessible to physical measuring instruments, but whose existence may nevertheless be inferred from observable effects. Materialist philosophers such as Daniel Dennett are right to point out the severe problems attached to claims that energy can be expended by anything 'non-physical',[9] and thus it is unhelpful in the context of yoga physiology to draw any definite distinction between that which is 'physical' and that which is 'non-physical'. Notions such as that of the kośas, and of sthūla and sūkṣma 'bodies' (śarīra), represent attempts to overcome an inflexible 'physical' versus 'non-physical' (or 'supra-physical') dichotomy, and to present phenomenal reality as a continuum of evolving substance, characterised by distinct, though mutually influencing, levels of 'density'.

The biologist Lyall Watson has poignantly remarked that 'Organisms are alive, but life is not something "in" them. Organisms are "in" life';[10] and it is perhaps this sense of 'life' as an organising or informational 'field'—like Scott's 'patterning field-force'—that comes closest to capturing the Indian notion of prāṇa.

With regard to the texts of haṭha-yoga, *prāṇa* is usually best translated as 'vital force', and is held to surge through the human organism at a level more subtle than that of the bodily fluids such as blood and lymph with which we are more familiar. Some modern commentators have equated this force or energy with the *chi* known to Chinese martial and medicinal arts (called *ki* in Japanese), and it is certainly true that the concepts are very similar.[11] Prāṇa or vāyu is subdivided into sev-

---

[8] *Ib.*: 50.

[9] See, e.g. Dennett 1991: 35.

[10] Watson 1995: xiv.

[11] This study is not the place for a detailed comparison. Cf., e.g. Svoboda

eral types, which are deemed to control or influence the functioning of certain aspects of the human organism, and to circulate in specific regions of the body associated with these functions. The *Śiva-Saṃhitā* hints at there being innumerable modes of prāṇa, but names only the ten principal ones (*ŚS* 3.3-5). These same ten are listed in the *Gheraṇḍa-Saṃhitā* (2.60), five being primary—i.e. associated with fundamental life-processes—and called *prāṇādi* (vital airs/forces), and five being secondary—i.e. associated with more superficial processes—and called *nāgādi* (bodily airs/forces). The five prāṇādi vāyus are:

1. *prāṇa*[12]—the upward-moving vital force, situated in, or associated with, the heart centre; governor of in-coming energy, especially via the breath;
2. *apāna*—the downward-moving force, associated with the region of the anus; governor of out-going energy, i.e. expulsion, excretion and parturition;
3. *samāna*—force circulating in the abdominal region and governing digestion and assimilation;
4. *udāna*—force moving upwards from the throat, governing speech;
5. *vyāna*—force circulating throughout the whole sūkṣma-śarīra and governing the integrity of all vital processes.

The five nāgādi vāyus are:

1. *nāga*—which expels gas in the form of belching;
2. *kūrma*—which operates the eyelids;
3. *kṛkara*—which expels dust and mucus through sneezing, as well as inducing appetite;
4. *devadatta*—which instigates yawning;
5. *dhanaṃjaya* (lit. 'victory prize')—which circulates throughout, and maintains the integrity of, the whole

1998: 40.

[12] This is *prāṇa* in its narrow sense, denoting a particular *mode* of vital force. In its broader sense, *prāṇa* signifies *all* the vital forces.

sthūla-śarīra, and remains with the physical body when it is cast off at death.

It can be seen, then, that each of these prāṇa-vāyus—whether designated as prāṇādi or nāgādi—represents an aspect of the body's innate 'intelligence', and is held to regulate a particular process that is ordinarily unconscious though entirely necessary for the preservation and flourishing of life. These processes may come increasingly under conscious control through the practice of yoga, as breathing techniques are combined with bodily contractions and mental concentration to, first, cleanse the nāḍīs through which vital force flows, and then to intentionally direct that flow. While there is almost certainly a very intimate connection between the various prāṇas and the bioelectrical impulses that run along the fibres of the human nervous system, the precise nature of this relationship is a contentious matter. The theory that nerves and nāḍīs are identical, which will be discussed below (pp. 179-83), is interesting but far from satisfactory. The concept of prāṇa encompasses far more than mere nerve impulses, as it is held to move through, and bridge the gap between, multiple 'levels' of the human being.

Of the ten main types of prāṇa, it is prāṇa and apāna that are regarded as the 'highest agents' (*ŚS* 3.6), and hence it is the operations of these two which haṭha-yogins are most concerned to bring under their volition. It is the ordinary tendency of apāna—as the governor of excretory functions—to flow downwards and out of the body, while prāṇa flows upwards and is expelled with the breath. By means of the specially designed postures (āsanas), bodily 'seals' and 'locks' (mudrās and bandhas), and breath-retentions (kumbhakas),[13] the yogin aims to prevent the escape of this vital force and to unify and retain it within the central channel of suṣumnā-nāḍī.

The conscious retention of prāṇa within the body for longer and longer periods is held to be a way of suspending the oth-

---

[13] See Chapter 8 below.

erwise relentless movement towards death and decay. 'As long as vāyu stays in the body,' declares *Gorakṣa-Śataka* 91, '*jīva* ("life") remains. Its departure [results in the] death [of the body]. Therefore vāyuṃ nirodhayet should be practised.' *Vāyuṃ nirodhayet*, as noted already (p. 113), refers to the process of suspending the flow of prāṇa, in order that its power can be 'harnessed' and utilised for higher purposes.

Nāḍīs

Nāḍī is the feminine form of *nāḍa*, both terms denoting a tube, stalk or channel.[14] Such channels may include veins, arteries, nerve fibres and other bodily vessels, but, in the context of yoga physiology, *nāḍī* refers specifically to conduits of prāṇa (*prāṇa-vāhinya* [*GoŚ* 26]).

The number of nāḍīs in the subtle matrix permeating the human organism is given variously in the manuals of haṭha-yoga as 350,000 (*ŚS* 2.13), 300,000 (*GoŚ* 13), 200,000 (*Gorakṣa-Paddhati* 12), or as uncountable, 'like the veins of an *aśvattha* leaf' (*Triśikhibrāhmaṇa-Upaniṣad* 76). Most commonly agreed upon, however, is the figure of 72,000, which is given in *HYP* 3.123, *Gorakṣa-Śataka* 25, *Śiva-Svarodaya* 32, and elsewhere. All 72,000 nāḍīs are said to emanate from a central point or subtle organ called the *kanda* ('bulb'), which, according to *HYP* 3.113, is like a soft, white rolled cloth. It is said to be 'four *aṅgula*s in breadth' and situated 'twelve *aṅgula*s above [the anus]', an *aṅgula* being the breadth or width of one finger. Brahmānanda, quoting Yājñavalkya, adds that 'Two aṅgulas above the anus (*guda*) and two below the penis (*meḍhra*) is the centre of the body (*deha-madhya*)... Nine aṅgulas from [i.e. above] the centre of the body is the *kanda-sthāna* ("seat of the kanda") in men. It is egg-shaped and enveloped in a membrane (*tvag*, "skin")' (*J* 3.113). On this account, the kanda should be located in the region of the subtle body corresponding approximately to the navel, or just below it, a

[14] Cf. Monier-Williams 1963: 534.

positioning supported by several other texts, including the *Śiva-Svarodaya*, in which *kanda* and *nābhi-sthānaka* ('navel region') are equivalent terms (*ŚSv* 32; cf. *GoŚ* 23).[15]

The kanda is sometimes alternatively said to be located in the region corresponding to the perineum, a claim made, for example, in Kālīcaraṇa's commentary on the *Ṣaṭ-Cakra-Nirūpaṇa*, translated in Arthur Avalon's *The Serpent Power*. Kālīcaraṇa quotes an unspecified work as saying that 'Two fingers above the anus and two fingers below the Meḍhra [penis] is the Kanda-mūla ["bulbous root"], in shape like a bird's egg'.[16] This appears to be a corruption of the quotation attributed to Yājñavalkya in *Jyotsnā* 3.113 (quoted above), the main difference being that Kālīcaraṇa's version neglects to mention that the kanda is nine aṅgulas *above* the midpoint between penis and anus and not *in* that place. Consequently, Avalon assumes the kanda and mūlādhāra-çakra to be adjacent rather than roughly a hand's breadth apart.[17] Such confusion is understandable, since in certain Tantric texts the seat of Kuṇḍalinī-śakti is given as the pericarp of the mūlādhāra-cakra (e.g. *ṢCN* 10-11), while in others, including several haṭha treatises, she (Kuṇḍalinī) is said to 'sleep above the kanda' (*HYP* 107). The *Śiva-Saṃhitā* adds to the puzzle by ignoring the kanda altogether and stating that fourteen principal nāḍīs emanate from mūlādhāra-cakra itself (*ŚS* 2.29). More will be said about this matter in the discussion of Kuṇḍalinī below (pp. 171ff.).

Gorakṣa-Śataka 26 states that, of the seventy-two thousand nāḍīs, seventy-two are noteworthy and, of these, ten are most important (cf. *ŚSv* 36ff.). These ten are named, and their respective locations vis-à-vis gross and subtle aspects of the body given, as follows:[18]

---

[15] It is interesting to note that, in the healing arts of Japan such as Shiatsu, the centre of human vital energy (*ki*) is also held to be situated in the abdomen (*hāra*), the acupressure point three finger-breadths below the navel being known as the 'sea of ki'.

[16] *ṢCNC* 1.

[17] See, e.g. Avalon 1974: 115.

[18] *GoŚ* 29-31; cf. *ŚSv* 37-41.

1. *Iḍā*—situated on the left side of the central spinal channel (suṣumṇā-nāḍī).
2. *Piṅgalā*—on the right side of suṣumṇā.
3. *Suṣumṇā*—in the mid-region (between iḍā and piṅgalā).
4. *Gāndhārī*—terminating in the left eye.
5. *Hastijihvā*—terminating in the right eye.
6. *Pūṣā*—terminating in the right ear.
7. *Yaśasvinī*—terminating in the left ear.
8. *Alambuṣā*—terminating in the mouth.
9. *Kuhū*—in the region of the liṅga (phallus, genital organ).
10. *Śaṁkhinī*—in the anal region or at the perineum (*mūla*, 'root').

Apart from these very brief descriptions of location, little else is said about the majority of these nāḍīs in the haṭha literature, the exceptions being the first three—*iḍā*, *piṅgalā* and *suṣumnā*—towards which considerable attention is directed in haṭha-yoga practice. These three channels are held to correspond to, or be 'presided over by', the deities Soma, Sūrya, and Agni respectively (*GoŚ* 32), who, on the physical plane, manifest as moon, sun and fire.

In some visual representations of the three main nāḍīs, iḍā and piṅgalā are pictured, respectively, to the left and right of suṣumnā all the way from mūlādhāra-cakra at the perineum to ājñā-cakra in the centre of the brow; other representations, meanwhile, portray iḍā and piṅgalā as strands that intertwine like a double helix around the central column of suṣumnā in a way reminiscent of the Hermetic *caduceus*, which shows a winged staff enwrapped by a pair of snakes (see Appendix A, p. 251). Within suṣumnā, there are considered to be three main obstructions called *granthi*s (lit. 'knots') which must be 'pierced' by Kuṇḍalinī-śakti as she rises upwards; and some commentators assert that the granthis are junctions where suṣumnā is crossed by iḍā and piṅgalā, a claim which favours the 'intertwining' representation of the three main nāḍīs. The meeting points of the three principal nāḍīs are held to coincide with mūlādhāra-, anāhata- and ājñā-cakra, and the three knots formed there are commonly referred to as *Brahma-granthi* (knot of Brahmā), *Viṣṇu-granthi* (knot of Viṣṇu) and *Rudra-granthi* (knot of Rudra [Śiva]).[19] Avalon states that it is in the granthis that māyā is particularly strong,[20] māyā being an aspect (or sometimes a synonym) of Śakti, the emanative power of Brahman. Māyā is productive of the phenomenal universe and thus serves to 'mask' or 'veil' the Reality behind the phenomena.

Alongside the theory of nāḍīs is a conception of 'tides' or 'currents' of prāṇa, these currents being held to govern the appropriate times for engaging in certain activities. The study of this aspect of vital force is often termed *svara-yoga*, *svara* meaning 'sound' and referring both to the subtle sound made by prāṇa as it passes in and out of the body and to the prāṇa itself.[21] A major treatise on svara-yoga is the *Śiva-Svarodaya*, in which can be found remarkably detailed accounts of the times of day when the svara is channeled most strongly through iḍā and piṅgalā respectively. The purpose of such information is to assist the yogin in coordinating his or her activities with the alternating current of vital force, it being stated that, 'during the day or night, according to whether one wishes to perform excellent or less excellent (*aśubha*) actions, one should observe the flow of the nāḍīs' (*ŚSv* 101). The predominance of flow in iḍā is held to be conducive to 'placid work' (*ib.* 60), and, when the current is strongest in piṅgalā, then 'difficult work should be done' (*ib.* 61). The aim of haṭha-yoga prāṇāyāma and svara-yoga is to first regulate and balance the flow of prāṇa along iḍā and piṅgalā nāḍīs, and then to transfer that flow into the central

---

[19] Cf. Feuerstein 1990a: 121; Sastri 1953: 350-51. It should be noted that, according to the *HYP* (4.70ff.), the three granthis are alternatively positioned in the heart, throat and brow centres respectively.

[20] Avalon 1974: 137.

[21] Swami Satyananda Saraswati defines *svara-yoga* as 'the ancient science of pranic body rhythms which explains how the movement of prana can be controlled by manipulation of the breath' (in Muktibodhananda Saraswati 1984: xi).

channel of suṣumnā. It is this transference of current—the concentration and purposeful channeling of vital force—that is implied when haṭha-yoga is said to involve the 'union of sun (*ha*) and moon (*ṭha*)', and it is the internal 'heat' generated by the activity of prāṇa in suṣumnā-nāḍī that is, in turn, held to arouse Kuṇḍalinī from her slumber.

The name of the central channel, *suṣumnā*, can mean 'very gracious or kind', a definition which Monier-Williams finds in the *Ṛg-Veda.*[22] According to *HYP* 3.4, its synonyms include:

śūnyapadavī—place of the void,
brahmarandhra—hollow of (or entrance to) Brahman,
mahāpatha—the great path,
śmaśāṇa—the crematorium, or burning ground,
śāṃbhavī—the consort (or power) of Śambhu (Śiva),
madhyamārga—the central path.

Several of these terms refer to the effect which is held to result from prāṇa's being successfully channeled up through this nāḍī. *Śūnyapadavī*, for example, is suggestive of the falling away of one's identification with phenomenal entities, leaving that which is 'empty' or 'void' of phenomenality (i.e. the true Self), while *śmaśāṇa* relates to the 'burning' of saṃskāras (habitual tendencies) which occurs during the various stages of samādhi. Further names and epithets for the central channel are contained in other texts, such as the *Varāha-Upaniṣad* (29-30), wherein, as B. K. S. Iyengar has noted, suṣumnā is described as 'blazing and shining (jvalanti),...sound incarnate (nādarūpiṇi)' and 'the "Supporter of the Universe" (Viśvadhāriṇī...)'.[23]

In the *Ṣaṭ-Cakra-Nirūpaṇa* (*ṢCN*), suṣumnā-nāḍī is said to contain within it a more refined channel called *vajrā-* or *vajriṇī-nāḍī*, which term derives from *vajra*, meaning 'thunderbolt' or 'adamantine'; and, within vajriṇī, is said to be a still more subtle channel known as *citrā-* or *citriṇī-nāḍī*, the hollow

[22] Monier-Williams 1963: 1237.
[23] Iyengar 1981: 33-34.

of which is *brahma-nāḍī*—the 'path' or 'channel' of Brahman.[24] The words *citrā* and *citriṇī* are both feminine forms of *citra*, meaning 'brilliant', 'bright', 'clear', and also 'variegated' or 'multicoloured'. Additionally, Monier-Williams notes that, in the *Ṛg-Veda*, the term may refer to a clear *sound*.[25] All of these definitions are in accordance with the use of the term in the *ṢCN*, wherein citriṇī is described as being 'lustrous with the lustre of the Praṇava...[and] subtle as a spider's thread' (*ṢCN* 2). Her (i.e. citriṇī's) nature or essential form (*svarūpā*) is said to be *śuddha-bodha*, meaning roughly 'pure intelligence', 'pure wisdom' or 'pure awareness'. Hence we see that the nature of this innermost nāḍī is identified with the experience that occurs as the vital force is channeled up through 'her' centre. She is characterised as partaking of the nature of the supreme Goddess (Devī), who is experienced as the nāda (inner sound). In its highest form, as the seat of one's identity rises to the force-centre in the region of the brow (ājñā-cakra), this sound is heard (internally or 'psychically') as the fundamental and universal vibration, *om*. The praṇava or *oṃ* may be likened (to a limited extent) to the divine *logos* or 'word of God' mentioned in the Christian New Testament (in the opening verse of St. John's gospel), since, on the yogic view, the 'word' (*vāk* or *śabda*) or 'sound' (nāda) is regarded as the primal manifestation or emanative medium of Īśvara ('the Lord'), and it is by means of this vibratory mechanism that the universe is held to be stirred from a pacific state into a dynamic and evolving one. In yoga symbology, however, nāda—*qua* Īśvara's 'power' and the instrumental cause of universal transformation—is personified as the Goddess (Devī), a characterisation that does not, of course, appear in traditional Christianity.

---

24 Avalon emphasises that brahma-nāḍī is not separate from citriṇī, but is 'The interior of the latter' (1974: 111).

25 Monier-Williams 1963: 396.

Cakras

Along citriṇī-nāḍī are said to be strung the major 'force centres' called cakras. The term *cakra* means 'wheel', and may refer to the wheel of a vehicle, or to certain other circular objects such as the discus that Viṣṇu is commonly characterised as spinning upon one of his fingers. Circles and spirals, and the notions of whirling and turning, are fundamental to Indian cosmology, as cosmic evolution is held to be of a spiral nature; and hence, when the cosmos—or a particular aspect of it—is represented in diagramatic or symbolic form, this too may be called a *cakra*.[26] Other terms for such models or diagrams include *maṇḍala* (circle, disc, sphere) and *yantra* (instrument, tool, symbol), the latter term suggesting the functional value of these images. Cakras of this sort, which may take the form of a two-dimensional geometric design or a three-dimensional sculpture, are used as aids for meditation, and they usually have a central focal point towards which, or 'into' which, the meditator's attention is drawn. They represent not simply the immediately perceptible world, but the multiple levels of reality that are present in the universe as a whole and within the human being.

In the context of human subtle physiology, *cakra* signifies a 'centre' or 'vortex' of 'force' or 'energy' situated at various junctions throughout the subtle matrix of nāḍīs. It is considered that, just as there are thousands of nāḍīs, so also are there thousands of cakras, although comparatively few of these are mentioned in the yoga literature. Avalon cites a Sanskrit work by Brahmānanda-Svāmī entitled *Advaitamārtanda* ('Undivided light/sun'), in which many cakras situated along the cerebrospinal axis are named, including twenty that are listed in what is believed to be their correct order.[27] Six of these—located at intervals from the perineum to the centre of the brow—are generally held to be of major importance in haṭha-yoga, with

[26] An extract from *Bhairava-Yāmala*, quoted by P. R. A. Śāstrī in Avalon (1974: 145), reads, for example: 'O Supreme One, the whole Cosmos is a Śrī-cakra [glorious cakra] formed of the twenty-five Tattvas...'.
[27] Avalon 1974: 151.

certain so-called 'minor' cakras receiving occasional references in the literature.

Several of the Yoga Upaniṣads provide varying descriptions of the cakras, as do certain Tantras. Of this latter category of texts, one of the most notable and comprehensive is the already mentioned *Ṣaṭ-Cakra-Nirūpaṇa* ('Exposition of the six cakras'). Composed (presumably from earlier sources) around 1577 C.E. by Pūrṇānanda-Svāmī, it was rendered into English, along with Kālīcaraṇa's commentary, by John Woodroffe in his work *The Serpent Power*, first published in 1919 under the pseudonym Arthur Avalon. The *SCN* describes the cakras as being strung along citriṇī, the most refined conduit residing within suṣumnā-nāḍī; and it is up through citriṇī that Kuṇḍalinī-śakti is held to surge, activating the major cakras as she penetrates each one in turn, breaking through the three granthis located at the base-, heart- and brow-centres.

The descriptions of the cakras in the *SCN* are highly elaborate, each being represented as a lotus flower (*padma*) with a specified colour and number of petals.[28] Each cakra, or padma, is also assigned a central geometric shape, which itself has a particular colour, plus an animal or mythological creature, a tattva (existent principle) and a bīja-mantra (seed sound). Within the *bindu* of each bīja-mantra—i.e. the dot which, when placed above a Devanāgarī character, indicates that the sound is nasalised—is said to reside a male deity (deva); and abiding in each lotus is an aspect of the Goddess (Śakti). In addition to the central 'seed mantra', monosyllabic mantras are also attributed to the lotus petals, and these correspond to fifty characters of the Sanskrit alphabet (or syllabary). The tattvas associated with the first five cakras (counting from mūlādhāra upwards) are the five mahābhūtas (gross elements)—earth, water, fire, air and ākāśa (roughly 'space' or 'ether')—while the ājñā-cakra consti-

---

[28] Avalon notes (1974: 16) that 'the number of the petals of any specific lotus is determined by the disposition of the...Nāḍīs around it.' In other words, the number of petals indicates the number of nāḍīs that are thought to 'meet' or 'cross' at that place.

tutes the seat of 'mind' (antaḥkaraṇa) or its most refined aspect (mahat, buddhi).

Brief descriptions of the six main cakras are given below, and several of their numerous associations listed. (Illustrations are to be found in Appendix A.)

Mūlādhāra-cakra

Definition and location: Mūla means 'root' or 'base', and *ādhāra* means 'support', thus *mūlādhāra* denotes the 'foundational' or 'root-support' cakra. Its location is said to be 'below the genitals and above the anus' (*ṢCN* 4), corresponding to the centre of the perineum in the sthūla-śarīra.[29]

Number and colour of petals: four, crimson.

Petal mantras: vaṃ, śaṃ, ṣaṃ, saṃ.

Geometric shape: yellow square.

Tattva: pṛthivī (earth).

Animal: the elephant Airāvata.

Bīja-mantra: laṃ.

Deva: Śiśuḥ sṛṣṭikārī ('Child creator/emanator', i.e. Brahmā), seated upon Haṃsa, the 'Great swan'.

Śakti: Ḍākinī.

Additional information: The *ṢCN* (8-11) describes a 'lightning-like triangle' that 'constantly shines' within the pericarp of mūlādhāra-cakra. The triangle is red and downward-pointing, and has the 'form of love' (*kāmarūpa*). Inside the triangle is Svayaṃbhu-liṅga, around which Kuṇḍalinī is said to be coiled three and a half times.

Svādhiṣṭhāna-cakra

Definition and location: Sva means 'own' or 'ownmost', and *adhiṣṭhāna* means 'standing place' or 'abode', thus *svādhi-*

[29] Buddhananda (1984: 21ff.) is more precise, stating that mūlādhāra corresponds to the perineal body, which is 'a small fibromuscular node about one to one and a half inches in front of the anus and approximately two inches inside the body.' In women, mūlādhāra is placed at the top of the cervix, just below the entrance to the womb.

ṣṭhāna denotes one's 'ownmost abode'. Its location corresponds to 'the root of the genitals' (*ṢCN* 14).

Number and colour of petals: six, vermilion.

Petal mantras: baṃ, bhaṃ, maṃ, yaṃ, raṃ, laṃ.

Geometric shape: white crescent moon.

Tattva: jala (water).

Animal: Makara (the body of a fish with a head resembling that of a crocodile).

Bīja-mantra: vaṃ.

Deva: Hari (Viṣṇu), seated on Garuḍa, a mythical bird-man.

Śakti: Rākiṇī.

Maṇipūraka-cakra

Definition and location: Maṇi means 'jewel', and *pūraka* means 'filling up', 'completing' or 'flooding', thus *maṇipūraka* (sometimes simply *maṇipūra*) denotes the region that is 'jewel-filled'. *ṢCN* 19 places this cakra 'at the root of the navel', as does the *Gorakṣa-Śataka* (23), and hence it may be referred to as *nābhi-padma*, the 'navel lotus'.

Number and colour of petals: ten, 'the colour of heavy-laden rain-clouds' (*ṢCN* 19).

Petal mantras: ḍaṃ, ḍhaṃ, ṇaṃ, taṃ, thaṃ, daṃ, dhaṃ, naṃ, paṃ, phaṃ.

Geometric shape: downward-pointing red triangle.

Tattva: tejas (fire).

Animal: ram.

Bīja-mantra: raṃ.

Deva: Rudra (Śiva), seated upon Nandin, a white bull.

Śakti: Lākinī.

Anāhata-cakra

Definition and location: Anāhata means 'unstruck', which refers to the 'sacred inner sound' (śabda or nāda) that is 'heard' during deep introspective meditation 'without the striking of any two things together' (*ṢCNC* 22). It is said to reside 'in the heart', which is the region associated with the upward-moving prāṇa (*ṢCN* 22).

Number and colour of petals: twelve, 'the shining colour of the Bandhūka flower' (i.e. red) (*ṢCN* 22).

Petal mantras: kaṃ, khaṃ, gaṃ, ghaṃ, ṅaṃ, caṃ, chaṃ, jaṃ, jhaṃ, ñaṃ, ṭaṃ, ṭhaṃ.

Geometric shape: hexagram (two overlapping triangles, one pointing upwards, the other downwards), 'of a smoky colour'.[30]

Tattva: vāyu (air, wind, breath).

Animal: black antelope.

Bīja-mantra: yaṃ.

Deva: Īśa (Śiva).

Śakti: Kākinī.

Additional information: Anāhata is the second of three cakras to be represented with a Śiva-liṅga in its pericarp, the first being mūlādhāra and the third being ājñā. The presence of the liṅga, referred to in this centre as *bāṇa-liṅga* (*bāṇa*: arrow), signifies special potency.

A minor cakra, possessing eight red petals and described as containing 'the Kalpa Tree' and a 'jewelled altar surmounted by an awning and decorated by flags and the like', is situated just below Anāhata.[31]

Viśuddha-cakra

Definition and location: Viśuddha means 'pure' or 'cleansed' both in a hygienic and a moral sense. This cakra is sometimes called *viśuddhi*, which is the feminine form of the same word. It is located 'At the base of the throat' (*kaṇṭha-mūle*).[32]

Number and colour of petals: sixteen, smoky purple.

Petal mantras: [all of the Sanskrit vowels:] *aṃ, āṃ, iṃ, īṃ, uṃ, ūṃ, ṝṃ, ṛṃ, ḷṃ, ḹṃ, eṃ, aiṃ, oṃ, auṃ, aṃṃ, aḥṃ.*

Geometric shape: a white circle within a downward-pointing triangle.

---

[30] Avalon 1974: 382.

[31] *Ib.*: 383.

[32] *Ib.*: 391.

Tattva: ākāśa (space, ether).
Animal: white elephant.
Bīja-mantra: haṃ.
Deva: Sadāśiva ('Eternal Śiva').
Śakti: Sākinī.

Ājñā-cakra

Definition and location: Ājñā means 'command' or 'order', and it is when one's attention is centred in this cakra that direct communication with the guru is said to occur;[33] in other words, one 'hears' the 'command' of one's guru, or of the 'inner guru', the supreme Self.[34] The term may also indicate that this is the 'command centre', instrumental in controlling bodily operations. Its location is that of the 'eye of Śiva' (or 'third eye'), in the centre of the brow, just above the bridge of the nose.
Number and colour of petals: two, white.
Petal mantras: haṃ, ksaṃ.
Geometric shape: downward-pointing golden triangle, within which is the third, or 'other' (*itara*) Śiva-liṅga.
Tattvas: mūla-prakṛti (root-substance) and antaḥkaraṇa (the 'inner instrument' or 'mind').
Bīja-mantra: oṃ.
Deva: Viṣṇu.
Śakti: Hākinī.

The number of associations made with the various cakras is not exhausted by the above lists, although these are the ones that tend to be the most commonly mentioned. In his book, *Chakras: Energy Centers of Transformation*, Harish Johari presents further associations with the cakras, including such things as behavioural characteristics, hand gestures (known as *mudrā*s), and the seven 'higher' *loka*s ('worlds' or 'planes').[35]

---

[33] Cf. *ṢCNC* 32; Avalon 1974: 10n.
[34] It is perhaps for this reason that Feuerstein (1974b: 190) translates *ājñā* as 'insight'.
[35] Johari 1987: 92ff.

This latter correlation is particularly significant as it emphasises and illuminates the *experiential* nature of the cakras, which are, first and foremost, centres of perception or awareness (*cit*, *citi-śakti*). Like the kośas discussed in the previous chapter, they stand for different modes of 'seeing' and of self-identification; and, when this is borne in mind, their actual locations in relation to the physical body become of only secondary importance. The seven lokas are: (1) *bhū-*, (2) *bhuvar-*, (3) *svarga-*, (4) *mahar-*, (5) *jana-*, (6) *tapo-*, and (7) *satya-loka*, and these correspond to the cakras from mūlādhāra up to the sahasrāra-padma.[36] Bhū-loka is the 'gross', 'physical' or 'earthly' plane, i.e. the plane of existence that is accessable to the ordinary physical senses, and of which the sthūla-śarīra is an integral part. With regard to the cakras, when one's self-identity is centred in the gross physical world, then one may be said to be operating from the perspective of mūlādhāra. This is not, of course, meant to imply that the awareness of such a person is literally centred in the region of the perineum, but, rather, that the dominant elements in that awareness will be the gross physical phenomena of which the root cakra is emblematic. *Bhuvar-loka*—corresponding to svādiṣṭhāna-cakra—roughly translates as the 'atmosphere' or 'world of air', but it really refers to a plane of existence which is more 'refined' or 'subtle' than that of gross physical objects. Svarga-loka is the 'celestial realm' or 'plane of light'; mahar-loka, the 'plane of greatness';[37] jana-loka, the 'generative plane'; and tapo-loka, the 'plane of heat'; each loka being yet more ethereal than the one before. The highest plane is, of course, satya-loka, *satya* meaning 'truth' or 'reality'; this is the sphere of clear perception and absolute knowingness.

The lokas are not so much alternative 'worlds' as alternative 'levels' of *the* world. One's awareness of the lokas develops as one's perception becomes more acute; and this process is char-

---

36 Cf. *ib.*: 96.

37 Johari refers to this as *manas-loka* (*ib.*: 92), 'mind-world'.

acterised in haṭha-yoga as the 'opening' or 'piercing' of the cakras by the ascending force of Kuṇḍalinī.

Also connected with the cakras are certain vṛttis, which, as noted in Chapter 5, are 'modifications' or 'turnings' of the mind-field, and may include thoughts, emotions, attitudes, and other mental phenomena. According to yoga philosophy, the presence of any vṛtti influences one's mode of perception, facilitating a more or less distorted impression of reality. Avalon cites a text called the *Adhyātma-viveka* ('Discernment of the Supreme Self') as mentioning the contiguity between vṛttis and cakras. In this work, several vṛttis—which tend here to fall into the categories of either moral qualities or mental dispositions—are linked to each cakra (according to the number of its 'petals'), beginning with svādiṣṭhāna and going up to the *soma-cakra*, which is one of the minor (though nevertheless important) centres located between the ājñā-cakra and sahasrāra-padma. 'It is stated', reports Avalon, 'that particular Vṛttis are assigned to a particular lotus, because of a connection between such Vṛtti and the operation of the Śaktis of the Tattva at the centre to which it is assigned. That they exist at any particular Cakra is said to be shown by their disappearance when Kuṇḍalī [= Kuṇḍalinī] ascends through the Cakra.'[38] In moral terms, the vṛttis associated with higher cakras are more 'virtuous' than those associated with lower ones, and hence it is held to be the basest elements of human nature that are first to 'disappear', followed by those which are more honourable.[39] Rather than 'disappearing', however, it would be more appropriate to think of the vṛttis as being systematically *transcended*, in the sense that one is no longer *affected* by them. One's moods, emotions, mental attitudes, moral predilections, etc.

---

[38] Avalon 1974: 139-40.

[39] Vṛttis associated with svādiṣṭhāna-cakra include: 'Credulity, suspicion, disdain, delusion,' etc.; maṇipūraka: 'Shame, treachery, jealousy,...ignorance [*moha*],' etc.; anāhata: 'Hope, care or anxiety, endeavour, mineness,' etc.; and soma: 'Mercy, gentleness, patience or composure, dispassion [*vairāgya*],' etc. Other associations are made with the remaining cakras (see Avalon 1974: 138-39 for a fuller exposition).

may be said to 'dissolve' back into the waters of consciousness from which they arose, but they still exist in a latent form, to be utilised when required. The important point is that, as one's sense of self moves closer to its true home, the vṛttis—of whatever kind—cease to constitute the 'visor' through which one perceives the world (in a distorted form).

Although discussions about the cakras typically draw attention to the elaborate symbolism used to describe them, an issue which is frequently neglected—perhaps because of its complexity—is that of the nature of the *relationship* between that symbolism and the cakras themselves, between, that is, these 'centres', 'accumulators', or 'transformers' of vital force in the subtle body and the signs by which they are represented. At the very least, such signs or symbols provide considerable assistance to the yogin insofar as they facilitate the concentration of attention upon, or within, a particular region of the subtle matrix. In the absence of such imagery, there would be much less to focus upon and to 'draw the mind inwards'. At the same time, however, it should be recognised that the symbolism is not intended to be *solely* heuristic; the specific shapes, colours, sounds, and so forth, connected with each cakra are held to furnish an accurate representation—albeit in comparatively 'gross' form—of the essential character of that cakra. According to the philosophy upon which much Tāntrika practice is based, there is no such thing as an isolated sense-experience which does not involve all of the other sensual faculties; every object of perception is held, rather, to have a stimulating effect upon all five senses. Thus, on this view, it is impossible to hear a sound without simultaneously 'feeling' it, 'seeing' it, 'tasting' it, and 'smelling' it. By this, far more is meant than the obvious fact that, if I hear, for example, the roar of a tiger, the sound will be accompanied by mental impressions of a tiger corresponding to the other four senses. Rather, what the idea is meant to convey is that the *sound itself* provokes the other sensual impressions, and that these impressions are not necessarily *of* the object which produced the sound (in this case, a tiger). A roar may indeed have *emanated* from a tiger, but that roar has a sound—a quality, frequency or vibration—and hence a 'character', of its own, which is connected to, but also potentially abstract from, the tiger from whom it emanated. Furthermore, there is considered to be a *hierarchy* of sensual impressions, according to which auditory impressions 'give rise to' palpatory ones, which in turn generate visual images, and so on. Sound is regarded as the initial vehicle, or mechanism, of manifestation, which is why the universe, including the human form, is held to be constituted by śabda (word, utterance), this being internally perceptible in the form of nāda or mantra. As Avalon points out, according to Tantra philosophy, 'The whole human body is in fact a Mantra, and is composed of Mantras.'[40]

Crucial for understanding the relevance of the cakra-related symbols is the notion that every sense-datum perceived by the ordinary physical senses is only the *grossest manifestation* of a whole chain—or multilayered fabric—of signification, beginning with a disturbance in the equilibrium of the three guṇas (fundamental 'strands' of phenomenality). Thus, underlying any audible sound, there is held to be a series of progressively more subtle vibrations which are imperceptible to the auditory faculties of the sthūla-śarīra, but which correspond to the more subtle levels of one's own being and are therefore *potentially* audible. The same applies to the other four senses; thus for every visible image there exist a number of potentially-visible ones, for every taste, more 'subtle' tastes, and so on. Of course, to describe—or even to conceive—what a 'subtle taste', for example, might be *like* is probably an impossible task, but the mechanism by which it could be experienced is precisely that of yoga *per se*, or, more specifically, saṃprajñāta-samādhi, in which the aim is to identify with increasingly rarified aspects of one's being, and to cultivate the 'inner' or 'psychic' perception of the subtle elements corresponding to those aspects.[41]

---

[40] Avalon 1974: 166.

[41] Cf. Chapter 5 (pp. 116ff.) above. As an aside, it is interesting to note that accounts of those who have had 'out-of-the-body experiences' (OOBEs)—and

The written or spoken bīja-mantra of any ćakra is, then, only the outward expression, and thus the grossest manifestation, of a far more subtle vibrational quality. It is the *vaikharī* (uttered speech) dimension of śabda, which exists simultaneously in three more refined modes known respectively as *madhyamā* (intermediate), *paśyantī* ('perceiving' [with the 'inner faculty']) and *parā* (highest, other).[42] The attribution of mantras—whether to the cakra as a whole or to its several 'petals'—is far from arbitrary; on the contrary, these sounds are regarded as 'incarnations' of the śakti (power) which is the generative force underlying the cakra. In fact, the idea that mantras are 'attributed' to the cakras is itself misleading, since a cakra cannot exist independently of its mantras. As its name suggests, a bīja-mantra represents the 'seed' that gives birth to, and informs, a particular cakra; and the minor mantras radiating out from this 'seed'—and written as syllables upon the lotus petals—stand for certain qualities of that cakra. Similarly, the geometric shape associated with any particular cakra is held to be a visible manifestation of that cakra's śakti, as is its colour. The sound, form and colour are inseparable, for the presence of the one implies the (real or potential) existence of the others, all of them having emanated from the presiding śakti, who is, her-

---

may thus be said to have been temporarily operating at a level other than that of the sthūla-śarīra—often mention extraordinary 'sensual' episodes. Prescott Hall, a researcher into the subject, writes, for example, that, during OOBEs, the experiencer hears

> a hissing or whistling, as of escaping steam; single musical notes; musical phrases, generally new to the hearer; human tunes; the sound of a bell or bells, sometimes in harmony; and metallic noises like the striking of an anvil... A very peculiar sensation is as if someone unseen were blowing in one's face. It is as if some unseen finger-tip touched one about the throat, mouth and nose, causing a 'tickling' sensation. (Quoted in Murphy 1992: 223-24n.)

Such accounts perhaps hint at what the experience of 'subtle phenomena' might be like.

[42] Cf. Avalon 1974: 48; 165: 'Letters when spoken are...the manifested aspect in gross speech of the subtle energy of the Śabdabrahman as Kuṇḍalī. The same energy which produces these letters manifesting as Mantras produces the gross universe.'

self, only an aspect of the supreme Śakti or Devī—the 'power' of Śiva.

To fully appreciate the significance to the cakras of particular animals, as well as that of the presiding śaktis and devas as they are variously represented, one would need to delve deep into Indian mythology; and even then it is likely that many mysteries would remain. The principle of non-arbitrariness still obtains, however, as all the imagery connected with the cakras is held to emanate from the essential nature of the cakras themselves; that is, from the nature of the *experience* as these centres are 'opened' by the awakened Kuṇḍalinī-śakti. Discrepancies between the descriptions of cakras given in different texts may be accounted for by the existence of variations in the personality-matrices of yogins; for, while every human being is held to have a common origin in Śakti, we nevertheless constitute unique networks of gross and subtle structures, which act as more-or-less distorting prisms of perceptual data. In other words, the very *faculties* of perception may serve to qualify the image of the object perceived in ways which vary from one individual to another, and this is almost bound to result in different descriptions being given of what is basically the same object, especially in the case of such subtle phenomena as those associated with the cakras. It is for this reason that the cakra pictograms provided in the *ṢCN* and elsewhere are perhaps best regarded as yantras or maṇḍalas of the kind mentioned in the opening paragraph of this section; that is, as diagramic models which *approximate* to a certain aspect of reality and act as gateways between human and cosmic levels of experience.

Any discussion of the cakras would be incomplete without some mention of those said to reside above the ājñā-cakra. These include the *manas-cakra*, which is ascribed six petals (corresponding to the five ordinary senses plus the 'internally generated' sense responsible for dreams and similar experiences), and the sixteen-petalled *soma-cakra*, already noted with regard to the vṛttis.[43] Still higher, at the very apex of citriṇī-

---

[43] Cf. Avalon 1974: 127-28.

nāḍī, is the cakra or lotus of twelve petals (*dvādaśārṇa*), said to be situated in the pericarp of the highest centre of all, namely *sahasrāra-padma*, the 'thousand-petalled lotus'. The sahasrāra is not typically regarded as a cakra in the strict sense, since, whereas the cakras stand for particular loci of self-identity, or 'rungs', as it were, on the ladder leading to Self-realisation, the sahasrāra represents the very pinnacle of yogic attainment, and the transcendence of all other centres. Like the cakras, however, it is symbolised as a lotus-flower, and on its thousand petals are said to be written the letters of the Sanskrit alphabet twenty times over, thereby implying the absorption of all the qualities of sound. Synonyms for the sahasrāra are, inevitably, legion; as verse 44 of the *ṢCN* states:

> The Śaivas call it the abode of Śiva [*Śiva-sthāna*]; the Vaiṣṇavas call it Parama Puruṣa [Supreme Self]; others again call it the place of Hari-Hara [Viṣṇu-Śiva, sustainer and dissolver]. Those who are filled with a passion for the Lotus feet of the Devī [Goddess] call it the excellent abode of the Devī [*padaṃ devyā*]; and other great sages (Munis) call it the pure place of.Prakṛti-Puruṣa.[44]

In short, the sahasrāra-padma is the place where the static pole or universal principle is rejoined by the active or emanative pole. These principles—personified, or deified, as Śiva and Śakti respectively—are commonly represented as reunited lovers engaged in intimate and potent embrace, with the resultant orgasm leaving the yogin, whose body has provided the instrument for this union, in a state of 'Eternal and Transcendent Bliss' (*nityānanda-mahodayāt*) (*ṢCN* 53). Śakti is also, of course, frequently portrayed as the she-serpent Kuṇḍalinī, about which more shall now be said.

Kuṇḍalinī

> Spirals are the natural curve of life and uniform growth. They are always growing and yet never cover the same ground. They are the

---

[44] Trans. Avalon *ib.*: 438.

> only form of curve in which one part differs from another in size, not in shape. Spirals work both ways, coming from and going to their source. They define and illuminate what has already happened, as well as leading inevitably on to bigger things and new discoveries.[45]

In the above quotation from his book *Dark Nature* the biologist Lyall Watson concisely and poetically draws attention to the significant and recurring phenomenon of the spiral in the natural world. This phenomenon has not been missed by the traditional philosophers of India; indeed, the notion of the spiral infuses their concepts of evolution on both an individual and a cosmic level. At the heart of haṭha-yoga is the idea of Kuṇḍalinī-śakti, a coiled serpent in the form of a spiral, representing the reservoir of potential force or power which is, in principle, available to every one of us.

Kuṇḍalinī means 'she who is coiled' and *śakti* means 'power'; hence *Kuṇḍalinī-śakti* stands for the 'coiled' or 'spiral power'. Like the compressed spring of a jack-in-the-box, she lies dormant yet potent with energy, ready to expand upwards as soon as the lid is released and the pathway is clear. She is referred to as feminine because, from the yogic perspective, Kuṇḍalinī is identical to the supreme Goddess (Devī), who is the power, and hence the 'consort', of Śiva. Her nature is *sṛṣṭi-sthiti-layātmikā*; *sṛṣṭi* meaning 'emission', 'production', or 'emanation'; *sthiti* denoting 'existence' or 'preservation'; and *laya*, 'absorption' or 'dissolution'.[46] Hence she stands for the three guṇas or trimūrti rolled into one.

Synonyms of *Kuṇḍalinī* listed in *HYP* 3.104 include: *Kuṭalāṅgī* (crooked bodied), *Bhujaṅgī* (she-serpent), *Śakti* (power), *Īśvarī* (owner, possessor, female Lord), and *Kuṇḍalī* (coiled); and, in the succeeding verse (3.105), it is stated that haṭha is the means and Kuṇḍalinī the key with which the yogin may unlock the 'door to liberation' (*moksa-dvāra*).

---

[45] Watson 1995: 10.
[46] Cf. Avalon 1974: 15-16.

As mentioned in the above discussion of the nāḍīs (pp. 153ff.), there is some controversy concerning the 'seat' of Kuṇḍalinī in the human subtle body. The *Gheraṇḍa-Saṃhitā* (3.9), for example, states that 'The supreme Goddess (*paradevatā*) Kuṇḍalī—power of the Self (*ātma-śakti*)—[resides in] mūlādhāra', and references can be found in other relevant sources that concur with this designation (e.g. *ṢCN* 10-11). The *HYP* and *Gorakṣa-Śataka*, however, are clear in their placement of Kuṇḍalī/Kuṇḍalinī 'above the kanda (*kandordhve*)' (*HYP* 3.107, *GoŚ* 47), the kanda being, according to these texts, in the region of the lower abdomen. It is instructive that one of the key techniques described in the *HYP* (3.114-16) involves applying physical pressure to the abdomen with the heels and sides of the feet—the heels pressing into the navel and the balls of the feet into the solar plexus—and stimulating Kuṇḍalinī by firmly contracting 'the sun' (*bhānu*, i.e. the solar plexus).[47]

Rather than thinking in too literal a way about a serpent curled up in a particular bodily centre, it is perhaps useful to bear in mind that what is being discussed in the case of Kuṇḍalinī is a force so powerful and all-pervasive as to be considered the source of all manifestation. There is more than one specific locus in the bodily matrix that harbours a strong potential for stimulating or accessing that force, and one or other of such loci may be the object of attention in particular haṭha techniques. The presence of a range of 'power access points' could be one reason for disagreements in haṭha texts concerning Kuṇḍalinī's initial location.

The aim of haṭha-yoga is to first purify the nāḍīs to facilitate the improved flow of prāṇa, and then to induce the arousal and upward-movement of Kuṇḍalinī. The activation of this otherwise latent but extremely powerful force is held to engender a profound transformation of the yogin, and to precipitate the subtilisation and sublimation of his or her ordinary sense of

---

[47] This posture, illustrated on p. 266, is referred to as *vajrāsana* (thunderbolt posture) in *HYP* 3.114 and 115, and as *kandāsana* (kanda posture) in later manuals (e.g. Iyengar 1991: 348). Cf. p. 201 below.

identity. Key stages in this transformative process are regarded as coinciding with the 'piercing' or 'opening' by Kuṇḍalinī of the various cakras located along citriṇī-nāḍī within the channel of suṣumnā,[48] and her dramatic arrival at the pericarp of sahasrāra-padma (in the region of the cerebrum) marks the yogin's 'divinisation', i.e. the realisation of his identity as Brahman. In the following lively passage, Ramaswami Sastri presents a number of factors indicative of Kuṇḍalinī's activation:

> When there is a throbbing in mūlādhāra, when hair stands on its root, when uḍḍīyāna-, jālaṃdhara- and mūla-bandha come involuntarily... When the breath stops without any effort, when kevala kumbhaka [complete retention (of prāṇa)] comes by itself without any exertion, know that Kuṇḍalinī-śakti has become active. When you feel currents of prāṇa rising up to the sahasrāra, when you experience bliss, when you repeat Om automatically, when there are no thoughts of the world in the mind... When in your meditation the eyes become fixed on trikute, [between] the eye-brows, when the śāmbhavī-mudrā operates, know that Kuṇḍalinī has become active... During meditation when you feel as if there is no body, when your eye-lids become closed and do not open in spite of your exertion, when electric-like currents flow up and down the nerves, know that Kuṇḍalinī has awakened.[49]

American psychiatrist and ophthalmologist Lee Sannella has made a detailed study of the psychological and physiological characteristics of what he calls the 'kundalini experience', and notes that 'such physical sensations as itching, fluttering, tingling, intense heat and cold, photisms (perceptions of inner lights) and the perception of primary sounds, as well as the occurrence of spasms and contortions, seem to be "archetypal"

---

[48] It should be noted that, in most practically-oriented haṭha treatises, such as the *HYP*, *GS*, etc., the more refined nāḍīs within suṣumnā are not distinguished from suṣumnā itself, and therefore Kuṇḍalinī's ascension is described as taking place through suṣumnā rather than citriṇī (see, e.g. *HYP* 3.117-118).

[49] Sastri 1953: 347 (the transliteration of Sanskrit terms has been slightly emended).

features of the process, or at least of certain phases of it.'[50] He further observes that the 'clinical picture' of Kuṇḍalinī's awakening, constructed on the basis of his own research, differs from the 'classical model' presented in the Indian texts. While the latter suggest that 'the kundalini awakens, or is awakened, at the base of the spine, travels straight up the central axis of the body, and completes its journey when it reaches the crown of the head', 'the clinical picture is that the kundalini energy travels up the legs and the back to the top of the head, then down the face, through the throat, to a terminal point in the abdominal area.'[51] Sannella coins the term 'physio-kundalini cycle' to distinguish the experiences of his own research subjects from that described in the traditional yoga literature, and cautions that 'It is quite feasible that the physio-kundalini is a separate mechanism that may be activated as part of a complete kundalini awakening. It is too early to draw any final conclusions.'[52]

Many accounts of experiences associated with the Kuṇḍalinī phenomenon—whether of the 'classical' or the 'physio' variety—include sensations of intense heat, especially in the region of the spine. Among Sannella's numerous case studies, for example, is that of a 41-year-old woman whose practise of meditation gave rise to just such sensations, accompanied by the perception of 'light inside her skull' and 'all the way down her spine as well.' The experience was ongoing over a period of weeks, during which time the woman 'felt that if she did not meditate, the heat flowing in her body would grow so intense as to damage her system.' Nor were the sensations entirely subjective, as 'Other people could feel excessive heat when they touched her lower back.'[53] The occurrence of such tangible symptoms implies a causal continuum between subtle and gross aspects of the human organism, as does the fact that, in haṭha-

---

[50] Sannella 1987: 24.
[51] *Ib.*: 106.
[52] *Ib.*: 107.
[53] *Ib.*: 72.

yoga, mechanisms of the sthūla-śarīra (gross body)—such as breathing and muscular contractions—are utilised for the stimulation of Kuṇḍalinī. On the yogic view, the activities of the various 'layers' of one's being are intimately woven together into one psychophysical matrix. Only at the point of physical death is the outermost layer, the sthūla-śarīra, cast off.

In a discussion of 'The Manifestations of the Kundalini Awakening', Marshall Govindan describes the internal perception of 'a great light' in the region of ājñā-cakra, similar to that reported by Sannella's acquaintance above, as a 'preliminary stage' in the arousal of Kuṇḍalinī. During this stage, he continues, 'The mind becomes calmer and the appetite reduced. The breath flows simultaneously through both nostrils for a number of days, indicating that the [iḍā and piṅgalā nāḍīs] are in equilibrium.'[54] Eventually comes the 'explosive' animation of Kuṇḍalinī, the experience of which Govindan describes as akin to 'an electric shock from the base of the spinal column, travelling all the way up to the [sahasrāra-padma].'[55] Govindan adds that musical sounds (nāda) may be heard, and that suppressed feelings may be temporarily stirred up from the 'subconscious mind'. The physical body will be paralysed for the duration of the initial awakening, and both breath and pulse may cease, giving the appearance of physical death;[56] 'but if one opens the eyelids, one will find that the eyes are glowing like diamonds with [prāṇic] energy',[57] and the corresponding 'inner', or supra-physical, experience will be one of blissful illumination. Offering practical advice, Govindan warns that,

> If [someone] in the [samādhi] state has not come back by the twenty-first day, one should gently try to bring the person back to physical consciousness. However, it is for them to decide whether

---

[54] Govindan 1991: 166.

[55] *Ib.*

[56] Cf. pp. 226ff. below. The balance of scientific evidence existing on this matter supports the view that the heart rate may be dramatically decelerated but not altogether stopped during samādhi.

[57] Govindan *ib.*

to go or to come back. Beyond twenty one days it will not be possible to bring the person back to life.[58]

As mentioned with regard to the notion of jīvanmukti in Chapter 6 above, the state of physiological suspension in samādhi need not signify the end of one's psychological and physical life, but should, on the contrary, furnish the highest possible enrichment of that life. The peak experience of Kuṇḍalinī's initial upsurge is held to open up a permanent pathway in the suṣumnā-nāḍī (or, more accurately, within citriṇī-nāḍī enclosed by suṣumnā), through which prāṇa may flow (*HYP* 3.118). Then, as *SCN* 53 evocatively puts it, when 'The beautiful Kuṇḍalinī [has drunk] the excellent red nectar issuing from Para-Śiva, [she] returns from there where shines Eternal and Transcendent Bliss [*nityānanda-mahodayāt*] in all its glory along the path of Kula [= brahma-nāḍī], and again enters the Mūlādhāra.' According to Govindan, repeated occurrences of Kuṇḍalinī's ascension will engender, perhaps over several lifetimes, a gradual transformation of the person's mental and physical faculties. 'Ultimately, even the physical cells become charged with divine incorruptibility' and the body radiates 'a characteristic golden hue' (which is, he notes, too 'subtle' to be captured on photographic film).[59]

Since Kuṇḍalinī is said to 'throw open the mouth to suṣumnā, so that prāṇa is able to move freely through it' (*HYP* 3.118), it is clear that a distinction is made in haṭha theory between Kuṇḍalinī and prāṇa. While both terms denote a primal 'force' or 'energy', they are not thought of as identical. Swami Rama, founder of the Himalayan Institute, characterises Śakti (Kuṇḍalinī) as 'an impulse...that produces motion,' and vāyu (prāṇa) as 'a medium of action'.[60] He describes the relationship

---

[58] *Ib.* This claim would seem to be placed in some doubt by the example of Haridas who, according to credible evidence, remained in a state of suspended animation (or *virtual* suspended animation) for forty days (see pp. 235-37 below).

[59] Govindan *ib.*: 167.

[60] Rama 1986: 29.

between the two as akin to that between potential, or latent, energy and kinetic, or dynamic, energy. Hence, while prāṇa is 'the most basic unit of energy',[61] Kuṇḍalinī provides the 'static background' which supports, or gives rise to, that energy.[62] Kuṇḍalinī, then, is not a 'unit of energy', but the source, or 'mother', of *all* energy, one of her many titles being *Prāṇa-devatā* (Goddess of prāṇa), which suggests her *priority* over prāṇa.[63] It may seem paradoxical to talk of Kuṇḍalinī as a 'static background' when she is commonly represented as the *active* pole of the Śiva-Śakti duad, but the paradox arises only when the stratified nature of the universe, as presented by yoga metaphysics, is forgotten. This 'stratification' does not consist of layers of different substances, such as one might find if one were to dig down below the earth's surface for example, but of a *single substance* in different 'stages', as it were, of its own evolution. Nor do we need to go back in time to discover 'earlier' manifestations of this primal substance, for, according to the *sat-kārya-vāda* (doctrine of the pre-existent effect), most commonly associated with the Sāṃkhya darśana, any effect must be pre-existent in its cause, and, similarly, the cause—both material and efficient—continues to exist in its effect (*SK* 9). This means that, with regard to the schematic of twenty-five tattvas described in the Sāṃkhya philosophy, when it is stated that one tattva 'gives rise to' or 'issues forth' another, the second tattva is not held to replace the first, but is, rather, the *same* substance perceived at a 'denser' (or 'grosser') level of manifestation. Hence, for example, when one reads, in *Sāṃkhya-Kārikā* 22, that 'From *prakṛti*...issues *mahat*...; from this issues *ahaṁkāra*...; from which proceed the "set of sixteen" [i.e. manas, plus five sense capacities, five action capacities, and five *tanmātra*s (subtle elements)]; from five of this "set of sixteen" [i.e. the five tanmātrās] proceed the five elementary sub-

[61] *Ib.*: 79.
[62] *Ib.*: 132.
[63] Cf. Avalon 1974: 15-16.

stances [*mahābhūtas*]',[64] it should not be understood as an account of a linear evolutionary process; what is being described is not a temporal sequence but a hierarchy of 'states' or 'levels' of substance, with prakṛti standing for substance in its most primitive and imperceptible condition, and pṛthivī (earth), being the last of the five mahābhūtas, denoting the densest manifestation *of* prakṛti.

It is my contention that the satkāryavāda is implicitly accepted in the manuals of haṭha-yoga, wherein *Kuṇḍalinī* takes the place of *prakṛti* as the term denoting substantiality *per se*, and *prāṇa* is the medium of force through which all activity takes place.[65]

The above digression into the Sāṃkhya doctrine of causality is intended to shed some light upon the matter of how Kuṇḍalinī may be regarded as both static and dynamic. In her unmanifest state as *potential* energy/matter she is passive, whereas, in her various levels of manifestation, she appears as though active. In both states, she stands for the *power* of Śiva; and, as Śiva is held to be infinite, so is his power. As it takes only a relatively tiny fraction of that power to maintain the process of cosmic evolvement, a fathomless reservoir remains latent, and it is into this reservoir that the yogin is considered to tap when he or she brings about the elivation of Kuṇḍalinī.

The nerve-nāḍī identity theory

Attempts have been made by several interpreters to relate the phenomena of thc subtle bodily matrix to those with which modern biological science is more familiar. Avalon has noted,

---

64 Trans. Jha in Radhakrishnan and Moore 1957: 434.

65 Sāṃkhya philosophers speak of the five prāṇādi-vāyus as constituting 'the common function of the [antaḥkaraṇa]' (Vācaspati Miśra, *Tattva Kaumudī* 29, trans. Jha *ib.*: 436); hence, on this view, *prāṇa* may be defined as an impulse emanating from the mind, though ordinarily at a level below conscious awareness. This definition is at least partially compatible with the use of the term in haṭha material, although Sāṃkhya texts are typically more precise, consistent, and therefore more narrow, in their terminological application.

for example, that, while the cakras are 'not to be identified with the physical ganglia and plexuses' of the nervous system, they are nevertheless 'connected with, and in a gross sense represented by them.'[66] Others, however, have gone further and have indeed tried to draw an equation between the nāḍīs and cakras on the one hand, and the fibres and plexuses of the physical nervous system on the other. In his book *Kundalini—The Secret of Yoga* (1992), Gopi Krishna, founder of the Kundalini Research Institute, sets out to 'clear the cobwebs that have grown around the subject' of the cakras so that 'the existence of the power reservoir of [Kuṇḍalinī]' may be established 'on a scientific basis, acceptable to a strictly rational mind'.[67] In practical terms, this means divesting the doctrine of its more 'superstitious' and 'mysterious' appendages, which are held to be mere hang-overs from 'an earlier [pre-scientific] stage in the development of the human mind,'[68] and to bring it into conformity with a biological understanding of the human organism. Krishna thus rejects the notions of presiding deities, Sanskrit syllables, seed mantras and other symbolic associations as 'fabricated' ritualistic elements, 'unacceptable to common-sense'.[69] In an earlier work (1976), Krishna says of the cakras that 'To assume their existence [as centres of subtle force] even for an instant in these days of physiological knowledge and research would mean nothing short of an insult to intelligence', and suggests that they be regarded solely as heuristic devices for meditative visualisation, with the lotus having been chosen as a symbol due to its association with 'chastity' and purity.[70]

On Gopi Krishna's theory, then, the notion of a subtle bodily matrix, imperceptible to normal scientific methods of observation, can be dispensed with; the web of nāḍīs can be equated with the physical nervous system, the cakras with 'clusters of

---

[66] Avalon 1974: 164.
[67] Krishna 1992: 52.
[68] *Ib.*: 60.
[69] *Ib.*: 53-54.
[70] Krishna 1976: 139.

intersecting nerves',[71] and prāṇa with nerve energy.[72] The same view is taken by an earlier commentator, Brojendranath Seal, whose Appendix to Professor Sarkar's *Positive Background of Hindu Sociology* is quoted at some length by Avalon.[73] Seal is more precise than Krishna insofar as he (Seal) identifies specific nāḍīs with known nerve channels. He states, for example, that 'Suṣumnā is the central cord in the vertebral column' and that 'The two chains of sympathetic ganglia on the left and right are named Iḍā and Piṅgalā respectively.'[74] He then proceeds to list eleven further nāḍīs named in Tantric sources, identifying each with a particular nerve.[75] However, even if Seal were right to equate certain nāḍīs with nerve fibres, the locations he ascribes to them do not concur with descriptions given in the haṭha manuals (e.g. *GoŚ* 29-31).

With regard to the cakras, Seal equates mūlādhāra with 'the sacro-coccygeal plexus', svādhiṣṭhāna with 'the sacral plexus', and maṇipūraka with 'the lumbar plexus'. Anāhata, he continues, is 'possibly the cardiac plexus', and 'Bhāratī-Ṣthāna ["abode of Bhāratī (goddess of speech)", i.e. viśuddha-cakra], the junction of the spinal cord with the medulla oblongata'. Ājñā-cakra is the cerebellum; manas-cakra, the sensorium; and soma-cakra, 'a sixteen-lobed ganglion, comprising the centres in the middle of the cerebrum, above the sensorium'. Finally, Seal asserts that sahasrāra is 'the upper cerebrum with its lobes and convolutions'.[76] Such a comparison between the cakras and the various cerebro-spinal and sympathetic nerve centres is insightful, as it at least suggests the possibility of significant correspondences between gross and subtle aspects of the bodily matrix. However, to go further than mere comparative analogy, and to imply, as Seal does, direct equivalence between these

---

[71] Krishna 1992: 56.

[72] *Ib.*: 58.

[73] Avalon 1974: 112-14, 154-158.

[74] Quoted in Avalon *ib.*: 113.

[75] The list of fourteen nāḍīs enumerated by Seal comprises the ten listed on p. 155 above, plus: *sarasvatī*, *payasvinī*, *vāruṇā* and *viśvodarā* (*ib.*: 114).

[76] *Ib.*: 155-56.

different centres, is to oversimplify what is, in actual fact, a highly complex and elaborate schematic of the human being.

It is perfectly consistent with haṭha theory that a relationship should exist between the physiological processes of the sthūla-śarīra and the operations of the subtle matrix; indeed, if the two were not intimately linked, then the techniques of haṭha wherein gross physical mechanisms are utilised—i.e. the postures, muscular contractions and breathing methods—would be pointless, considering that the explicit intention is to effect change on a more subtle level; but the relationship is not at all straightforward. Bearing in mind the satkāryavāda mentioned above (pp. 178-79), the network of nāḍīs and cakras may be regarded as comprising a more 'primal' mode of substance, which 'gives rise to', or 'manifests as', certain physiological organs on the gross level; but it is far from clear exactly which organs correspond to which cakras. As Avalon notes, according to the *ṢCN*, the cakras are situated *within* suṣumnā-nāḍī, 'and not in the nerve plexuses which surround it.'[77] 'It is only therefore (if at all) in the sense of being the gross outer representatives of the spinal centres [cakras] that we can connect the plexuses and so forth with the Cakras spoken of in the Yoga books.'[78] The nervous system may, then, be characterised as a more tangible counterpart to (or, perhaps, expression of) the web of nāḍīs, but not as its equivalent.

Returning briefly to Gopi Krishna; perhaps the major problem with his reasoning is that he allows for only two possibilities: either (a) the nāḍīs and cakras are coterminous with physical channels and centres already known to biological science, or (b) they are entirely non-physical (i.e. insubstantial). Since the second of these possibilities is, according to Krishna, incompatible with statements in yoga texts that describe the nāḍīs and cakras in terms of physical locations, he concludes that the nāḍīs must be nerves and the cakras nerve-plexuses. Any inconsistencies between yogins' accounts of nāḍīs and

---

[77] Avalon 1974: 159.
[78] *Ib.*: 161-62.

modern information about the nervous system is explained away by Krishna on the basis that 'the structure of the body was an unfathomable mystery in their time'.[79] An 'unfathomable mystery' it may have been to the general population, but I would not be so quick to judge the level of physiological knowledge possessed by yogins, who were, after all, competent enough to develop a profound quality of insight into the workings of their deeper nature. A third possibility, which Gopi Krishna ignores, is that the nāḍīs and cakras are neither physical nerves nor entirely non-physical, but consist, rather, of a level of substance more ethereal than do the cells known to biology. It is, broadly speaking, this condition of 'ethereality' that should, I submit, be understood by the term 'subtle' in the context of yoga physiology.

As I remarked earlier, the notion of the subtle bodily matrix and its full significance in haṭha-yoga is a subject too broad and deep to be exhaustively covered in a single chapter, or even in a whole study. I trust, however, that the discussion presented here has succeeded in opening up some useful ways for thinking about the subject. It remains an unfortunate fact that the phenomena associated with the human being below the level of the sthūla-śarīra are generally unsusceptible to physical measurement, and hence, for those who have not yet acquired, by means of yoga, direct perception (*pratyakṣa-viṣayāni*) of the subtle organs—and who are not naturally gifted with psychic abilities—the existence of such phenomena can only be inferred or accepted on faith. Whether one accepts their existence or not, however, if only to gain a clear theoretical understanding of haṭha-yoga, it is vital that some familiarity with the notion of subtle organs and forces be developed; for it is principally at this level of being that the haṭha techniques described in the following chapter are designed to effect transformation.

---

[79] Krishna 1992: 59.

Part Three

PRACTICAL ASPECTS OF HAṬHA-YOGA

8

Haṭha Techniques

While it is important to understand the theory that underlies the practice of haṭha-yoga—and indeed haṭha theory and practice are intimately bound up together—it is the practice itself that is most strongly emphasised in the haṭha treatises. In the *HYP* (1.65-66), for example, it is stated that *yoga-siddhi* (perfection in yoga) will be attained neither by merely reading the śāstras (scriptures) nor by talking about the subject, nor yet by taking on the appearance of a yogin—'only [one who] acts (*kriyā-yukta*) will achieve siddhi.'

In this chapter I shall examine and descriptively outline the preliminary requirements and main techniques of haṭha-yoga. The principal textual source here is the *HYP*, although in discussing the ṣaṭ-karmāṇi (six [cleansing] acts) I also draw extensively upon the first chapter of the *Gheraṇḍa-Saṃhitā*. The information contained in this chapter will, I hope, help to dispel the still widely held belief that haṭha-yoga is solely concerned with physical fitness and not with the so-called 'higher' aspects of yoga discipline. It may be the case that, in modern society—and especially, though not exclusively, in western countries—the form in which haṭha-yoga is most likely to be encountered is that of an exercise regime, in which the strongest emphasis is placed upon the benefits to the physical body; but, although its postures and breathing techniques do indeed provide an excellent programme of physical exercise, haṭha-yoga is incalculably more than that. In its traditional form, haṭha-yoga works primarily with prāṇa, aiming to harness and channel this vital force, and to progressively increase the duration of time for which it can be retained within the subtle body. By means of kumbhaka (retention [of prāṇa]) and mudrā ('sealing', i.e. containing prāṇa), the haṭha-yogin endeavours to intensify the 'inner heat', and to thereby arouse the latent Kuṇḍalinī-śakti; and as this 'serpent power' ascends through suṣumnā-nāḍī, the yogin's concentration becomes fixed on her 'sound' (nāda), in which his mind is absorbed and carried towards the 'soundless state' of Brahman-identity.

Abhyāsa and vairāgya

Before moving on to an examination of specific haṭha techniques, it is worth pausing to consider the two principal aspects, or 'poles', of yoga discipline set forth in the *Yoga-Sūtra* (1.12-16). These poles, which are equally necessary for the attainment of citta-vṛtti-nirodha, are (a) *abhyāsa* and (b) *vairāgya*. Feuerstein notes that *abhyāsa* 'is composed of the prefix *abhi* or "unto" and *ās-a* or "sitting", thus meaning "sitting for" or "applying oneself to".'[1] The term is usually translated as 'practice', which, as the *Yoga-Sūtra* points out, is most effective in steadying the mind when carried out regularly, for a long period, and with earnest dedication (*YS* 1.13-14). *Vairāgya* may be translated as 'non-attachment', having, as Feuerstein again comments, a comparable meaning to '*vitrsna* "thirstlessness", *tyāga* "abandoning" and *saṃnyāsa* "renunciation".'[2] It can be seen as the 'negative' pole of yoga in contrast to the 'positive' pole of abhyāsa. Whereas the latter involves diligent engagement in (certain modes of) activity, designed to condition the mind in a way that brings enhanced 'steadiness' (*sthitau*, *YS* 1.13), vairāgya consists in a systematic *de*-conditioning of the mind, centring on a detachment from, or disidentification with, the various modes of phenomenal existence (prakṛti). These two poles, of practice and non-

---

[1] Feuerstein 1974b: 35.
[2] *Ib.*

attachment, are intended to lead to *puruṣa-khyāti*—'vision of the Self' or 'Self-revelation'—which is itself the highest state of non-attachment (*YS* 1.16).

Whenever the term non-attachment is used in the context of yoga praxis, it should not be understood to imply that the practitioner of yoga is seeking a passionless state of indifference towards worldy events. It may be the case that a yogin will retire from social activity for longer or shorter periods of time, but this is only an incomplete 'outer', and usually temporary, withdrawal. The true 'detachment' is that which occurs on an 'inner'—i.e. psychological—level. It is not that one becomes insensitive, or that the emotions 'dry up'; indeed, the yogin is held to become more compassionate, to see more clearly than anyone the unsatisfactoriness and suffering inherent in saṃsāra. 'To the discerning one (*vivekin*)', says Patañjali, 'all is duḥkha' (*YS* 2.15); that is, everything within the sphere of material existence is recognised to be unsatisfactory. The yogin *perceives* the suffering, but knows himself—and the ultimate Self of all—to be *beyond* that suffering; he has (or she has) not suppressed or extinguished his emotions, but has disidentified with them, recognising his true nature as *prior to* those emotions. This process of detachment from emotional vṛttis leads to a state of greater calmness, which in turn calms the vṛttis themselves, the result being that action becomes guided by discerning awareness (*viveka*), as opposed to blind passion.

As mentioned above, abhyāsa and vairāgya constitute broad categories of yoga discipline; the more specific techniques of yoga are outlined in the second and third chapters ('Sādhana-pāda' and 'Vibhūti-pāda') of the *Yoga-Sūtra*; and more detailed still are the instructions provided in the haṭha-yoga texts with which the present study is chiefly concerned.

In his commentary on the *HYP*, Brahmānanda describes the process of haṭha-yoga in terms of a gradual cessation of ordinary human activity. The āsanas (postures) engender control over the physical body, thereby enabling one to hold a static posture for an extended period of time. By means of kumbhaka, the yogin then proceeds to regulate and eventually arrest the flow of prāṇa, which, in turn, facilitates the one-pointed attention required to still the vṛttis of the mind. On the haṭha view, it is from increasingly prolonged kumbhaka that the final stages of aṣṭāṅga-yoga flow, namely pratyāhāra, dhāraṇā, dhyāna, and saṃprajñāta-samādhi (*J* 4.11). Eventually, says Brahmānanda, even 'the activities of buddhi (the most refined aspect of the mind) become still', and puruṣa alone remains (*ib.*).

Preliminary requirements

The soteriological system of haṭha-yoga is respectful of the comprehensive eightfold schema layed down in the *Yoga-Sūtra*,[3] and thus is conceived as a discipline whose teachings embrace every stratum of a person's life. B. K. S. Iyengar adopts the metaphor of a tree to describe the limbs of Pātañjala-yoga, and, at its roots and trunk he places yama and niyama respectively, as these are held to be the very foundations of yoga.[4] Derived from the verbal root *yam*—'to hold up, sustain'[5] —*yama* may be translated as 'restraint', in the sense of, for example, the reining of horses.[6] In the context of yoga, the term denotes certain ethical principles that ought to be cultivated in the aspiring yogin, and which must be present, at least to some degree, before he is likely to be accepted by a guru and before any significant progress can be made. *Niyama* denotes a lesser degree of 'restraint' and consists in a number of principles that concern one's attitude to life. In the *Yoga-Sūtra* (2.30-45) five yamas and five niyamas are mentioned, whereas in haṭha texts the number of each is generally ten. *HYP* 1.16 gives the following lists:

---

[3] Lists of the eight 'limbs' appear on pages 10 and 35 above.
[4] Iyengar 1988: 48-51.
[5] Feuerstein 1974b: 75.
[6] Cf. Monier-Williams 1963: 846.

Yamas:

1. *ahiṃsā*—harmlessness;
2. *satya*—truth, truthfulness;
3. *asteya*—non-stealing;
4. *brahmacarya*—continence (lit. 'moving in Brahman'[7]);
5. *kṣamā*—patience, forbearance;
6. *dhṛti*—fortitude, resolve;
7. *daya*—mercy, compassion;
8. *java*—swiftness, dexterity (of mind);
9. *mitāhāra*—moderate appetite;
10. *śauca*—purity, cleanliness.

Niyamas:

1. *tapas*—inner heat;
2. *saṃtoṣa*—contentment;
3. *āstikya*—'orthodoxy'; i.e. conviction in the authority of the Vedas;
4. *dāna*—charity;
5. *īśvara-pūja*—worship of Īśvara ('the Lord');
6. *siddhānta-vakya-śravaṇa*—listening to the exposition of *siddhānta* (= *vedānta*, 'Vedic knowledge');
7. *hrī*—modesty, humility;
8. *matī*—discernment;
9. *japa*—repetition (of mantras);
10. *huta*—sacrifice.

The translations provided in the above lists are inadequate to convey the full meaning of each term, but they will suffice for the purposes of the present study. Although mentioned as necessary components of yoga discipline, the majority of these principles are not further discussed in the haṭha treatises themselves; exceptions to this are the ninth and tenth yamas—mitāhāra and śauca—about which a little more will be said below.

---

[7] Cf. *Darśana-Upaniṣad* 1.14: 'The orientation of the mind towards the state of *brahman* is *brahmacarya*' (trans. Feuerstein 1974b: 78).

It is noteworthy that three of the niyamas (numbers 3, 5 and 6) place haṭha-yoga very firmly within the religious tradition of the Vedas, for it is still sometimes claimed that haṭha, and the Tāntric or Āgamic Śaiva philosophy on which it draws, is somehow antagonistic to orthodox Vedism. This, as was suggested in the first part of this study, is very definitely not the case. It is similarly false to assume that the yoga tradition is indifferent to socio-ethical mores. As Feuerstein rightly points out, 'Again and again the Yoga texts emphasise that moral integrity is an indispensable precondition of success. The acquisition of power must be counter-balanced by a simultaneous growth of one's sense of responsibility.'[8]

With regard to diet, the *HYP* provides specific instructions as to which foods the yogin should eat and which are best avoided. Suitable foods include: wheat, rice, barley, *saṣṭika* (a type of grain), milk, ghee, brown sugar, butter, sugar-candy, honey, dry ginger, *paṭolaka* (a vegetable), five pot-herbs, green gram, and pure water (*HYP* 1.62). Those that are unsuitable include: things which are bitter, sour, pungent, salty or burning, (most) green vegetables, oil, sesamum, mustard, alcohol, fish, flesh, curds, buttermilk, horse-gram, the fruit of the jujube, oil cakes, asafoetida, garlic, reheated or dry food, etc. (*HYP* 1.59-60). It is further stated that food should be consumed as an offering to Śiva, and that one quarter of the stomach should be left empty for ease of digestion and passage of 'air' or vital force (*J* 1.58).

The final yama, śauca (which is listed as a niyama in the *Yoga-Sūtra* [2.32]), constitutes an injunction to purify both the body and mind. Mental clarification is precisely what the techniques of yoga are designed to engender, and, for the body, six specific exercises are prescribed, referred to collectively as *ṣaṭ-karmāṇi* or *ṣaṭ-kriyā*.

Ṣaṭ-karmāṇi

The ṣaṭ-karmāṇi prepare those with excessive phlegm (*śleṣman*)

---

[8] Feuerstein 1974b: 76.

and fatty deposits (*medas*) for the challenging discipline of prāṇāyāma. If the three *doṣa*s (humours)—namely *vāta*, *pitta* and *kapha*—are already well balanced then these six preliminary cleansing techniques are unnecessary (*HYP* 2.21).[9] Respectively called *dhauti*, *vasti*, *neti*, *trāṭaka*, *nauli*, and *kapālabhāti*, the ṣaṭ-karmāṇi are described in the first chapter of the *Gheraṇḍa-Saṃhitā* (1.12-60) and in the second chapter of the *HYP* (2.21-35). The most extensive accounts are to be found in the former of these two texts, and thus the descriptions that follow are largely based thereon.

1. *Dhauti* means 'washing' or 'cleansing', and refers to a number of bodily purification techniques, of which four principal types are: (a) *antar-* (internal-), (b) *danta-* (dental-), (c) *hṛd-* (heart-), and (d) *mūla-dhauti* (root-cleansing) (*GS* 1.13).
   (a) Antar-dhauti comprises four procedures, namely *vātasāra* (air-flowing), *vārisāra* (water-flowing), *vahnisāra* (fire-motion) and *bahiṣkṛta* (expulsion). The first of these, vātasāra, involves shaping the mouth 'like a crow's beak' (*kākacañcū*)[10] and drawing air into the stomach, wherein it is made to circulate before being sent downwards and expelled via the anus (*GS* 1.15). In vārisāra, which is said to be the 'highest (*paraṃ*) dhautī', water is intentionally moved through the digestive tract and then expelled (*GS* 1.17-19). Vahnisāra (also called *agnisāra*) consists in drawing in the abdomen after a vigorous exhalation until the 'navel knot' (*nābhi-granthi*) is against the spinal column, and then pumping the abdominal muscles in and out numerous times,[11] thereby massaging the ab-

---

[9] *Vāta* roughly translates as 'air' or 'wind', and is a synonym of *prāṇa*. *Pitta* is variously translated as 'gall' or 'bile', but does not necessarily refer to the physiological secretions known by these names. *Kapha* or *śleṣman* denotes 'phlegm' or 'mucus', but again not necessarily in a literal (i.e. gross physical) sense.

[10] Cf. description of *śītalī-kumbhaka* below (p. 206).

[11] 'One hundred times' according to *GS* 1.20.

dominal organs and intensifying the 'gastric fire' (*jāṭharāgni*) (*GS* 1.20). The first stage of bahiṣkṛta is performed in the same manner as vātasāra, only the air is retained in the stomach for 1½ hours (half of one *yāma*) before being expelled. Then, however, the practitioner is required to stand (or squat) in water and draw out the *śakti-nāḍī* (lit. 'tube of power')—which term denotes the large intestine—so that it can be thoroughly washed, and then draw it back in (*GS* 1.22-23).[12]

(b) Danta-dhauti includes cleaning the 'root of the teeth' (*danta-mūla*), the 'root of the tongue' (*jihvā-mūla*), the ears (*karṇa*) and the 'hollow of the skull' (*kapāla-randhra*) (i.e. the frontal sinus). The teeth are rubbed with earth or powder (*GS* 1.27), and the base of the tongue is scrubbed by using the first three fingers; the tongue is then massaged with butter before being pulled out and stretched with metal pliers (*GS* 1.29-32), a procedure that is necessary preparation for *khecarī-mudrā* (see pp. 210-11 below). Fingers are used to clean the ears, and the sinuses are cleared by vigorous rubbing of the *bhāla-randhra* (brow-hollow) between the eyebrows with the right thumb (*GS* 1.33-34).

(c) Hṛd-dhauti, although literally meaning 'heart-cleansing', is concerned with maintaining cleanliness of the oesophagus and stomach. The *Gheraṇḍa-Saṃhitā* (1.36-41) describes three techniques, the first of which—*daṇḍa*-dhauti[13]—involves inserting a stick (e.g. plantain, turmeric or cane stalk) into the throat and then drawing it out again. The second is called *vamana*-dhauti, *vamana* meaning 'vomiting'. Theos Bernard, who trained under haṭha instructors in India, reports that it requires the drinking of 'eight or nine glassfuls of water, or enough so that it backs up into the throat. This will create a feeling of nausea, making it easy to empty the stomach of its en-

---

[12] Cf. Vasu 1976: 10.

[13] *Daṇḍa*: 'staff', 'stick'.

tire contents.'[14] The third is *vāso*-dhauti (cloth dhauti), in which the practitioner swallows a long thin strip of cloth while keeping hold of one end, and then slowly pulls it out. Of all the various dhautis, vāso-dhauti is the only one to be mentioned in the *HYP* (2.24-25),[15] wherein it is stipulated that the cloth should be the width of four fingers (*catur-aṅgula*) and the length of fifteen hand-spans (*hasta*) and should be moistened before swallowing. *Jyotsnā* 2.24 suggests that the beginner swallow only one span the first day, two the second, and so on.

(d) Mūla-dhauti (or mūla-*śodhana*[16]) is designed to assist the flow of apāna, and involves cleaning the rectum by applying water with either the middle finger or a plant stalk (daṇḍa).

2. *Vasti* literally means 'bladder', the name likely deriving from the fact that an animals' bladder was originally used to administer an enema, which is what this procedure resembles.[17] As described in *HYP* 2.26, vasti is performed by squatting on the heels in navel-depth water with a tube inserted into the rectum, and then drawing water up the tube by contracting the anus. The *Gheraṇḍa-Saṃhitā* (1.46) calls this *jala-vasti* (water vasti), and also mentions a 'dry' version (*śuṣka-* or *sthala*-vasti), in which the practitioner sits in *paścimottāna* (called *paścimatānāsana* in *HYP* 1.28 [see p. 199 below, esp. fn. 25]) and draws air into the rectum by contracting and dilating the anal sphincter.[18]
3. Neti is the practice of cleaning the nasal passages with a fine thread (*sūkṣma-sūtra*). The practitioner keeps hold of one end of the thread while passing the other up through one nostril at a time and pulling it out through the mouth (*HYP* 2.29, *GS* 1.50). A variation is *jala*-neti, in which water is

---

[14] Bernard 1968: 37.

[15] An equivalent process to vamana-dhauti is described in *HYP* 2.38, but is termed *gajakaraṇī* ('elephant process') rather than dhauti.

[16] *Śodhana*: 'cleansing', 'purification'.

[17] Cf. Gerson 1993: 102-3.

[18] This movement is called *aśvinī-mudrā* (lit. 'horse seal').

poured into one nostril and ejected through the other nostril or through the mouth.

4. Trāṭaka involves gazing intently at a small or 'subtle' object (*sūkṣma-lakṣya*) without blinking until tears well up in the eyes, the purpose being to cleanse the eyes and improve the ability to concentrate, which is necessary for practices such as *śāṃbhavī-mudrā* (see p. 215-16 below). It is also said to facilitate *divya-dṛṣṭi*, which may be translated as 'clear vision', 'light-seeing', or 'clairvoyance' (*GS* 1.54).
5. Nauli is the act of drawing in the abdomen, projecting the rectus abdominis muscles forward and expanding and contracting them in such a way as to resemble the waves of the sea.[19] Called *laulikī* in the *Gheraṇḍa-Saṃhitā* (1.52), the technique provides a powerful massage to the intestines and digestive organs, and is held to increase the 'bodily fire' (*deha-anala*). It may also be noted that, in scientific observations made by M. V. Bhole and P. V. Karambelkar,[20] nauli has been shown to be extremely effective at producing sub-atmospheric pressure in various internal cavities, thereby effecting the uptake of fluid into the colon and bladder required for both vasti and *vajrolī-mudrā*.[21]
6. Kapālabhāti ('shining skull') is described in the *HYP* (2.35) as breathing in and out rapidly like a bellows (*bhastrā*), a technique also employed in *bhastrikā-kumbhaka* (p. 206 below). The *Gheraṇḍa-Saṃhitā*, however, distinguishes three alternative varieties of kapālabhāti, namely *vāma-krama* (left process), *vyut-krama* (inverted process) and *śīt-krama* (hissing process). Vāma-krama is so-called because one begins by breathing in through the left nostril and expelling the air through the right, after which one breaths in through the right and out through the left and then repeats the whole sequence several times. The process is described as breathing in through iḍā- and out through piṅgalā-nāḍī,

---

[19] *Nauli* literally refers to the 'rolling' movement of a boat upon a rough sea.
[20] 1971: 26-32.
[21] See pp. 212-15 below.

and vice versa (*GS* 1.56), thereby emphasising the fact that it is the subtle energy underlying the physical breath with which the yogin is most concerned, one of the effects of the exercise being to repeatedly reverse the flow of prāṇa. Vyut-krama involves drawing water up through both nostrils and slowly ejecting it via the mouth, and śīt-krama is the opposite, i.e. sucking water in through the mouth and ejecting it via the nostrils. All versions of kapālabhāti are said to relieve the symptoms of diseases caused by an excess of kapha-doṣa (phlegm).

Once a certain degree of internal bodily hygiene has been acquired through the performance of the above techniques, it is claimed that one is ready for prāṇāyāma (*HYP* 2.36).

The central techniques

The central techniques of haṭha-yoga are āsana, kumbhaka, mudrā, and meditation upon an internal object (usually either manifestations of light or sound). In the *HYP* (which is the basic textual source of information for this section) āsaṇas are chiefly discussed in the opening chapter, kumbhaka in the second, mudrā in the third, and nādānusandhāna ('sound meditation') in the fourth.

Āsana

Āsana derives from the verbal root *ās*, meaning 'to be present; to exist; to inhabit, dwell in; to make one's abode in...; to sit quietly, abide, remain;...to continue in any situation'.[22] In the *Bhagavad-Gītā* (6.11-12) it denotes a 'seat' used in meditation, while in haṭha-yoga—where āsana is the first major 'limb' (*aṅga*, *HYP* 1.17)—the term refers to any bodily posture that may be maintained for a prolonged period. The postures are primarily intended to provide stable and compact foundations for the various breathing techniques which lead to the retention

[22] Monier-Williams 1963: 159. It may be noted that the Sanskrit term for the buttock region, *āsa*, has the same verbal origin.

of prāṇa in kumbhaka, although some have particular stimulatory effects in themselves and are remarkably good for improving stamina, balance and general health. Modern manuals on haṭha-yoga often feature a wide variety of postures, and popular forms of the discipline have tended to focus on āsana almost to the exclusion of its other elements. While āsana is an integral part of haṭha-yoga, providing, as it were, the 'setting' for its other aspects, if it is practised in isolation from the other components then the term *haṭha-yoga* is not strictly applicable.

As noted in Chapter 2 above, little is said about āsana in the *Yoga-Sūtra* beyond the fact that it should be 'steady and comfortable' (*YS* 2.46) and that it may be mastered 'by reducing the restless tendency and by meditation on [or "identifying with"] infinity (*ananta*)' (*YS* 2.47). Vyāsa's commentary mentions the names of thirteen sitting positions (*YB* 2.46), but it is only in the haṭha treatises that detailed instructions are provided regarding the performance of these or similar postures.

HYP 1.33 declares the number of āsanas propounded by Śiva to be eighty-four, and adds that, of these, four are most important.[23] In total, Svātmārāma's text describes fifteen āsanas, less than half the number in the *Gheraṇḍa-Saṃhitā* (wherein thirty-two are discussed).

Though it would be possible to spend a considerable amount of time describing the many āsanas that exist and the numerous physical benefits that may be acquired from their practice, the extensive coverage of this subject in other books makes such an exercise unnecessary.[24] Here, I shall simply list the āsanas that are explicitly mentioned in the *HYP*, and shall limit the discussion to the final four, which constitute the core sitting postures of haṭha-yoga. (Photographs illustrating a selection of these āsanas are included in Appendix A.)

---

[23] Cf. *ŚS* 3.84: 'There are eighty-four āsanas, and these are of various sorts. Out of them, four should be practised.'

[24] Probably the most comprehensive guide to yoga postures is B. K. S. Iyengar's *Light on Yoga* (Aquarian Press, 1991).

1. *Svastikāsana*—auspicious posture (*HYP* 1.19);
2. *Gomukhāsana*—cow's face posture (*ib.* 1.20);
3. *Vīrāsana*—heroic posture (*ib.* 1.21);
4. *Kūrmāsana*—tortoise or turtle posture (*ib.* 1.22);
5. *Kukkuṭāsana*—cock posture (*ib.* 1.23);
6. *Uttāna-kūrmāsana*—upright or 'raised up' tortoise posture (*ib.* 1.24);
7. *Dhanurāsana*—bow posture (*ib.* 1.25);
8. *Matsyendrāsana*—posture of Matsyendra (*ib.* 1.26-27);
9. *Paścimatānāsana*—back stretch posture (*ib.* 1.28);[25]
10. *Mayūrāsana*—peacock posture (*ib.* 1.30-31);
11. *Śavāsana*—corpse posture (*ib.* 1.32);
12. *Siddhāsana*—adept posture (*ib.* 1.35-43), also referred to as *vajrāsana* (thunderbolt posture), *muktāsana* (posture of release) and *guptāsana* (esoteric posture) (*ib.* 1.37);
13. *Padmāsana*—lotus posture (two variations described [*ib.* 1.44-49]);
14. *Siṃhāsana*—lion posture (*ib.* 1.52);
15. *Bhadrāsana*—blessed or auspicious posture, also called *Gorakṣāsana* (*ib.* 1.53-54).

Of all the āsanas in the above list, siddhāsana is said to be the finest (*HYP* 1.38), presumably because of its relative ease and suitability for prāṇāyāma. Two variations of siddhāsana are described, the first being performed by pressing the heel of one foot into the perineum (*yoni*) and placing the other foot firmly upon the penis (*meṇḍha*), effectively clamping the male member between the two feet (*ib.* 1.35). In the second variation,

---

[25] *Paścima* literally means 'west', which in Indian parlance stands for the back of the human body, the front being the 'east', the left side being 'north', and the right being 'south'. *Tān* means 'stretch'. Elsewhere (e.g. *GS* 2.16), the name of this posture is spelt *paścimottānāsana*, i.e. *paścima* (back) + *uttāna* (intense stretch) + *āsana* (posture). Iyengar notes that 'Ut is a particle indicating deliberation, intensity. The verb tān means to stretch, extend, lengthen out' (1991: 92).

both heels are above the penis (*ib.* 1.36).[26] Bodily orifices are closed in such a forceful manner in order to aid the retention of prāṇa during intense kumbhaka, and it is also for this reason that bandhas ('locks') are applied.[27] With the perfection of siddhāsana, the three major bandhas—namely *jālaṃdhara*, *mūla*, and *uḍḍīyāna*—are said to be instituted 'effortlessly of their own accord' (*ib.* 1.42) (cf. pp. 208ff. below).

Padmāsana—the well-known 'lotus posture'—is also of two kinds. Both versions involve placing the feet soles-upward upon their opposite thigh, but, in the first, the arms are crossed behind the back and the big toes clasped by the hands (*ib.* 1.44), whereas in the second the hands are rested upon one another in the lap and the chin lowered onto the chest (*ib.* 1.45-46). Following the descriptions of padmāsana in the *HYP* is the injunction to the yogin to draw the apāna upwards and to descend the prāṇa, thereby intensifying the abdominal fire that arouses Śakti (*ib.* 1.37, *J* 1.37). The posture is not so named because it in any sense resembles a lotus flower; its title derives, rather, from the manifold associations attached to the lotus in yoga symbology. The lotus represents, for example, the ability to remain steady and buoyant upon the surface of the phenomenal world, while only its slender stem extends down into the murky and sometimes turbulent depths. Also, of course, the raising of Kuṇḍalinī is supposed to open the several 'lotuses' situated along suṣumnā-nāḍī, thereby permitting the sublimation of the yogin's sense of self-identity.

Siṃhāsana is one of the many haṭha postures named after an animal. In this case it is the lion, which is held to embody qualities of strength and fearlessness. The posture involves sit-

---

[26] Avalon notes (1974: 203) that some yogins are capable of withdrawing the penis and testes up into the pubic arch.

[27] The descriptions given here—as in the haṭha treatises themselves—apply principally to men. It may be noted, however, that, in a booklet on mūlabandha produced by the Bihar School of Yoga, Buddhananda mentions a female version of siddhāsana called *siddha-yoni-āsana*. It is the same posture as siddhāsana, only the lower heel should be placed 'inside the labia majora of the vagina' (1984: 85).

ting on the heels with the ankles crossed, so that the heels press into the perineum on either side of the scrotal 'seam' (*sīvana*). The palms of the hands are placed upon the knees with the fingers well spread, and the eyes looking towards the bridge of the nose. The mouth is open wide and the tongue projected out (*ib.* 1.50-51). In modern haṭha practice this posture is usually combined with a forceful and prolonged exhalation through the mouth, which empties the lungs of stale air, although this is not mentioned in the *HYP*.

Bhadra refers to that which is 'excellent', 'virtuous', 'beautiful', 'auspicious', etc., and *bhadrāsana* is the name of the fourth of the principal haṭha āsanas. Again the ankles are situated so that the heels press into either side of the seam between anus and scrotum, only this time the soles of the feet are together and the knees out to the sides, the hands firmly clasping the feet (*ib.* 1.53-54).

An additional posture, called vajrāsana, appears in the description of *śakticālana* ('raising Śakti') (*HYP* 3.104ff.). Despite *vajrāsana*'s being one of the synonyms of *siddhāsana*, the posture that is described here is different, and involves clasping the ankles with the hands and pressing the feet against the kanda, which procedure is thought to assist the arousal of Kuṇḍalinī (*HYP* 3.114-115). If the position of the kanda is accepted as being between the navel and the pubis, then this version of vajrāsana must involve pressing the feet firmly into the abdomen, as illustrated in Appendix A below (p. 266). In his *Light on Yoga*, B. K. S. Iyengar refers to this posture as *kandāsana*.[28]

The ideal haṭha practice, according to *HYP* 1.43, involves positioning oneself in siddhāsana, maintaining kevala-kumbhaka (complete retention [of prāṇa]) and khecarī-mudrā, and meditating upon the nāda. Ultimately, as Usharbudh Arya has remarked, 'Hatha yoga is the conquest of the body',[29] and this means being aware and in control of physical posture at all times. Arya notes that, to acquire bodily poise and control, in-

[28] Iyengar 1991: 348-51.

[29] Arya 1985: 24.

tense 'mindfulness' or 'self-observation' is required; one must cultivate 'the habit of being a witness to one's own physical functions, aware of whatever it is that we are doing with our bodies, whether it be the external surfaces of the body or internal things like muscle tension, heart rate, and breathing.'[30] From this point of view, mental attention is not only very much a part of āsana; it is the foundation of it.

Contrary to popular misconceptions of yoga āsanas, they are not intended to be excrutiatingly disagreeable or physically taxing. Patañjali's dictum that āsana should be 'steady (*sthira*) and comfortable (*sukha*)' (*YS* 2.46) is applicable whether one is sitting cross-legged on the floor or standing on one's head. Āsana is, however, an extremely precise art form, and hence, even when considerable flexibility and stamina have been achieved, there is always 'work to be done' in a posture. Since all aspects of haṭha practice are mutually reflexive—that is, improvement in one aspect engenders improvement in others—āsana is not to be viewed as something to be perfected *prior to* one's engaging in prāṇāyāma, for the purification of the nāḍīs and retention of prāṇa will aid the practice of āsana just as āsana aids such purification and retention; neither, however, is it something to be taken lightly or overlooked altogether. In haṭha-yoga, the body is truly regarded as the temple of the spiritual Self, and, if Self-realisation is to be achieved, then the temple must be made a worthy abode.

Prāṇāyāma and kumbhaka

> That [steady āsana] having been attained, the movements of inspiration and expiration are discontinued (*viccheda*), [this being] prāṇāyāma. (*YS* 2.49)

Prāṇāyāma is the technique of haṭha-yoga *par excellence*, and the key aspect of prāṇāyāma is kumbhaka. *Prāṇāyāma* is derived from *prāṇa* ('vital force') plus *āyāma*, which Iyengar defines as 'stretch, extension, expansion, length, breadth, regu-

---

[30] *Ib.*: 4.

lation, prolongation, restraint or control';[31] hence *prāṇāyāma* may be rendered as 'extending (the period of holding) prāṇa'. As is often the case with technical terms in yoga, *prāṇāyāma* may refer to both a goal and a practice; the goal being to retain prāṇa within the suṣumnā, and the means to achieve it being the progressive prolongation of that retention, which is effected by the performance of certain very powerful breathing exercises combined with muscular contractions and concentrated mental focus.

HYP 2.71 states that prāṇāyāma is a threefold practice, the three parts being *recaka* (exhalation), *pūraka* (inhalation), and *kumbhaka* (retention). During recaka and pūraka there is movement of air, prāṇa and thought—all of these being intimately connected—whereas in kumbhaka the cessation of movement is held to facilitate the stillness and ultimate dissolution of mental modifications (*citta-vṛtti*). Kumbhaka itself is divided into two kinds, namely *sahita* (supported) and *kevala* (complete, total). Sahita-kumbhaka is the retention of breath and prāṇa as part of a cycle of inhalations and exhalations, and may be further divided into *antara*-kumbhaka ('inner retention', i.e. retention with the breath held in) and *bāhya*-kumbhaka (retention with the breath held out). Kevala-kumbhaka, on the other hand, involves holding the breath for an indefinite period, without the requirement to inhale or exhale. In this state, prāṇa is fully retained within the nāḍī-matrix and is forced into the central channel of suṣumnā.

The *Śiva-Saṃhitā* distinguishes four levels of intensity in kumbhaka, each of which is characterised by certain external indicators. During the first stage the yogin's body perspires profusely, and the sweat produced, it is stated, should be rubbed into the skin (*ŚS* 3.40; *HYP* 2.12-13). The second stage involves the trembling of the body,[32] and the third, 'jumping

---

[31] Iyengar 1981: 13.

[32] Aurobindo has stated that 'The body, accustomed to work off superfluous energy by movement, is at first ill able to bear this increase [of prāṇa brought about by prāṇāyāma]...and betrays it by violent tremblings' (1970: 510).

like a frog'; the fourth is called *gagane-cara*, literally 'moving in the sky' (*ŚS* 3.41), and this is claimed to effect *vāyu-siddhi* ('air power' or 'conquest of the air'), the text implying that the persistent yogin is literally able to 'rise into the air while remaining in padmāsana' (*ŚS* 3.42). It is possible, however, to interpret such a statement figuratively as an oblique reference to a state of consciousness in which a vast 'ocean of space' or 'voidness' is experienced; and, since this particular practice is claimed to 'remove the veil from saṃsāra' (*ib.*), thereby altering one's perception of the world, it seems reasonable to place the stronger emphasis upon the symbolic interpretation.

Brahmānanda, in his attempt to integrate the haṭha doctrine with the aṣṭāṅga schematic of the *Yoga-Sūtra*, quotes from the *Yoga-Cintāmaṇi* of Śivānanda Sarasvatī to the effect that pratyāhāra, dhāraṇā, dhyāna and samādhi are merely extensions of prāṇāyāma (*J* 2.12). On this account, pratyāhāra is said to consist in retaining prāṇa within the brahmarandhra for 25 *pala*s, one pala being equivalent to about 24 seconds.[33] Retention of prāṇa for 5 *ghaṭikā*s (= 2 hours) is dhāraṇā; 60 ghaṭikās (24 hours) is dhyāna; and one who maintains such a kumbhaka for twelve days is said to be in samādhi (*ib.*).

Strictly speaking, *kumbhaka* denotes the *cessation* or *suspension* of the flow of prāṇa and breath; however, there are a variety of breathing techniques which precede and follow such cessation (in the case of sahita-kumbhaka), and which lead up to complete retention (in kevala-kumbhaka), and these techniques are themselves referred to as types of kumbhaka. The *HYP* describes eight such techniques, which are briefly outlined below. In each one, to induce prāṇa into the brahma-nāḍī (the innermost channel of suṣumnā), jālaṃdhara- and mūla-bandha (chin lock and 'root' lock respectively [see below]) should be performed after inhalation (pūraka), and these two plus uḍḍīyāna-bandha (abdominal lock) should accompany bāhya-kumbhaka (*HYP* 2.45-46).

---

33 *J* 2.12 states that 1 pala = 6 *mātrās*; 1 mātrā = the time taken for one inhalation and one exhalation during deep sleep (i.e. about 4 seconds).

1. *Sūrya-bhedana-kumbhaka*
Sūrya (sun) stands for piṅgalā-nāḍī (in the sūkṣma-śarīra) and the right nostril (in the sthūla-śarīra), and *bhedana* derives from the root *bhid*, 'to pierce or pass through',[34] hence *sūrya-bhedana* denotes the practice of breathing in solely through the right nostril, and breathing out through the left (iḍā-nāḍī) (*HYP* 2.48). The ring and little finger of the right hand are traditionally used to block off the left nostril, and the thumb of the same hand to block off the right. The same digits may be used to restrict the air-flow through the open nostril during inhalation and exhalation in order to prolong the breathing cycle. Both nostrils are closed during antara- and bāhya-kumbhaka.

2. *Ujjāyī-kumbhaka*
This is the 'victorious' or, more literally, 'uplifting' retention, performed by breathing in and out through both nostrils while constricting the throat—i.e. slightly closing the glottis—enough to enable an audible deep hissing sound to be made. The abdominal muscles are contracted during inhalation as well as exhalation, thereby preventing the abdomen from over-inflating. On a subtle level, the drawing in of the abdomen is believed to force prāṇa upwards, aiding its retention. *HYP* 2.53 notes that ujjāyī may be performed while moving (*gacchatā*) or remaining still (*tiṣṭhtā*).

3. *Sītkārī-kumbhaka*
Sīt (or, sometimes, *śīt*) is an onomatopoeic term that means 'hissing', and *kārī* means 'maker'; so this is the 'hiss-making kumbhaka'. It involves inhaling through the mouth with the lips slightly apart, teeth gently touching, and tongue freely suspended. After retention, the breath is exhaled through the nose (*HYP* 2.54).

---

[34] Iyengar 1981: 203.

4. *Śītalī-kumbhaka*
Śītalī ('that which cools') is performed like sītkārī, except that the sides of the tongue are curled over to form a tube, which protrudes between the lips, and through which air is sucked in (*HYP* 2.57). This facial posture is termed *kākī-* (crow's beak) *mudrā*.

5. *Bhastrikā-kumbhaka*
Bhastrā is the term for the bellows used by a blacksmith, and bhastrikā is breathing 'like a bellows', i.e. rapidly, with a forceful pumping action of the upper abdomen. It is noted in *HYP* 2.67 that this technique is particularly effective for breaking through the three granthis within suṣumnā.

6. *Bhrāmarī-kumbhaka*
Bhrāmarī signifies 'that which belongs to a bee (or beetle)', especially its sound, and this technique is so called because the in- and out-breaths are accompanied by a humming sound (*HYP* 2.68). Iyengar mentions that it may be practised in conjunction with *ṣaṇmukhī-mudrā*, in which the thumbs are used to close the ears and the fingers to close the eyes.[35] This intensifies the effect of the humming. In the *Gheraṇḍa-Saṃhitā* (5.78-79), however, *bhrāmarī* denotes one of a number of internal sounds which spontaneously become audible during contemplative prāṇāyāma performed in a quiet place.

7. *Mūrcchā-kumbhaka*
Mūrcchā means 'swooning', and, as described in *HYP* 2.69, this technique consists simply in applying jālaṃdhara-bandha and exhaling slowly. Alternatively, the *Gheraṇḍa-Saṃhitā* (5.83) states that it involves fixing one's attention between the eyebrows (i.e. on ājñā-cakra) and thereby conjoining or merging manas (mind) with the ātman (Self). Referred to as *manomūrcchā*, this 'fainting' or 'intoxication of

---

[35] *Ib.*: 152.

the mind' is not intended to be a state of unconsciousness, but, on the contrary, one of heightened awareness, in which everything that is not the Self dissolves.

8. *Plāvinī-kumbhaka*

   Plāva means 'floating', and *plāvinī*, 'that which floats'. In *HYP* 2.70, this kumbhaka is described as enabling one to float 'like a lotus leaf' on the surface of water, due to the filling of the body with air (and prāṇa). This has sometimes been taken to mean that the technique should be performed in water,[36] but the term is likely to be figurative, indicating that the yogin may feel himself to be 'floating' above the 'sea' of saṃsāra. Exactly how the technique is performed is not made clear, and more recent authorities such as Iyengar also regard it as mysterious.[37]

Mudrā

> What else of substance can I say, O Caṇḍa, than that nothing in this world brings prompt success (*kicit-siddhi*) like the [practice of] mudrā? (*GS* 3.100)

In each of the kumbhakas described in the above section, the breath is retained by the application of certain mudrās. *Mudrā* means 'seal' and refers to something that is used to form a closed circuit. In the context of yoga, *mudrā* denotes (a) a kind of hand position or gesture, and (b) a muscular contraction or other physical position which facilitates the retention of prāṇa within the body and/or focuses awareness on a particular point. The principal contractions are called *bandha*s, meaning 'lock' or 'binding'. The haṭha texts do not provide much information regarding hand positions, although occasional references to hands appear in the descriptions of āsanas.[38] Mudrās of the second sort, however, are given considerable attention, the list

---

[36] See, e.g. Hewitt 1987: 107.

[37] Iyengar 1981: 154.

[38] For example, it is stated (*HYP* 1.45) that, in one version of padmāsana, the hands should be placed palms upwards in the lap.

of such techniques in the third chapter of the *Gheraṇḍa-Saṃhitā* extending to twenty-five. The *HYP* mentions ten main mudrās in its third chapter, plus one other (*Śāṃbhavī*) in Chapter 4, and all of these are outlined below. These eleven are included in the *Gheranda-Saṃhitā*, though with some minor variations (and a major variation in the case of *vajrolī-mudrā* [see below]).

1. *Uḍḍīyāna-bandha*—'flying up lock'
The lungs are emptied of air and the abdomen drawn back strongly towards the spine and up towards the thorax, thereby forcing prāṇa upwards along suṣumnā (*HYP* 3.55).

2. *Mūla-bandha*—'root lock'
The *yoni* is pressed with the heel and contracted so that the apāna, or downward-flowing prāṇa, is forced upwards. *Yoni* may, in certain instances, refer to the female genitalia, but here denotes the perineum or, more specifically, the muscular tissue between the anus and the posterior part of the external genitalia (corresponding to mūlādhāra-cakra). The intention is to unite apāna with prāṇa, thereby intensifying bodily heat (*jvalano deha*), which in turn arouses the 'sleeping' (*suptā*) Kuṇḍalinī, who uncoils 'like a snake struck by a stick' (*HYP* 3.68).

3. *Jālaṃdhara-bandha*
Jāla is both a noun meaning 'web' or 'net', and an adjective meaning 'watery' or 'fluid'; and, according to *HYP* 3.71, both meanings are implied in the name of this mudrā:

> Because it 'binds' (*bandhāti*) the network of subtle channels (*sirā-jāla*) and [dams up] the downward-flow of 'moon-fluid' (*nabhojala*), this bandha, which prevents diseases of the throat, [is called] jālaṃdhara.

The technique involves drawing the chin in and pressing it down towards the jugular notch (between the collar bones), thereby preventing the passage of air through the throat, and stemming (*stambha*) the flow of prāṇa through iḍā and piṅgalā (*HYP* 3.73). To the instructions given in the traditional texts, Theos Bernard adds that he 'was taught always to simulate the act of swallowing a couple of times' before applying jālaṃdhara.[39]

4. *Mahā-mudrā*—'great seal'
The yoni is pressed with the left heel, while the right leg is extended and the toes clasped. Jālaṃdhara- and mūla-bandha are simultaneously applied. This is then repeated with the opposite leg extended (*HYP* 3.10-15).

5. *Mahā-bandha*—'great lock'
The perineum is pressed with the left heel, and the right foot is placed sole-upwards on the left thigh. Mūla-bandha is applied, along with either jālaṃdhara- or *jihvā*-bandha, the latter being the 'tongue lock' in which the teeth are clenched and the tongue pressed firmly against them. Again the posture is repeated with the legs swapped over (*HYP* 3.19-23).

6. *Mahā-vedha*—'great penetration'
Vedha (sometimes *bheda*) here refers to the 'piercing' of the cakras and granthis within suṣumnā-nāḍī, which is held to result from the perfection of this technique. It involves assuming the mahā-bandha while placing the hands flat on the ground on either side of the buttocks; the weight of the body is then taken upon the hands and the buttocks repeatedly struck upon the ground, thereby giving stimulation to the mūlādhāra-cakra (*HYP* 3.26-29). Due to the difficulty of raising the the lower foot off the ground when it is tucked beneath the perineum (as in mahā-bandha), many teachers recommend that one sit in padmāsana (lotus posture) instead when performing mahā-vedha.

---

[39] Bernard 1968: 71.

7. *Khecarī-mudrā*

Kha[40] is a synonym of *ākāśa*, which is variously translated as 'space'; 'sky', 'ether', etc.; it refers to the most refined of the five 'gross elements' (mahābhūtas), out of which the other four are said to arise. *Carī* is the feminine form of *cara*, meaning 'moving in', and thus *khecarī* may be rendered as 'moving in space', and *khecarī-mudrā* as 'the seal [which engenders or involves] moving in space'.[41] While this phrase may be simplistically interpreted to imply that the mudrā engenders some form of levitation, *HYP* 3.41 states that siddhas refer to it as khecarī because it involves the 'moving in space' of both the mind (citta) and the tongue. The mind 'moves in space' in the sense that attention is focussed upon the 'space' in the centre of the brow, i.e. ājñā-cakra; and the tongue is said to do so because, in this mudrā, it is turned back and lodged in the space behind the soft palate. The purpose of this tongue position is to stem the tide of bindu (or soma), the vital 'nectar' whose downward flow is held to cause loss of energy and eventual death. Bindu is thought to condense into seminal fluid due to the influence of sexual desire, and therefore, in order for it to be retained in the soma-cakra without one's experiencing agitation or frustration, khecarī-mudrā must go hand-in-hand with the transcendence of erotic impulses. Because this mudrā obstructs the passage of air into the lungs, it can only be successfully performed by yogins who have mastered the art of kevala-kumbhaka, that is, of holding prāṇa and breath in the body for an extended or even indefinite period of time.[42]

---

[40] The 'a' in *kha* becomes an 'e' when it is followed by 'c'.

[41] Rieker claims (1989: 113n.) that 'The real origin of *khecari* is *khecar* = sun', but no reference is given to support this claim, nor does it seem particularly helpful for determining the word's meaning.

[42] Vasu notes in his Foreword to the *Gheraṇḍa-Saṃhitā* (1976: xii) that during hibernation certain animals, 'like frogs, etc.,...turn their tongues upward, closing the respiratory passage.'

In order to perform khecarī-mudrā successfully the tongue must be lengthened to the extent that it can reach the cavity behind the soft palate. To this end, the tongue is pulled out of the mouth and gradually stretched until its tip reaches the the space between the eyebrows. An additional procedure, designed to allow the tongue to turn back fully, is to slice through the fraenum linguae (which normally attaches the tongue to the bottom of the mouth) using a razor or sharp leaf. A hair's breadth cut will be made each day for approximately six months until the fraenum is completely severed. Bernard notes that the tongue position in khecarī is more effectively maintained if the soft palate has first been loosened, the most convenient method being

> to bend the end of the handle of an ordinary teaspoon enough to form a hook. Insert this in the back of the throat and draw it forward until it catches on the palate ridge. When a firm grip has been secured, repeatedly pull the palate toward the front part of the mouth. In time this membrane will become so flexible that it will be almost possible to touch the teeth with the soft palate.[43]

HYP 3.38 states that remaining with the tongue turned upwards in khecarī-mudrā 'even for half a *kṣaṇa*' (*kṣaṇa*: 'moment')[44] will bring about immunity from disease, etc.

8. *Viparītakaraṇī* —'reversing process'

This mudrā involves turning the body upside-down so that the soft palate, wherefrom the vital 'moon nectar' is held to flow, is situated below the navel centre. By doing so, the nectar is more easily retained in the soma-cakra as opposed to its being consumed by the microcosmic 'sun' (sūrya) located at the navel, and consequently the rapid march towards death is reversed. On the matter of how the mudrā is to be performed the *HYP* (3.78) remains relatively vague,

---

43 Bernard 1968: 67.

44 In Indian astronomy, one kṣaṇa = 48 minutes.

stating that the procedure should be learnt from one's guru and not from written texts. Several commentators, including Brahmānanda (*J* 3.81), interpret it as a version of the shoulder stand (*sarvāṅgāsana*), while, in the *Gheraṇḍa-Saṃhitā* (3.35), its description resembles the headstand (*śīrṣāsana*).[45]

9. *Vajrolī-mudrā*—'mighty', 'adamantine', or 'thunderbolt' seal
   Controversy surrounds this particular mudrā due to its involving sexual intercourse, something which is frowned upon by certain practitioners and textual interpreters of yoga.[46] Ślokas 3.84-103 are omitted from Vishnudevananda's translation of the *HYP* on the grounds that 'they describe Vajroli, Sahajoli, and Amaroli mudras, practices which are not followed in sattvic sadhana [i.e. "pure spiritual practice"].'[47] Such a statement would be amusing for its display of prudery were it not for the condescending way in which the translator and commentator treats his readers. Rieker adopts the same high-and-mighty tone, stating that 'In leaving out these passages, we merely bypass the description of a few obscure and repugnant practices that are followed by only those yogis who lack the will power to reach their goal otherwise.'[48] Similarly, in his translation of the *Śiva-Saṃhitā* (wherein the technique of vajrolī is termed *vajroṇḍī*) Vasu omits its description 'as it is an obscene practice indulged in by low class Tantrists.'[49] The position taken by Vasu, Vishnudevananda and Rieker is based on the assumption that ('sattvic') haṭha-yoga and sexual intercourse are incompatible since the latter involves indulgence in 'worldly pleasures'.[50] It is true that the yama (ethical pre-

[45] Photographs of both versions are included in Appendix A.
[46] The account given here does not apply to the version of vajrolī described in the *Gheraṇḍa-Saṃhitā* (3.11), wherein the practice resembles a handstand.
[47] Vishnudevananda 1997: 138.
[48] Rieker 1989: 127.
[49] Vasu 1996: 51.
[50] Rieker *ib.*

cept) of brahmacarya is integral to most yoga systems, including haṭha-yoga, and that this is often regarded in the narrow sense of 'continence' or 'celibacy'; but it is also the case that this particular vow may be interpreted more broadly to mean 'moving in—or being intent upon—Brahman', and in this sense it need not exclude an active sexual relationship.[51]

We may be thankful that the translators of the Adyar edition of the *HYP* were not so censorious, and that we can therefore read the ślokas omitted from other editions. Here we learn that vajrolī-mudrā may be practised by both men and women, and that it involves the voluntary prevention of ejaculation at the moment of orgasm. For the man, this is effected by firmly contracting the perineum (yoni) and 'sucking' the seminal fluid (bindu) up into the bladder; or, if ejaculation has already occurred, the bindu—mixed with female secretions (called *rajas*)—may be drawn back up through the urethra (*HYP* 3.87). Avalon condemns this practice 'as injurious to the woman who "withers" under such treatment',[52] but he neglects to mention that vajrolī may also be performed by a yoginī (female yogin) who has learnt, through diligent practise of the 'same contraction' (*samā-kuñcya*), to retain her own fluid and to draw up the male bindu (*HYP* 3.99).[53] More specific anatomical information is provided by Buddhananda, who writes that, 'In vajroli mudra the urogenital muscles including the transversi perinei superficialis, ischiocavernosus, bulbospongiosus, transversus perinei profundus and the sphincter urethrae are contracted. In the male the penis is slightly contracted inwards[;] in the female, the clitoris, lower vaginal muscles

---

[51] Cf. Iyengar 1991: 34-35.

[52] Avalon 1974: 201n.

[53] It should be remembered that *rajas* and *bindu* refer to the subtle essences that underly the gross sexual fluids as well as to the fluids themselves. (The female secretion known as rajas is not to be confused with the guṇa ['fundamental strand'] of that name in Sāṃkhya metaphysics.)

and the urethra are contracted.'[54] The technique may be practised alone by inserting a catheter into the urethra and then creating a (virtual) vacuum in the bladder, thus inducing the intake of air or liquid. Scientific studies[55] have shown that water is most effectively drawn up into the bladder when nauli (the fifth of the ṣaṭ-karmāṇi) is performed.

The *HYP* describes two further practices related to vajrolī, namely *sahajolī* ('strong', 'mighty') and *amarolī* ('immortal'). The first of these apparently involves both sexual partners besmearing their bodies with a mixture made from water and the ashes of burnt cow-dung. This should be done following sexual intercourse in which vajrolī has been performed and while sitting in a pleasant (sukha) frame of mind (*HYP* 3.93). It is stated that sahajolī is 'successful only [for those who are] virtuous, brave, truth-seeing (*tattva-darśinām*), and free from jealousy (*matsara*); and not for those who harbour jealousy' (*HYP* 3.95).

Amarolī consists in inhaling the odour of, and drinking, one's own urine on a daily basis. According to *HYP* 3.96, it is the middle part of the stream that should be absorbed, this being called *amarī* or *Śivāmbu* (water of Śiva) (*J* 3.96).[56]

Without denying that vajrolī and its supplementary practices may be performed in the literal manner implied above, it should be borne in mind that a symbolic interpretation is also possible; this is supported by the fourteenth śloka of the *caturthopadeśa* (fourth 'lesson' or chapter) of the *HYP*, which states that 'Citta's being equanimous and vāyu's travelling through the middle path (i.e. suṣumnā-nāḍī) give rise to amarolī, vajrolī and sahajolī,' thereby suggesting that these three mudrās involve internal states as opposed to (or in addition to) their being practices performed by two sexual

---

54 Buddhananda 1984: 22.

55 Bhole and Karambelkar 1971: 26-32; Wenger and Bagchi 1961: 312-23.

56 *Amarī* has the same meaning as *amṛta*—i.e. 'un-dying', 'immortal'—and both terms have come to refer to the 'elixir of life' or 'nectar of immortality' (cf. Feuerstein 1974b: 31).

partners. Since, on a subtle level, both rajas and bindu are held to exist in every individual, whether male or female, vajrolī can be interpreted as the process of 'uniting' these 'forces' or 'principles' within oneself, and not simply as mixing together semen and female secretions, which are, after all, held to be only the grossest manifestations of these vital fluids (cf. *J* 3.100). Similarly, sahajolī may be taken to refer to the *internal* savouring and distribution of these combined fluids following the blissful 'orgasm' of samādhi. As so often in yoga, the literal and the figurative interpretations need not exclude one another.

10. *Śakticālanī-mudrā*—'raising the Śakti'
Śakticālanī does not refer to one specific 'seal' or 'lock' but to the process of arousing and elevating Kuṇḍalinī (or Śakti). The account provided in the *HYP* (3.114-116) states that one should press the kanda (in the navel region) with the feet, perform bhastrikā-kumbhaka, and contract the 'sun' (*bhānu*) (corresponding to the solar plexus). Such powerful activity in the region of the abdomen is designed to generate sufficient heat to stimulate the serpent power and provoke her upward movement.

11. *Śāṃbhavī-mudrā*
Śāṃbhavī is another name for Śakti, and means 'of, or belonging to, Śaṃbhu (Śiva)'. The mudrā of this name is intended to engender the yogin's identity as *tattva*, which in this context means 'Truth' or 'Reality'[57] —the state enjoyed by Śaṃbhu (*HYP* 4.37). The practice does not involve any physical movement, such as a muscular contraction, but consists, rather, in fixing one's attention upon an 'internal object' (*antar-lakṣya*) (*HYP* 4.36). Brahmānanda proposes *saguṇa-īśvara*,[58] dwelling in anāhata-padma, as a suitable object (*J* 4.37), while the *Gheraṇḍa-Saṃhitā* (3.64) states

[57] *Tattva* literally translates as 'that-ness'.
[58] 'Lord with attributes', i.e. a personified deity.

simply that attention should be focussed in the 'inner eye' (*netrāntara*) and the vision of the Self (ātman) rejoiced in.

Nādānusandhāna

The purpose of the techniques so far mentioned is to bring about the retention of prāṇa within the body, thereby instigating the profound 'inner heat' which stirs the sleeping Kuṇḍalinī from her slumber. Then, as Kuṇḍalinī rises up through citriṇī-nāḍī, and pierces the cakras and granthis, the yogin in deep introspection is said to be able to hear a 'subtle' or 'inner sound' (*nādam-anta*) within the right ear (or the subtle equivalent thereof) (*HYP* 4.67). The nāda (or śabda) is considered to be Kuṇḍalinī-śakti herself manifested as sound or vibration, one of her titles being *Śabda-brahman* ('Brahman's sound/word'),[59] and, as she ascends, so the sound becomes increasingly refined and the yogin's mind more fully absorbed within it.

Anusandhāna (sometimes spelt *anusaṃdhāna*) roughly translates as 'aiming at', 'being intent upon' or 'attending to'; and thus the practice of nādānusandhāna (*nāda* + *anusandhāna*) has to do with fixing one's attention upon the inner sound.[60] The final purpose of the practice is equivalent to that of Pātañjala-yoga, that is, to bring about the dissolution of mental modifications (citta-vṛtti), the resulting state being referred to as *laya* (absorption). Although, according to *HYP* 4.66, the number of methods for achieving laya provided by Ādinātha (Śiva) is ten-and-a-quarter millions (*sapāda-koṭi*), nādānusandhāna is held to be the foremost of them all.

The method involves sitting in the 'posture of deliverance' (muktāsana, also called siddhāsana) and applying śāṃbhavī-mudrā, i.e. concentrating upon an inner object (*HYP* 4.67). The mind's attention should be withdrawn from externally-received sensual information, becoming focussed upon the nāda, a proc-

---

[59] Cf. Avalon 1974: 16.

[60] Feuerstein renders the expression as 'cultivation of the [inner] sound' (1990a: 228), but it is not so much the sound that requires cultivation as one's ability to concentrate upon it.

ess that is aided, according to *Jyotsnā* 4.68, by closing the ears with the thumbs of each hand and using the fingers to close eyes, nostrils and mouth.[61] The mind (citta), says *HYP* 4.90, should be as intent upon the nāda as a bee is intent upon collecting the nectar of flowers, remaining undistracted by their 'perfume' (i.e. by external sensual experiences).

The *HYP* (4.69ff.) identifies four principal stages (*avasthā*) of intrapsychic experience in yoga practice, and each of these is characterised by the audition of a particular mode of nāda. With each successive stage, a more subtle aspect of the sound is heard and the mind's absorption is intensified. The first stage—termed *ārambha*, which simply means 'commencing' or 'beginning'—is instigated by the piercing of Brahma-granthi in the heart lotus,[62] which event engenders a blissful state of 'space' or 'voidness' (*śūnya*).[63] Simultaneously, various musical sounds are perceived to emanate from within the body, along with the 'unstruck sound' (*anāhata-dhvani*), from which the heart cakra derives its name (*HYP* 4.70). It is claimed that, at the commencement of this śūnya state, the yogin comes to possess a fine-smelling and radiant 'divine body' (*divya-deha*) and a 'full heart' (*saṃpūrṇa-hṛdaya*) (*HYP* 4.71).

The second stage of nādānusandhāna is called *ghaṭa-avasthā*—a literal translation of which would be 'water jar stage'—and is characterised by the piercing of Viṣṇu-granthi in the viśuddhi-cakra, and by the hearing in that centre's *ati-śūnya* ('higher void') of a sound resembling a kettle-drum (*bherī*).

Next comes *paricaya-avasthā*—the 'stage of familiarity with (i.e. knowing) [the sound]'—wherein, it is said, the nāda is like the beating of a drum (*mardala*), and emanates from *mahā-*

---

[61] The closing of mouth and nostrils implies that kevala-kumbhaka must be effected.

[62] In other Tāntrika texts, such as the *Ṣaṭ-Cakra-Nirūpaṇa*, Brahma-granthi is located in mūlādhāra-cakra.

[63] The literal meaning of *śūnya* is 'empty', 'void', 'vacant'; but, when the term is applied to an intrapsychic state, these translations fail to capture its full significance. Like *ākāśa*, *śūnya* is best thought of as a condition of 'expansiveness' or 'space' that lacks individuated objective content.

śūnya (the 'great void'), 'abode (*samāśraya*) of all the siddhis' (*HYP* 4.74), which is located in the middle of the brow. Then the 'knot of Rudra' is broken through and, in the fourth stage, known as *niṣpatti* (completion), a sound akin to that made by a *vīṇā* (similar to a lute) is heard.

The four avasthās just mentioned may all be classified as varieties of saṃprajñāta-samādhi,[64] for the nāda provides an 'object of cognitive support' or 'focus of attention' for the mind, with each progressive stage witnessing the unveiling of a more subtle or refined (sūkṣma) aspect of that object (*HYP* 4.84). The nāda may also be characterised as a 'vehicle' that carries the mind through successive layers of self-identity and towards the ultimate state of soundless (*niḥśabda*) *Parabrahman* (Supreme Absolute), the realisation of the highest Self (*paramātman*) (*HYP* 4.101). This final state, beyond sound and all other phenomena, may be taken to be the asaṃprajñāta-samādhi spoken of by Vyāsa (*YB* 1.1), and the 'other' (*anya*) state mentioned by Patañjali (*YS* 1.18)—a condition in which no new saṃskāras are generated and where puruṣa or ātman dwells in its own nature.

We can see from the discussion of techniques in this chapter that haṭha-yoga is a comprehensive discipline, comprising an array of practices designed to carry the practitioner from the novitiate stage through to the highest goal of Self-realisation. The precise set of techniques that are suited to this task will vary from one practitioner to another, a personal guru being required to determine the appropriate methodology. For some, a rigorous routine of āsanas and purificatory exercises will form a necessary preliminary regimen, establishing improved physical hygiene and stamina prior to the practise of prāṇāyāma; others, meanwhile, already possessing the physical capacity and mental discipline needed for prāṇāyāma, can begin intensive breathing work at an earlier stage. Those commentators who wish to portray haṭha as a 'purely physical' discipline, useful

---

[64] 'Samādhi-with-cognitive-support' (see pp. 116ff. above).

for maintaining bodily health but having little to do with mental training and spiritual illumination, conveniently overlook such practices as nādānusandhāna, the principal aim of which is to achieve the highest state of samādhi. Haṭha-yoga has a systematic approach to spiritual unfoldment, progressively 'internalising' the practice—engaging the student in an inward journey from the gross body to the most refined mental structures, to eventually reveal an expanded and divinised sense of identity.

To some readers, the benefits to be derived from the more advanced stages of kumbhaka, in which the flow of air into and out of the body is drastically restricted for prolonged periods, may seem obscure, and the probability of such techniques actually being performed remote. In order to appreciate the yogin's belief in the feasibility and desirability of such practices, it is important to acknowledge the role of prāṇa, the subtle energy that is held to constitute a more fundamental source of nutrition than oxygen, food, or anything else that is ingested into the body. According to haṭha theory, the experienced yogin is able to control the breathing cycle to the extent that the breath is suspended for hours at a time precisely because he has learnt to retain prāṇa within the innermost core of his being—the suṣumnā-nāḍī—and to tap into the infinite reservoir of Kuṇḍalinī-śakti. Whether or not one subscribes to the theoretical explanations for yogic feats offered in the traditional literature, the fact that extraordinary instances of endurance and control over physiological processes do occur is beyond question. And this brings us to the effects of haṭha-yoga, a number of which will be examined in the following chapter, both from a traditional and a scientific perspective.

9

Effects of Haṭha-Yoga

The claims made on behalf of haṭha-yoga in the traditional texts are as extensive as they are remarkable. Descriptions of particular techniques, whether they be āsanas, kumbhakas or mudrās, are frequently accompanied by a declaration to the effect that observing the correct procedure will result in the 'removal of all diseases',[1] and/or will lead inexorably to emancipation (mokṣa).[2] If such claims are viewed as referring to individual techniques in isolation from haṭha-yoga as a holistic enterprise, they must surely be seen as exaggerations; could it really be the case, for example, that the sitting spinal twist known as Matsyendrāsana (posture of Matsyendra) is 'a weapon that destroys the whole sphere of terrible afflictions' (*HYP* 1.27)? If, however, such claims are considered with regard to each technique's proper place in the discipline as a whole—i.e. as concerning the technique's effect in combination with a full range of āsanas, mudrās, kumbhakas, and intense mental concentration—then they become a little more feasible.

Haṭha-yogins have rarely gone out of their way to seek 'objective' verification of the abilities they acquire; indeed, the most easily observable of such abilities usually relate to physiological processes, and are therefore regarded by the yogin as merely superficial, hardly worthy of verification. The most significant changes are those that occur at a subjective level—the transformations of perception, self-knowledge and

---

[1] E.g. *HYP* 1.27, 29, 44, 49.
[2] E.g. *HYP* 1.35.

one's notion of self-identity—and it is impossible to submit these for external scrutinisation. For the traditional practitioner, the only evidence required to demonstrate the effects of haṭha-yoga is that gained through personal experience; nothing else is considered either necessary or sufficient. There have, however, been a number of scientific studies carried out on haṭha-yogins and the effects of haṭha techniques, and this number is steadily growing. The bulk of the present chapter is concerned with such studies, the aim being to provide, not an exhaustive discussion of the data currently available, but, rather, a useful summary of the sorts of experiments that have been conducted, and a representative selection of the information gathered therefrom. Should anyone wish to take the subject further, all of the scientific papers mentioned in the main text and in footnotes appear in the Bibliography.

Before looking at haṭha-yoga through the lens of biomedical science, however, it is worth taking note of the discipline's effects as described in the traditional treatises. These effects are said to be evidenced in several 'special powers', acquired by the yogin through prolonged and assiduous practice, and commonly termed *siddhis*.

Siddhis

The term *siddhi* derives from the verbal root *sidh*, which itself is the weak form of *sādh*, meaning 'to perfect, attain, succeed, accomplish, fulfil'. From the same root come such terms as *sādhana* ('that which leads to the goal'), *sādhaka* (someone or something that is 'directed towards the goal'), *sādhu* (a title for a holy person), and *siddha* ('one who has achieved the goal'). In the context of yoga, *siddhi* has two principal meanings. Firstly it denotes the 'absolute success' or 'perfection' achieved by the yogin who has realised his or her true identity as Brahman; and secondly it has the sense of a more minor 'accomplishment' or 'special power' acquired on the way to ultimate success, such accomplishments being 'signposts', as it were, indicating that one is at least heading in the right direction.

In the *Yoga-Sūtra*, siddhis are said to be attained by sustained practice of saṃyama, which consists in the combined inner disciplines of dhāraṇā, dhyāna and samādhi. The third chapter of Patañjali's text is entitled 'Vibhūti-pāda', *vibhūti* meaning 'signal blessing', 'gift' or 'power' and thus being a virtual synonym of *siddhi.* Much of the Vibhūti-pāda is devoted to outlining the numerous siddhis accrued by one's performing saṃyama on specific objects. Sūtras 3.45-46, for example, state that

> By saṃyama on the gross and subtle elements and on their essential nature, correlations and purpose, mastery over them is gained. (*YS* 3.45)
>
> From that comes attainment of aṇima [diminution] and other siddhis, bodily perfection and the non-obstruction of bodily functions by the influence of the elements. (*YS* 3.46)[3]

Of all the siddhis mentioned, eight are held to be most important. These eight, generally referred to as the mahā- ('great' or 'major') siddhis, are the following:

1. *aṇiman*—the ability to become as small as (or to perceive the nature of) an atom;
2. *laghiman*—lightness of weight, implying the ability to levitate;
3. *mahiman*—the ability to expand infinitely;
4. *prāpti*—the power to reach everywhere;
5. *prākāmya*—freedom of will;
6. *vaśitva*—dominion over the universe;
7. *īśitṛtva*—the power to create;
8. *kāmāvasāyitva*—the gift of wish fulfilment.

In the descriptions of these eight siddhis offered by Vyāsa in *Yoga-Bhāṣya* 3.45, it is not made explicit whether those that involve a transformation of bodily state are associated with the sthūla-śarīra, or with the sūkṣma-śarīra alone. In the *Mahā-*

[3] Trans. Satchidananda 1984.

bhārata, however, Yājñavalkya is reported as saying that 'the eight excellences' (*guṇa*s)—which expression denotes the eight mahā-siddhis—'[pertain to] the subtle [body], not to the other [i.e. physical body].'[4] Kamil Zvelebil supports this 'subtle' interpretation of the siddhis, stating that, with regard to the siddha tradition of south India, powers such as 'travel through the air, passing unobstructed through walls, touching sun and moon, etc.' should be understood as referring, not to 'the body of "gross" matter, but a mind-made or mind-formed (*manomaya*) body which is produced from the physical body like "a sword from the sheath, pith from a reed, a snake from a basket."'[5]

The notion that siddhis obtain solely, or primarily, upon a 'subtle' plane is ambiguated, however, in the popular autobiography of Paramahansa Yogananda, in which the author provides numerous anecdotal accounts of 'miraculous powers' being exhibited by yogins, which powers include such things as bodily bilocation, levitation (apparently of the gross physical body), and materialisation of physical objects.[6] The explanation given for such abilities is that the respective yogin has gained extensive control over 'prāṇic force' or 'lifetrons', which regulate the 'vibratory variations in electrons and protons.'[7] Yogananda reserves the most spectacular descriptions of supranormal abilities for his guru twice removed, the immortal *mahāvatāra* (mahā-avatāra: 'great descended one') Babaji, who, among other things, is reported to have dematerialised and rematerialised his physical body, resuscitated a corpse, and materialised a palace in the high Himālaya.[8]

It should be noted that an ambivalent attitude is adopted by certain yogins towards the siddhis. Regarded as indications of a yogin's progress towards the highest goal, they are to be wel-

---

4 *Mahābhārata* 12.318.7, trans. Feuerstein 1974b: 126 (brackets are Feuerstein's).

5 Zvelebil 1996: 115.

6 Yogananda 1981: 23-24, 276, 46-47.

7 *Ib.*: 47.

8 *Ib.*: 300ff.

comed; but, at the same time, it is commonly held that one should be wary of their potentially distracting influence; for one who has not fully integrated the yamas and niyamas (moral dicta) into his life, siddhis may, it is believed, harbour seeds of pride and the corrupting temptation to misuse such powers for selfish ends.[9] For this reason, Patañjali warns that the siddhis 'are extraneous obstacles (*upasarga*) to samādhi', though, he adds, they are useful in worldly activities (*YS* 3.38). The following anecdote concerning Swami Sivananda of Rishikesh illustrates the nonchalance with which the siddhis are regarded by some gurus:

> A pupil once asked him how she could attain levitation. His answer was: 'Leave it alone, it only awakens curiosity in people and you would be likely to bang your head against the ceiling. Choose the middle way, that of Meditation, of control over your breath, of being motionless, of prayer, of love, of humility and of Self-realisation.'[10]

The point is not that siddhis should be altogether rejected, but that they should not become the exclusive aim of yoga sādhana. As Aurobindo remarks, 'We need not shun the siddhis and cannot shun them...; for these things are the natural action of the consciousness to which [the yogin] is rising, just as mental activity and physical motion are the natural action of man's ordinary life.'[11] Each siddhi represents a power or quality of the Absolute as viewed in its personal aspect as Īśvara, and hence the extent to which the siddhis are experienced depends upon the extent to which the yogin's own nature abides in that of 'the Lord'.

As already mentioned, in the *Yoga-Sūtra* the siddhis are held to be acquired through saṃyama, the components of which are essentially described as progressively prolonged and intense forms of mental concentration. In haṭha-yoga, however, the

---

[9] Cf. Yogananda 1981: 228n.
[10] Lindenberg, in Sivananda 1955b: xix.
[11] Aurobindo 1970-76 vol. 27: 366.

emphasis is placed more firmly upon the techniques of prāṇa-retention, specifically kumbhaka and mudrā. *HYP* 3.8, for example, states that the instructions in mudrā were delivered by Ādinātha (Śiva) and that their practise gives rise to 'the eight sovereign powers' or 'qualities of the Lord' (*aṣṭa-aiśvarya*) beloved by 'all siddhas' (*sarva-siddhānāṃ*). While these eight powers are not individually named in the *HYP* itself, Brahmānanda's commentary on an earlier śloka (1.11) provides a list corresponding to that described by Vyāsa (*YB* 3.45). The *Śiva-Saṃhitā* (3.54), on the other hand, enumerates nine alternative siddhis, namely:

1. *vāk-siddhi*—perfection in speech, speaking the truth;
2. *kāmacāri*—moving to where one desires, teleportation;
3. *dūradṛṣṭi*—'far-seeing', clairvoyance;
4. *dūraśruti*—'far-hearing', clairaudience;
5. *sūkṣma-dṛṣṭi*—'subtle seeing', i.e. perceiving subtle phenomena;
6. *parakāyapraveśana*—entering another's body;
7. *viṇ-mūtra-lepane svarṇama-dṛśya-karaṇa*—turning objects to gold by smearing them with one's feces and urine;
8. *bhavantyetāni sarvāṇi*—becoming completely invisible;
9. *khecara*—'moving in space'.

The method given in the *Śiva-Saṃhitā* (3.53) for acquiring these abilities is that of increasingly prolonging the duration of kumbhaka up to 'three *ghaṭikā*s' (one ghāṭikā = 24 minutes); 'thereby, the yogin permanently attains the siddhis' (*ib.*). A reference to the last siddhi mentioned, namely khecara, also appears in the *HYP* (4.27), wherein the power is said to arise as a consequence of 'binding (*baddha*) vāyu', i.e. retaining prāṇa within suṣumnā-nāḍī and, according to Brahmānanda's commentary, focusing it in the ājñā-cakra between the eyebrows (*J* 4.27). In some translations of haṭha texts, *khecara* is rendered as 'rising in the air',[12] thereby implying that a form of bodily levitation or flight is intended. More precisely, however, the term means 'moving in ākāśa', i.e. having one's being in, or identifying with, the most refined of the mahābhūtas; khecara may, therefore, be regarded as a particular meditative state as opposed to (or at least in addition to) a bodily power. The seventh siddhi listed above—i.e. turning objects to gold by smearing them with excrement—is especially hard to take literally, and should probably be understood as a figurative statement implying that even the waste products of a yogin become 'pure'.

To fully evaluate the siddhis, one would need to engage in a lengthy examination of data pertaining to 'psychic' or 'parapsychological' phenomena *per se*, and while such a project would doubtlessly prove interesting and worthwhile, it would take us too far from the immediate topic of haṭha-yoga. Here, therefore, I have merely endeavoured to outline the main claims made in the yoga texts themselves. Now let us turn our attention to the field of biomedical science, which, though having relatively little to say about the 'subtle' phenomena associated with the siddhis, can at least give us grounds for acknowledging haṭha-yoga's capacity to enhance human performance on many levels.

Scientific data

The last hundred years or so have seen the development of increasingly accurate and sophisticated methods for measuring and recording certain physiological processes, such as the breathing rhythm, heart rate, neuro-electrical activity, etc.; and these methods have been employed in a large number of scientific studies designed to investigate the physiological effects of yogic or quasi-yogic techniques. This section provides a brief summary of, and a selection of noteworthy examples from, the scientific literature, with an emphasis on those data that dem-

[12] E.g. Iyangar 1972: 66; Vasu 1996: 32; Vishnudevananda 1997: 164.

onstrate something about the effects of techniques most closely associated with the haṭha tradition.

Of the many physiological responses to haṭha-yoga that are susceptible to investigation, scientific studies have tended to be chiefly concerned with respiratory, circulatory, muscular-articular, and to a lesser extent endocrine and nervous system responses. The methodology adopted by experimenters has typically involved taking a group of volunteers—often young students—who are inexperienced in haṭha techniques and then having these volunteers trained in a variety of techniques for a period of several months. Measurements of one or more physiological process are taken before, after, and sometimes during, the period of training, and these data are compared with those acquired from equivalent measurements of a control group, i.e. a group of similar people (with regard to age, sex, body type, etc.) who have received no training in haṭha-yoga. Sometimes measurements are also taken of the haṭha-yoga group after a period of 'de-training', in which members are requested to desist from practising the techniques they have learnt.

Any conclusions drawn from such experiments are inevitably restricted by the limited span of time for which the subjects have undergone training. According to traditional haṭha texts, such as Brahmānanda's *Jyotsnā* (2.48), a serious haṭha-yogin will practise several āsanas and kumbhakas four times a day—before sunrise, at midday, before sunset, and at midnight—and continue this routine for a number of years under the instruction of a guru. It is therefore unrealistic to expect any dramatic results from someone who has practised only a few exercises once a day for a matter of months. Nevertheless, a number of such relatively short-term studies have successfully shown that significant physiological changes can occur as a result of one's practising haṭha-yoga, such changes including the following:

(a) Decrease in basal breath rate, i.e. the number of breaths taken per minute in a supine resting position. For example, a study by K. N. Udupa et al showed that, after training for six months in a selection of haṭha techniques, the average basal breath rate of twelve subjects had dropped from 16.8 to 13.4 per minute.[13] K. S. Gopal et al compared a group who had practised haṭha-yoga for six months with a group who had no yoga experience but engaged regularly in other forms of light exercise, and found the basal breath rate of the former group to be 10 breaths per minute as opposed to 23 per minute in the latter.[14]

(b) Increase in breath holding time. For example, M. V. Bhole and P. V. Karambelkar found that the breath holding time of physical education students could be extended by up to 22 seconds after only a three-week haṭha-yoga programme.[15]

(c) Increase in respiratory amplitude, i.e. the degree to which the lungs expand during respiration, thus indicating an increase in lung capacity.[16]

(d) Improvement in the smoothness of breathing.[17]

(e) Improved relaxation and flexibility of muscles. An obvious benefit of practising haṭha āsanas is increased muscular flexibility, and this has been demonstrated in several studies.[18] In addition to 'extent flexibility' and 'dynamic flexibility', a study by M. L. Gharote also measured such factors as 'explosive strength, dynamic strength, trunk strength, coordination, equilibrium and stamina', and found that overall fitness was improved after only a three-week training programme comprising āsanas, ujjāyī-prāṇāyāma, agnisāra-dhauti, kapālabhāti and nauli.[19] A method known as electromyography has been used in several studies to measure and record the electrical activity pre-

---

[13] Udupa et al 1971: 345-53; cf. Funderburk 1977: 50-54.

[14] Gopal et al 1973: 686-72.

[15] Bhole and Karambelkar 1971: 19-26; cf. Funderburk 1977: 54-56.

[16] Dhanaraj 1974: 'The Effects of Yoga and the 5BX Fitness Plan on Selected Physiological Parameters', Ph.D. dissertation, University of Alberta, USA, cited in Funderburk 1977: 57.

[17] See Datey et al 1969: 325-33; cf. Funderburk 1977: 56-57.

[18] See Funderburk 1977: 7-9.

[19] Gharote 1973: 31-35.

sent in certain areas of muscle during the performance of āsanas. Results have demonstrated that regular practise of haṭha-yoga postures reduces the amount of strain endured by muscles as they are being stretched.[20] In a particularly interesting study by P. V. Karambelkar et al, it was found that performing āsanas according to dicta outlined in the *Yoga-Sūtra*—i.e. the precepts to relax and 'meditate on the infinite (*ananta*)' (*YS* 2.46-47)—reduced still further the electromyographic readings (EMG), thus supporting the idea that a strong link exists between mental focus and the degree of tension experienced in the body.[21]

(f) Decreased heart rate. Experiments involving groups of young people who have received training in haṭha-yoga for only a matter of weeks or months have indicated that, while the heart rate—measured in beats per minute—generally increases during āsanas (except śavāsana [the supine 'corpse posture']) and vigorous prāṇāyāma, the heart rate in basal state consistently decreases.[22]

(g) Increased cardiovascular efficiency, i.e. 'the capacity of an individual to maintain strenuous activity of the whole body for a prolonged period.'[23] S. K. Ganguly and M. L. Gharote[24] studied eleven men (average age 26) before and after a haṭha training programme of eight months duration, comprising cleansing techniques, āsanas, prāṇāyāma performed with appropriate mudrās, as well as some meditation. Statistically significant results were obtained, demonstrating the capacity of haṭha-yoga practices to boost cardiovascular efficiency.[25]

(h) Change in blood composition. Among the components of the blood which chemical analysis has shown to *increase* as a

---

20 See, e.g. Gopal et al 1975: 3-11.

21 Karambelkar et al 1969: 1-13.

22 Dhanaraj 1974, cited in Funderburk 1977: 22; Udupa et al 1971: 345-53.

23 Funderburk 1977: 16.

24 Ganguly and Gharote (unpublished manuscript): 'Cardio-vascular Efficiency Before and After Yogic Training', cited in Funderburk 1977: 16.

25 The method used for measuring cardiovascular efficiency was the 'Harvard Step Test' (see Funderburk 1977: 16).

result of following a haṭha-yoga training programme are: red blood cells, haemoglobin, lymphocytes, and thyroxin. Those which have been shown to *decrease* include leukocytes (white blood cells) and cholesterol.[26]

In addition to the numerous studies of people who have practised haṭha-yoga in a limited capacity for a relatively short period of time, there also exist some data collected from experiments on more experienced haṭha practitioners. In 1957, for example, psychologists Bagchi and Wenger used an eight-channel electroencephalogram (EEG) plus other instruments to record respiration, finger blood-volume changes, and skin conductance and temperature of yogins in India.[27] Of particular interest here are their findings that, although the breathing rate of yogins slowed down during meditation, their heart rates, lower finger temperatures, palmar conductance and blood pressure increased considerably, suggesting, as Michael Murphy has commented, 'that for these yogins meditation was an active rather than a passive process.'[28]

In a study of seven Indian yogins, N. N. Das and H. Gastaut found, too, that during intense meditation the heart rates of their subjects accelerated, while breathing and general muscle tone relaxed.[29] Brain wave activity was shown to increase in proportion to heart rate, and then to slow down following samādhi. At some points the brain waves reached 40-45 Hz (cycles per second), which is far in excess of the normal beta rate of around 20 Hz exhibited in an average waking person. Upon cessation of the samādhi state, the brain waves returned to a slower rate in the alpha band.[30] In their conclusions, Das

---

[26] See Funderburk 1977: 41-46, 74-75.

[27] Bagchi and Wenger 1958: 193.

[28] Murphy 1992: 529.

[29] Das and Gastaut 1955: 211-19.

[30] Brain waves (i.e. electrical currents produced by neural activity) are divided into four principal categories: beta (14-30 Hz), alpha (8-13 Hz), theta (4-7 Hz) and delta (0.5-3.5 Hz). These are typically associated with the mental states of waking, resting/relaxing, dream-sleep, and deep dreamless sleep respectively (cf. Hocking 1993: 8ff.).

and Gastaut stated that 'supreme concentration of attention' is likely to be 'responsible for the perfect insensibility of the yogi during *samadhi*', which state is shown by the EEG results to be profoundly different to 'sleep, lethargy, anesthesia or coma.'[31]

After taking part in experiments at the Menninger Foundation in Kansas, USA, the yogin Swami Rama was so impressed with the EEG machines that he took some back to India, claiming that they would greatly assist with the training of yogins.[32] Swami Rama had used a breathing method consisting of 'deep and slow rhythmic [breaths] at a constant rate...with no pauses at the top and bottom of the breathing cycle', and was able to consciously alter his EEG pattern, producing theta waves simultaneously with beta and alpha waves.[33] He also exhibited remarkable control over blood flow and heart rate, in one experiment decreasing the flow of blood to the thenar (ball of the thumb) of his right hand while simultaneously increasing the flow to the hypothenar (palm above the little finger) of the same hand. This resulted in 'a temperature differential of ten degrees Fahrenheit between the two sides of his palm', the left side turning pink as it became warmer, the right turning grey as it cooled.[34] In another experiment, Rama produced 'a state of atrial flutter during which the heart ceased to pump blood for seventeen seconds' (after which time the Swami was requested by worried observers to return his heart to normal).[35] Swami Rama had not stopped his heart, but had accelerated 'its speed to such an extent (300 beats per minute) that it was not pumping any blood (since the ventricles had stopped and the atria merely fluttered). The effect on the circulatory system was thus the same as if the heart had completely ceased to beat.'[36] A professor of cardiology reported that such an electrocardiograph (ECG) record is 'sometimes seen in patients and is asso-

---

[31] Quoted in Murphy 1992: 530.
[32] Hocking 1993: 66.
[33] *Ib.*
[34] Rama et al 1976: 25; cf. Murphy 1992: 532.
[35] Rama et al 1976: 26.
[36] *Ib.*

ciated with loss of blood flow in fainting or death';[37] yet Swami Rama induced the effect without any strenuous muscular action, relying solely upon breath control and mental concentration, and with no physiological damage to himself.

Experiments by B. K. Anand et al have demonstrated the ability of certain yogins to remain in a relaxed state (typified by alpha brain waves) in the midst of intense sensory stimuli, such as loud noise and bright light, and with their hands submerged in ice-cold water for periods of up to 55 minutes.[38] Other researchers have studied Tibetan monks who are able to raise their body heat in order to withstand freezing temperatures at high altitudes. In 1982, for example, a paper by a team from the Harvard Medical School was published in the scientific journal *Nature* in which they described tests carried out on three *lāma*s (Tibetan Buddhist 'priests'), aged 46, 50 and 59 respectively, in upper Dharamsala (Himachal Pradesh, India). Using the practice known as *tummo* ('heating'), the lāmas exhibited the ability to raise finger temperature by between 3.15°C and 7.2°C, toe temperature by between 4°C and 8.3°C, and the temperature in other parts of the body by lesser amounts. To account for the remarkable increases in finger and toe temperature, the researchers posited vasodilation (i.e. widening of the blood vessels) as the most likely mechanism.[39]

There is certainly no shortage of data relating to breathing techniques characteristic of haṭha-yoga. In studying the effects of prāṇāyāma, Wenger and Bagchi,[40] for example, 'found that some of their subjects, especially experienced ones, could produce bidirectional changes in every autonomic variable the experimenters measured.'[41] With regard to heart rate in particular, B. K. Anand and G. S. Chhina[42] studied three yogins who combined 'intrathoracic pressure by forceful abdominal

---

[37] Quoted in Funderburk 1977: 32.
[38] Murphy 1992: 531.
[39] *Ib.*: 102-3.
[40] 1961: 312-23.
[41] Murphy 1992: 529.
[42] 1961: 90-94.

contractions [i.e. uḍḍīyāna-bandha] with closed glottis [i.e. jālaṃdhara-bandha] after inspiration or expiration' to produce a dramatic reduction of the arterial pulse.[43] By using an ECG and X-ray examination, Anand and Chhina were able to conclude that, although the yogins 'could not stop...their heart beats,' the muscular contractions they employed decreased venous return, which in turn 'greatly decreased their cardiac output'.[44] Even though such experiments cannot provide information regarding the more subtle effects of haṭha-yoga—such as, for example, the effect of prāṇāyāma and mudrās upon the flow of prāṇa—the fact that significant alterations in the heart's activity occur is suggestive of the potency of these kinds of techniques.

If looking for more spectacular illustrations of 'yogic powers', we may turn to the exceptional feats performed in front of scientific observers by Yogi Ramananda of Mysore, India; initially in 1957 at the age of 48, and then again in 1976. First, 'by concentrating all his energy on his fingers',[45] the yogin was able to slice through a rolled leaf, using his first and middle fingers like a pair of scissors and propelling one piece of leaf 'several feet away.'[46] Then, in a second demonstration, he had a chain made of iron wrapped around his waist and reconnected to itself to form a belt, with nine links left out in front. 'The ninth link', reports Funderburk, 'was connected to a metal bar on which the subject placed his feet, causing tension in the nine links.'[47] For two minutes, Ramananda's resting respiratory rate was measured, and was shown to be '6 breaths per minute.' Then he was instructed to break the chain, and, after increasing 'the respiratory rate to 18 breaths per minute for a duration of one minute...he took one breath...for 13 seconds' and, as he exhaled, the chain—which could withstand up to 650 pounds of tension before bending—snapped. 'Upon examination', writes

---

[43] Murphy 1992: 532n.
[44] Quoted in Murphy *ib.*
[45] Rao et al, quoted in Funderburk 1977: 13.
[46] Funderburk *ib.*
[47] *Ib.*: 14.

Funderburk, 'the link that broke was found to be severed in half, rather than bent open',[48] a result which suggests that Ramananda, who weighed a mere 106 pounds at the time of the demonstration, had brought some force other than brute strength to bear upon it.

Among the most impressive experiments carried out on yogins are those in which the subject is confined in an airtight or poorly ventilated container for an extended period of time. One such experiment was conducted by L. K. Kothari et al and published in the *American Heart Journal* in 1973. A yogin was wired up to a twelve-lead ECG and buried in an earthen pit for over seven days in the grounds of the Tagore Medical College and Hospital in Udaipur, India. Monitoring the ECG record from a nearby laboratory, the experimenters noted that, after twenty-nine hours of confinement, the yogin's heart rate had accelerated to as many as 250 beats per minute (as contrasted with the 106 per minute prior to the incarceration); then, suddenly, after thirty hours, the ECG from all twelve leads displayed 'a straight line with no electrical disturbance', and this 'continued for the next 5 days.'[49] Having suspected that the leads may have become disconnected, the experimenters were amazed when, half an hour before the pit was due to be opened, the ECG tracings reappeared, registering a rate of 142 beats per minute. Concluding his summary of this fascinating experiment, Murphy writes that,

> When the pit was opened, the yogi was found sitting in the same posture he had started in, but in a stuporous condition. In accounting for his remarkable [ECG] record, the experimenters argued that a disconnection of the [ECG] lead would have produced obvious markings on the tracings in their laboratory, as they found when they tried to simulate ways in which the yogi might have tinkered with it. Furthermore, the yogi was ignorant about such machines, and the pit was completely dark.[50]

---

[48] *Ib.*
[49] Kothari et al, quoted in Funderburk 1977: 33.
[50] Murphy 1992: 534-35.

Kothari et al conclude that 'the most likely cause of the straight line on [the yogin's] [ECG] tracing was a dramatic decrease in his heart's activity.'[51] However, bearing in mind Swami Rama's demonstration of 'atrial flutter' mentioned above, and given that the heart rate of the yogin in this particular experiment was seen to accelerate dramatically prior to the cessation of ECG tracing, it should be emphasised that this decrease—and perhaps actual stoppage—was itself probably induced by a rapid *increase* in heart activity. Recalling traditional haṭha theory, the speculation may be offered that such an increase in heart rate corresponds to—or is a gross physical manifestation of—the intense 'inner heat' created by the forced union of prāṇa and apāna within the sūkṣma-śarīra that precedes the arousal of Kuṇḍalinī-śakti.

Although predating the time of ECG machines and other technological recording methods, a still more impressive case of human burial and subsequent revival is that of the yogin Haridas, who was confined for 40 days in a small wooden box in 1837. What makes this case particularly valuable is, firstly, the fact that it is so well documented as to make the possibility of fraud extremely remote, and, secondly, the fact that Haridas employed some of the most advanced techniques described in the *HYP* and other manuals of haṭha-yoga. According to the detailed report of Sir Claude Wade,[52] the yogin was 'enclosed in a bag of white linen, fastened by a string over the head', and was interred in a padlocked 'wooden box, about four feet long by three broad, with a sloping roof'. The box was situated in 'a sort of cell' below the floor of a room which was itself sealed shut on all four sides. The building in which the demonstration took place belonged to the Mahārāja Runjeet Singh of Lahore, who took extreme precautions to guard against trickery, and had the building watched night and day by four sentries who were replaced every two hours.

---

[51] *Ib.*
[52] Cited in Murphy 1992: 472-474.

When the forty days were up, Claude Wade attended the disinterment of Haridas, along with Runjeet Singh and a servant of Haridas'. After the yogin's body was removed from the box, Wade tore open the bag, revealing a body with shrivelled and stiff limbs, and no palpable pulsation 'in the heart, the temples, or the arm.' The body appeared corpse-like, apart from 'a heat about the region of the brain,' a condition that concurs with descriptions of yogins in whom Kuṇḍalinī has ascended to the sahasrāra-padma.[53] Within half an hour, however, Haridas' pulse had returned, and he was breathing again and able to speak.

Wade's report received additional substantiation when a German physician named J. M. Honigberger published details about Haridas' remarkable yogic feat in 1851.[54] Honigberger's account, derived from 'the English general Ventura and other credible witnesses',[55] mentioned some of the preparatory measures taken by Haridas, which clearly place him within the haṭha tradition. These included the cutting of the fraenum beneath his tongue so that the tongue could be turned back to seal the air passage behind the soft palate (as in khecarī-mudrā), the swallowing of a long strip of cloth to clean the stomach (as in vāso-dhauti), and the use of enemas (as in vasti), all of which practices are described in hatha manuals such as the *HYP* (see Chapter 8 above). Summarising Honigberger's account, Murphy writes that:

> Before [Haridas'] burial, his ears, rectum, and nostrils were sealed with wax, and he was wrapped in a linen cloth that was also sealed. He was then laid into a chest, which the Maharaja locked, and lowered into the enclosure that Wade described. Upon his resuscitation...the yogi's attendant blew air into his throat and ears so that the wax plugs in his nostrils were loudly ejected. Having been

[53] Cf. Avalon 1974: 19-20.
[54] Cited in Garbe 1900.
[55] Murphy 1992: 474-75.

sealed up in this manner, Haridas had survived with virtually no ventilation.[56]

In Haridas, then, we have a well-documented example of someone's employing the haṭha-yoga cleansing techniques plus kumbhaka and mudrā to achieve a state of physiological suspension. Although scientific instruments were not available to record his brain wave-pattern, heart rate, breathing rhythm and other bodily processes, it is clear that, in order simply to survive the ordeal, the yogin must have slowed these processes down to an extremely low rate.

The dialogue between modern biomedical science and the traditional discipline of haṭha-yoga is an ongoing and fruitful one. Just as the former improves our understanding of the physiological mechanisms involved in haṭha practice, so the latter reveals to us the extent to which physiological processes can be voluntarily manipulated and enhanced, thereby shedding new light upon many mysteries associated with the body, the mind, and the complex relationship between the two. We have seen in Chapters 6 and 7 that the conception of the body in haṭha-yoga is far from being in conformity with that of mainstream biology, including as it does several 'levels' of organic reality that elude standard means of observation and measurement. This absence of conformity need not, however, be taken as evidence that the haṭha view is somehow more 'primitive' or 'superstitious' than that of modern science, for modern science clearly has much to learn from haṭha-yoga; and the two models can, in many ways, complement one another to provide a richer appreciation of the human being.

An essential strand of haṭha theory is the belief that the maximisation of physical health constitutes a necessary component of the Self-realisation process: the body must be purified and strengthened in order to efficaciously 'channel' powerful subtle forces (prāṇa), and to withstand the transformative

---

[56] *Ib.*: 475.

effects of Kuṇḍalinī-śakti. Although the majority of medical scientists remain publically sceptical about the existence of such subtle forces and supraphysical realms, the positive effects of haṭha's health-oriented techniques are hard to ignore. It is therefore as a method of health improvement that haṭha-yoga is becoming increasingly recognised and promoted throughout the world, and it is primarily at this level that the instructive exchange between biomedical science and the haṭha tradition can take place. Some of the people who are beginning to approach haṭha-yoga as a method of physical exercise and stress relief may be largely uninterested in the more philosophical aspects of the discipline discussed in this book; others, however, are finding that the discovery of haṭha's origins and primary purpose, i.e. as a systematic vehicle of self-unfoldment embedded within an initiatory pedagogical structure, is bringing an extra dimension to their practice, and is leading them towards an invigorated appreciation of the deep-rooted interrelatedness of physical and psychological well-being.

10

Conclusion

> I have no doubt whatever that most people live, whether physically, intellectually or morally, in a very restricted circle of their potential being...much like a man who, out of his whole bodily organism, should get into a habit of using and moving only his little finger. We all have reservoirs of life to draw upon, of which we do not dream. (William James)[1]

It is inevitable that no study of yoga, no matter how rigorous and comprehensive in its scope, can ever be finally satisfying; and nor should it be. Yoga is a theory-practice unity and a soteriological discipline, the full benefits of which require immense and unwavering dedication before they can be appreciated. It is not through ratiocination—not through exercising the cogs of citta (the conditional mind)—that the nectar of yoga can be tasted; but through diligent practice. And nor, therefore, is it possible for yoga's secrets to be revealed in a written form, for those secrets—those experiences beyond experience, and that knowingness beyond knowledge that so many mystics have endeavoured to point towards—transcend the limits of language and the logical grammatical structure on which it is based. Again and again the yoga texts stress the importance of practice:

> Success (siddhi) belongs to the one engaged in practice, but how to the non-practitioner? Yoga-siddhi is attained not by mere recitation (*pātha*) of the śāstra. Nor by wearing the garb [of a yogin] is

[1] Quoted in Murphy 1992: 231.

> siddhi brought about, and nor by discussing it. Practice alone causes siddhi. This, without doubt, is the truth. (*HYP* 1.64-65)
>
> *yogena yogo jñātavyo yogo yogāt pravartate | yo'pramattas tu yogena sa yoge ramate ciram.*
> (By means of yoga, yoga is known; from yoga, comes yoga. One who is assiduous in yoga rests in yoga for ever.) (*YB* 3.6)

This practical emphasis does not, however, mean that one should abandon the intellect; for the mind as much as the body is the tool of the yogin, and unless we 'think through' our spiritual practice—unless we utilise our critical faculties to the utmost—we are apt to make bad decisions about the techniques and path best suited for us, and we are unlikely to achieve a clear understanding of *why* we practise at all (if, indeed, we do). As noted in Chapter 5, the goal of yoga, as defined in the *Yoga-Sūtra*, is *citta-vṛtti-nirodha*—the 'dissolution of mental modifications'—so that one's true Self may 'abide in its own nature' (*YS* 1.2-3); it therefore ultimately involves the voluntary pacification of the mind in order that the Self (puruṣa, ātman) or Seer (draṣṭṛ) may 'shine forth'. To reach that goal, however, it is of no value to reject the mind and its powers of reasoning, for reason can be a helpful guide; the important thing is to be aware that, if scriptures and the testimony of yogins are to be believed, there is a way of perceiving and a way of *being* which relies not upon reason for guidance, but upon knowledge of a more immediate kind: a direct realisation.

Bearing in mind, then, the admitted limitations of intellection vis-à-vis a clear appreciation of yoga, it is my hope that, in writing this book, I have done more than to add extra dead weight to the already gravitous pile of verbiage on the subject. In my approach to, and engagement with, the haṭha tradition, I have endeavoured to treat the subject seriously and to explore the philosophical depths out of which the practice emerges; not to attempt to provide any definitive answers, but to explicate, contextualise, offer a few considered interpretations, and to bring together a disparate range of information which, by sharing a space between two covers, may shed a little light on other parts of the puzzle.

If any conclusions are to be drawn from the study, then I would propose that the following three are primary: First, the main lesson of Part 1 is that the theoretical background *and* practical techniques of haṭha antedate the best known systematic treatises on the subject by several hundreds and quite possibly thousands of years. While it remains impossible to place any accurate date upon the origins of haṭha-yoga, it is clear that this tradition should not be viewed as an exclusively Tāntrika development, i.e. as a variety of yoga that sprang up sometime during the period corresponding to the European Middle Ages. Haṭha is, rather, a branch or striation of Vaidika esotericism, with roots extending back far beyond the beginning of the Common Era. Firm conclusions cannot be drawn regarding the degree to which ṛṣis responsible for the Vedic Saṃhitās were familiar with techniques resembling those of haṭha-yoga, but we can at least find references to haṭha's core concepts and practical methods in certain of the Vedic Upaniṣads (see Chapter 1 above), including those which are old enough to precede the advent of Buddhism (*ca.* 500 B.C.E.).

Second, Parts 2 and 3 have demonstrated how haṭha-yoga should be regarded as a comprehensive soteriological system and not as merely a method of physical training which is auxiliary to some 'higher' or 'more refined' mode of yoga. The practices of haṭha include the cleansing of the physical body and the cultivation of strength, stamina and agility; but the haṭha view of health encompasses far more than flesh and bones. Its techniques are designed to work most potently on the level of the 'subtle body' (sūkṣma-śarīra), cleansing the vital channels (nāḍīs) and thereby enabling the vital force called prāṇa to flow uninhibitedly, and with a greater degree of voluntary control. The theory and practice of haṭha are inextricably bound together: without notions such as that of the human being as a multilayered organism, of a reflexive resonance between micro- and macrocosm, and of a subtle physiological matrix that governs and informs the gross physical body, haṭha practice would be unintelligible. These notions permeate the technical methodology of haṭha, and, in turn, haṭha's methodology provides access to realms of experience that give such notions a grounding. The haṭha system comprises ethical, gross-physical, subtle-physical and mental disciplines, uniting them in a complementary fashion and in a way that is clearly directed towards the final goal of Self-realisation. While certain passages in haṭha texts are often interpreted to imply that haṭha-yoga can take the practitioner only to a state of bodily perfection, after which point one must engage in the 'superior' discipline of rāja-yoga, I have shown that an alternative interpretation is possible.[2] On this alternative view, *rāja-yoga* denotes not a set of mental techniques which must be appended to haṭha-yoga, but the final goal of haṭha and of all varieties of yoga, i.e. the 'crowning glory' or 'radiant splendour' enjoyed in the final state.

The third, and perhaps most important conclusion, which has been alluded to above but bears re-emphasising, is that haṭha-yoga is immensely and unfathomably powerful, harbouring the potential to radically transform the human being on all conceivable (and inconceivable) levels. It is therefore also—both in its practices and its effects—profoundly *alien* to most people, even to many of those who claim to be its practitioners. The biomedical studies mentioned in Chapter 9 can only gesture towards the potency of haṭha—towards the force which can be harnessed by this discipline and the psychophysical changes that it can engender. Any science that strives to be 'objective' can help us to appreciate the profound benefits received by the haṭha-yogin on the physiological level, but it cannot reveal the still more profound transformations at the level of subjective insight which haṭha practice is designed to achieve. These changes, which involve the flowering of awareness and the dawning of new modes of perception and new ways of being, must, ultimately, be experienced to be appreci-

---

2 See Chapter 5, pp. 102ff. above.

ated. Haṭha-yoga—the 'forceful yoga', the yoga of 'determined effort'[3] —is powerful indeed; its purpose is the translocation of one's very sense of self-identity, shifting it, drawing it inwards, away from the gross shell of reality and towards the inner core. The paradox is that, once there, once the essence of self-hood—the spiritual Self—has been unveiled, it will be realised to encompass all that is: reality as oneness, 'absoluteness'. At least, this is the claim voiced in the haṭha texts, and by adepts of the discipline throughout the ages. The author of the *Gheraṇḍa-Saṃhitā* expresses the joyous realisation thus:

> I am Brahman (the 'Absolute'), nothing else am I. Brahman, indeed, I am, not one who suffers (*śokabhāk*). The form of truth-consciousness-bliss (*saccidānanda*) am I, eternally free, self-existent. (*GS* 7.4)

The novice practitioner should be aware of haṭha's potency, and should approach its more advanced practices with care and respect. It should be remembered that haṭha has traditionally been taught within an initiatory framework (discussed in Chapter 3), the guru being the constant mentor and guardian of the disciple, moulding his presentation of the subject to an intuited conception of the disciple's needs. It is therefore likely that any haṭha teachings encountered outside of such a framework will be incomplete and only partially appropriate for any individual.

But haṭha is, of course, a jewel with many facets, and may be approached from a variety of angles. For those who wish only to enhance their physical fitness and to prolong their life in the physical body, haṭha may be approached on this level. The āsanas will certainly improve one's physique and the flexibility of joints and muscles; and a basic prāṇāyāma routine will boost lung capacity and general breathing efficiency. All of this can be learnt by attending a good yoga class, as can the ability to relax and release tension in the body. It is for those who wish to take the practice a stage further, and who can find

---

3 Cf. Iyengar 1991: 22.

a suitably qualified teacher, that haṭha offers a set of tools—a coherent methodology—for building of oneself a temple, out of which may pour not only the sweat of intense and disciplined work, but also, and more importantly, the light of an awakened spirit.

The aim of haṭha-yoga is, then, precisely to enable the practitioner to tap into the 'reservoirs of life' to which the psychologist William James has alluded (see quotation above). More specifically, it is to integrate the 'solar' and 'lunar' aspects of vital force and to ignite the flame of undying power known as Kuṇḍalinī-śakti—to raise the Goddess and to hear her voice resonating within our heart. It is to unite Śiva and Śakti—pure, immutable consciousness and its transformative emanation of 'power' (energy-matter)—within the crucible of the human being. In less symbolically-laden language, it is to enable us to find answers to our most deeply troubling questions—about the nature of consciousness and perception, about the relationship between the experiencing self and the phenomenal world, about the causes of suffering and distress, and, ultimately, about who we really are. Not intellectual answers, but answers beyond reason, and therefore beyond doubt. Answers in the form of an awakening—a realisation of Truth.

OM NAMAḤ ŚIVĀYA[4]

OM ŚRĪ MAHĀ KĀLIKĀYAI NAMAḤ[5]

OM ŚĀNTIḤ ŚĀNTIḤ ŚĀNTIḤ[6]

OM

---

[4] 'Om, reverence to Śiva!'

[5] 'Om, the great auspicious Kālī—reverence to her!'

[6] 'Om, peace, peace, peace.'

Appendix A

Illustrations and photographs*

Representations of Śiva

Liṅga-yoni

* All illustrations are by Mikel Burley. The photographs on pp. 258-271 are of Mikel Burley and were taken by Sue Pomfrett.

Mahāyogin

Naṭarāja

Dakṣiṇāmūrti

Ardhanārīśvara

Haryardhamūrti

Nāḍīs and cakras

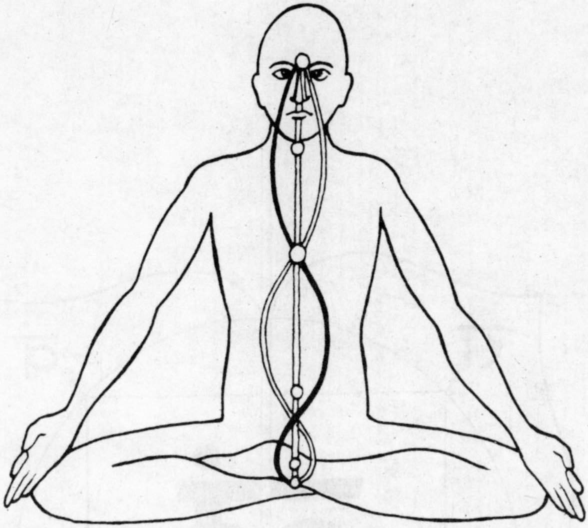

Diagram showing the approximate locations of the six major cakras and the three principal nāḍīs. Piṅgalā-nāḍī is here represented as black and curved, iḍā-nāḍī as white and curved, and suṣumnā-nāḍī as the central column.

The ancient Caduceus, symbol of Hermes in Greek mythology and of St Michael in that of Christianity. The close resemblance it bears to the imagery of the three principal nāḍīs has been observed by, amongst others, the Theosophist C. W. Leadbeater (1968: 22-23).

Mūlādhāra-cakra

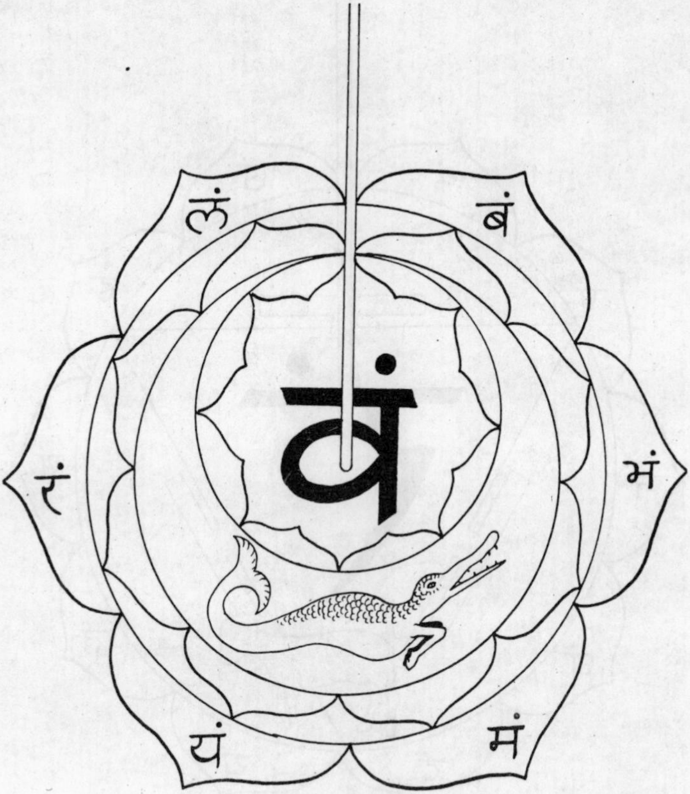

Svādiṣṭhāna-cakra

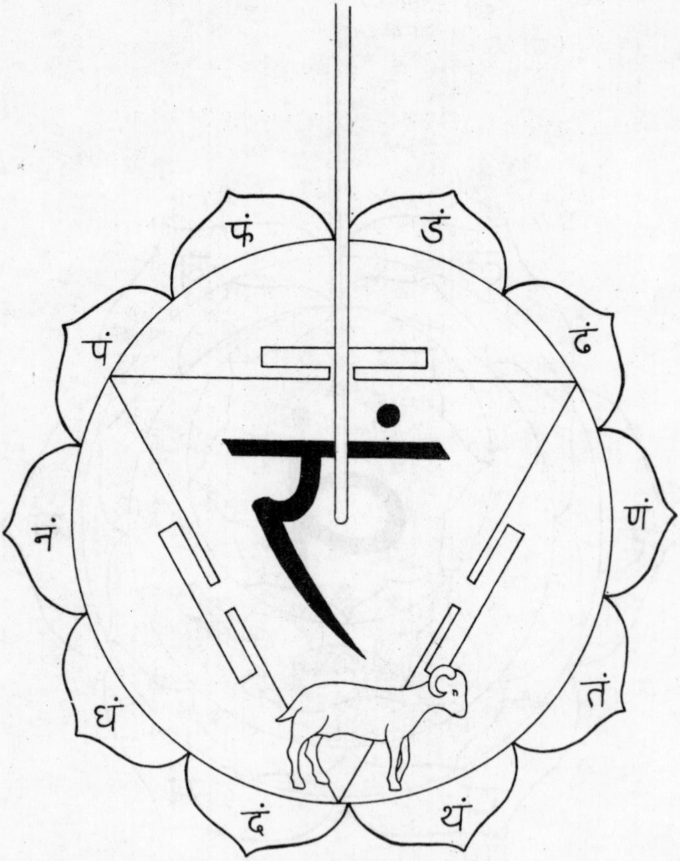

Maṇipūraka-cakra

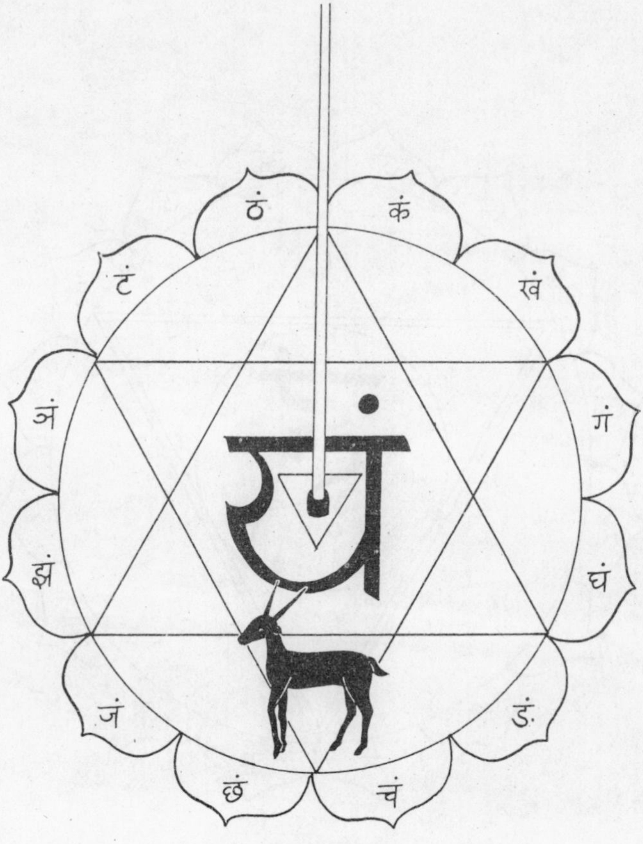

Anāhata-cakra

Viśuddha-cakra

Ājñā-cakra

A selection of āsanas and mudrās*

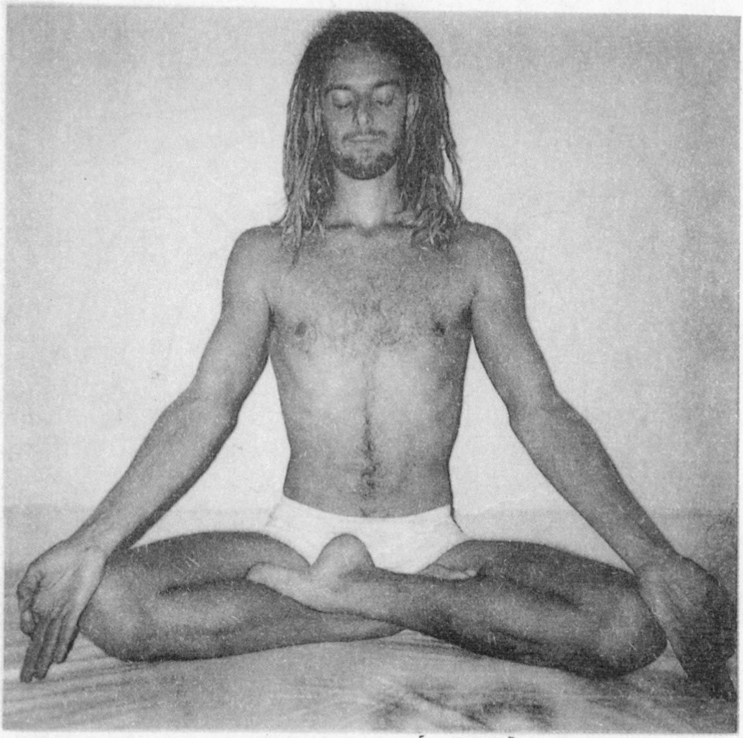

Svastikāsana (*HYP* 1.19)

(Note that both feet are trapped between the thigh and calf of the opposite leg, a fact which distinguishes this posture from Siddhāsana [p. 264 below].)

---

* The āsanas and mudrās pictured in this section are performed in accordance with their descriptions in the *Haṭha-Yoga-Pradīpikā* and *Jyotsnā* or the *Gheraṇḍa-Saṃhitā* (references are given in parentheses). They may, therefore, differ from those referred to by the same name in more recent haṭha manuals.

Gomukhāsana (*HYP* 1.20)

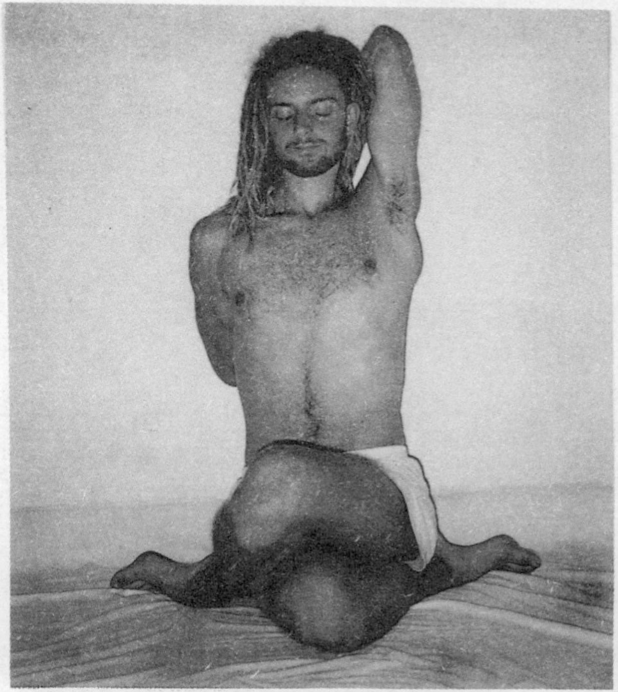

Gomukhāsana (variation)

Kukkuṭāsana (*HYP* 1.23)

Uttāna-kūrmāsana (*HYP* 1.24)

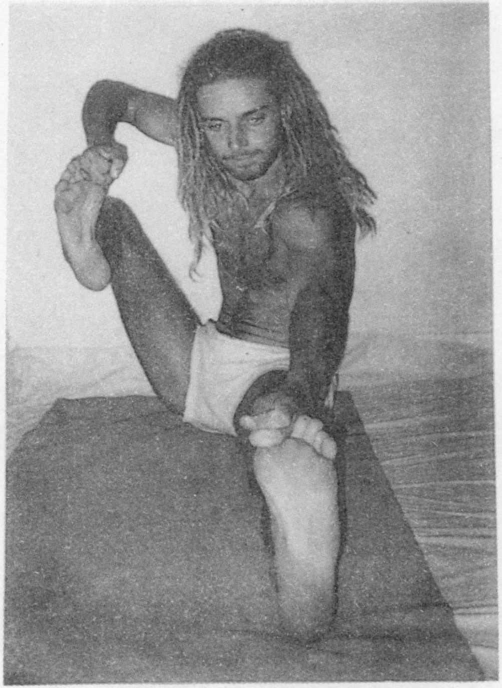

Dhanurāsana (*HYP* 1.25)

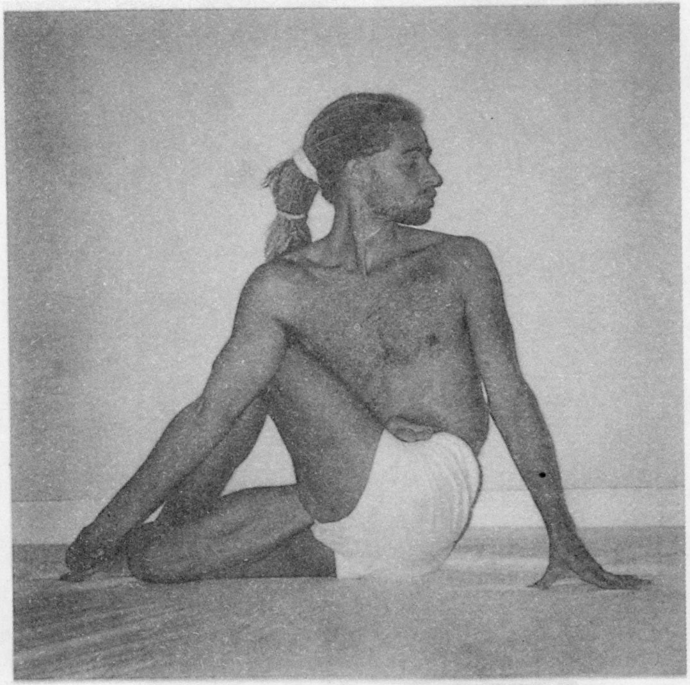

Matsyendrāsana (*HYP* 1.26-27)

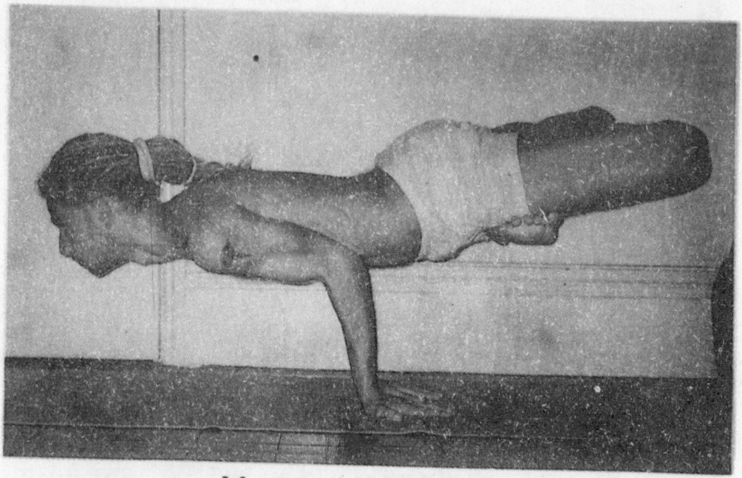

Mayūrāsana (*GS* 2.29-30)

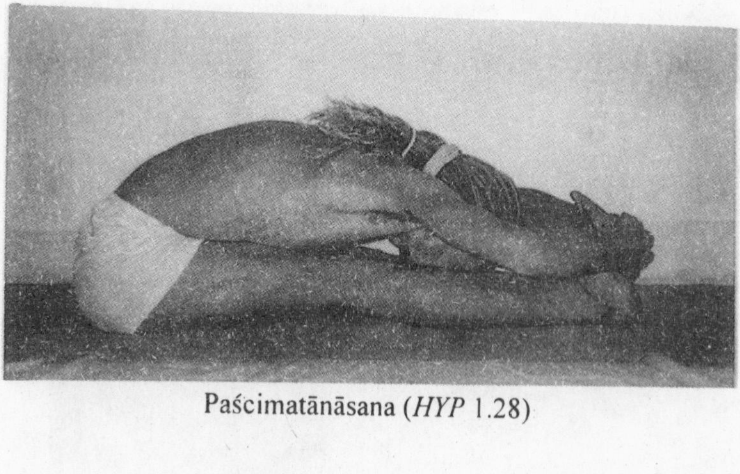

Paścimatānāsana (*HYP* 1.28)

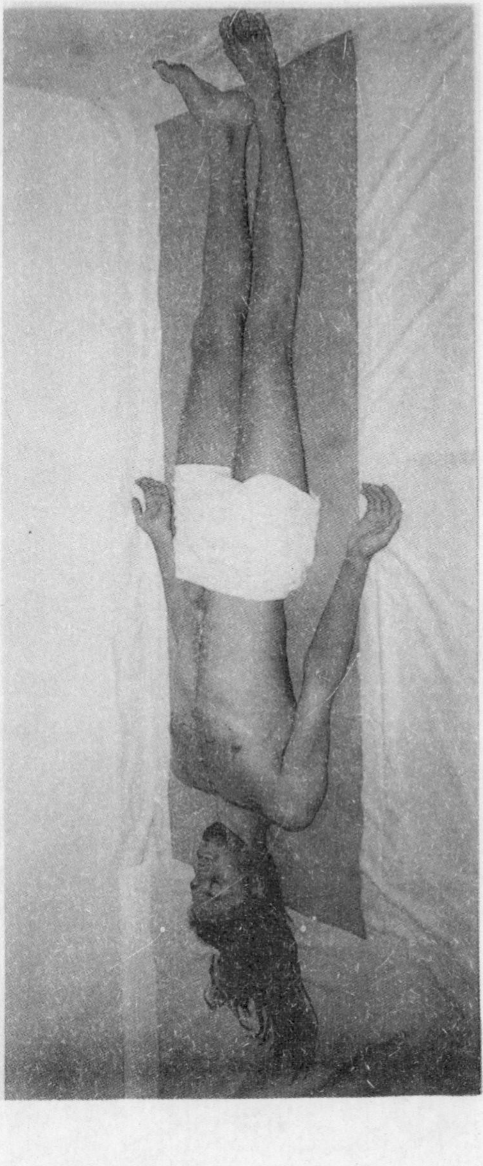

Śavāsana (*HYP* 1.32)

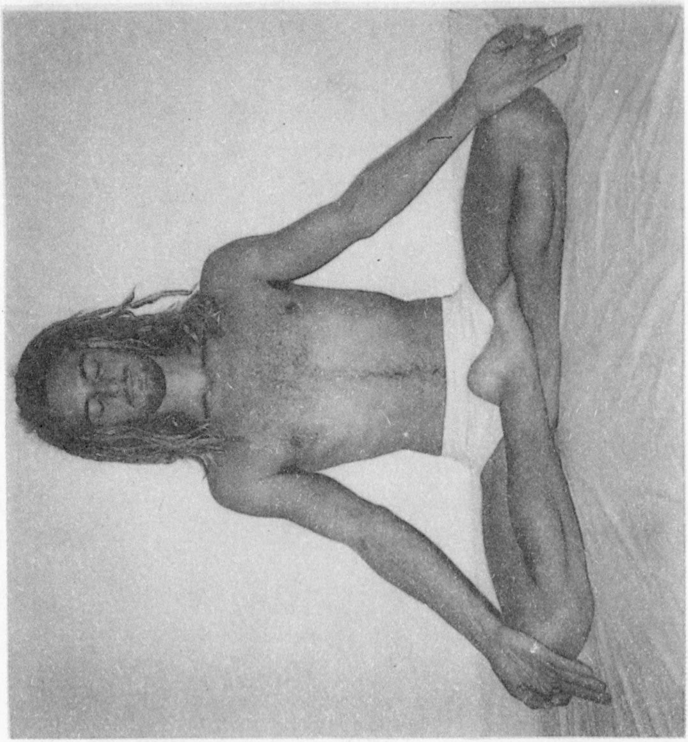

Siddhāsana (*HYP* 1.35)

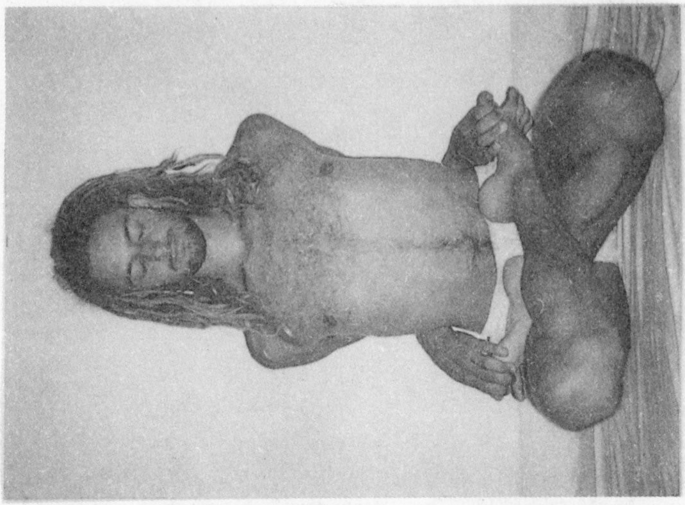

Padmāsana (*HYP* 1.44)

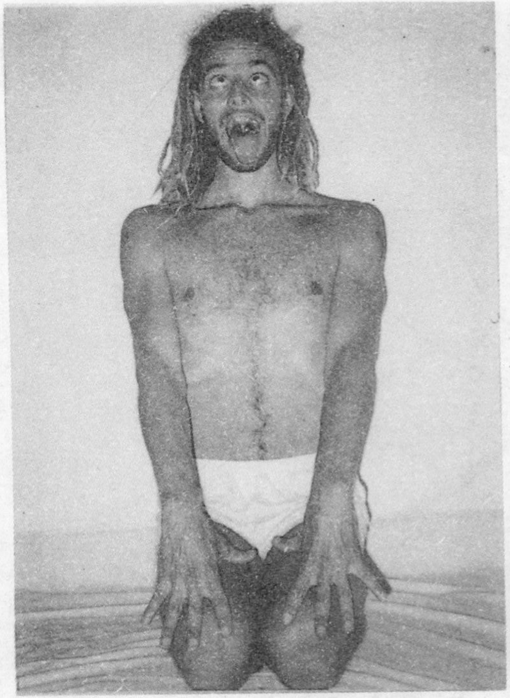

Siṃhāsana (*HYP* 1.52)

Bhadrāsana (*HYP* 1.53-54)

Vajrāsana (*HYP* 3.114-115)

(Known as kandāsana in more recent texts [see, e.g. Iyengar 1991: 348-51].)

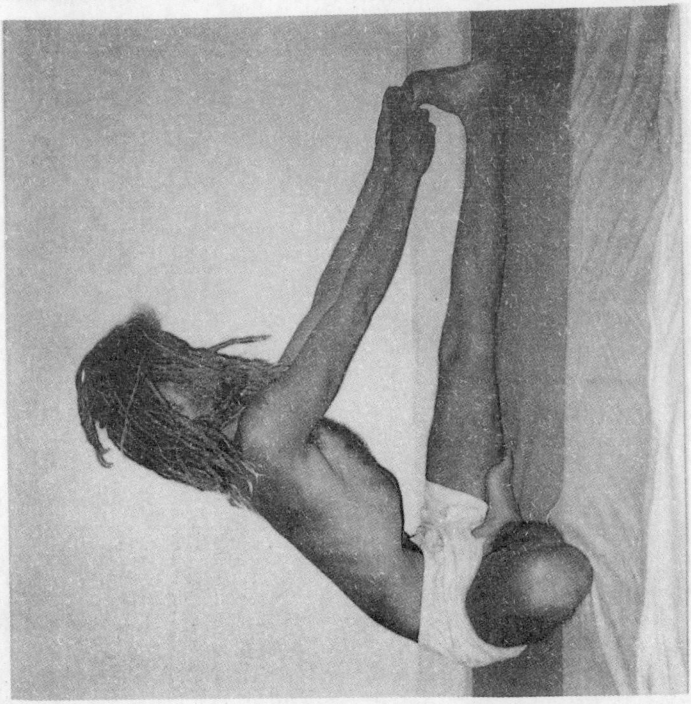

Mahāmudrā (*HYP* 3.10)

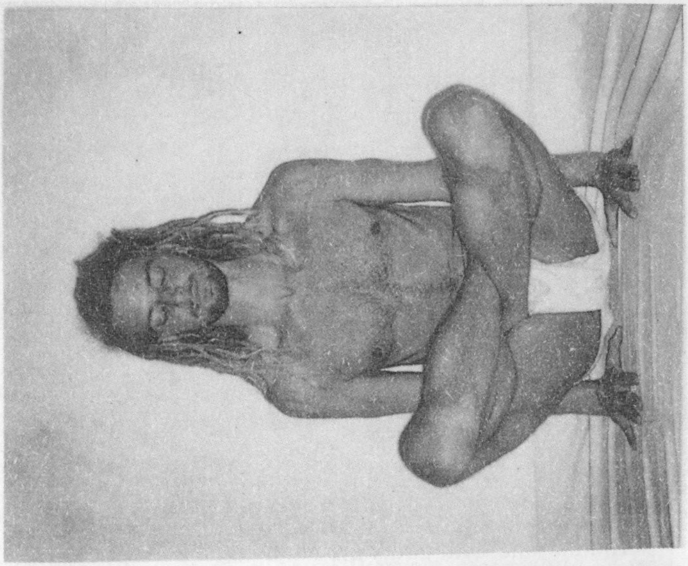

Mahāvedha (*HYP* 3.26-29)

Siddhāsana with uḍḍīyāna-bandha (*HYP* 3.55)

Viparītakaraṇī (*J* 3.81)

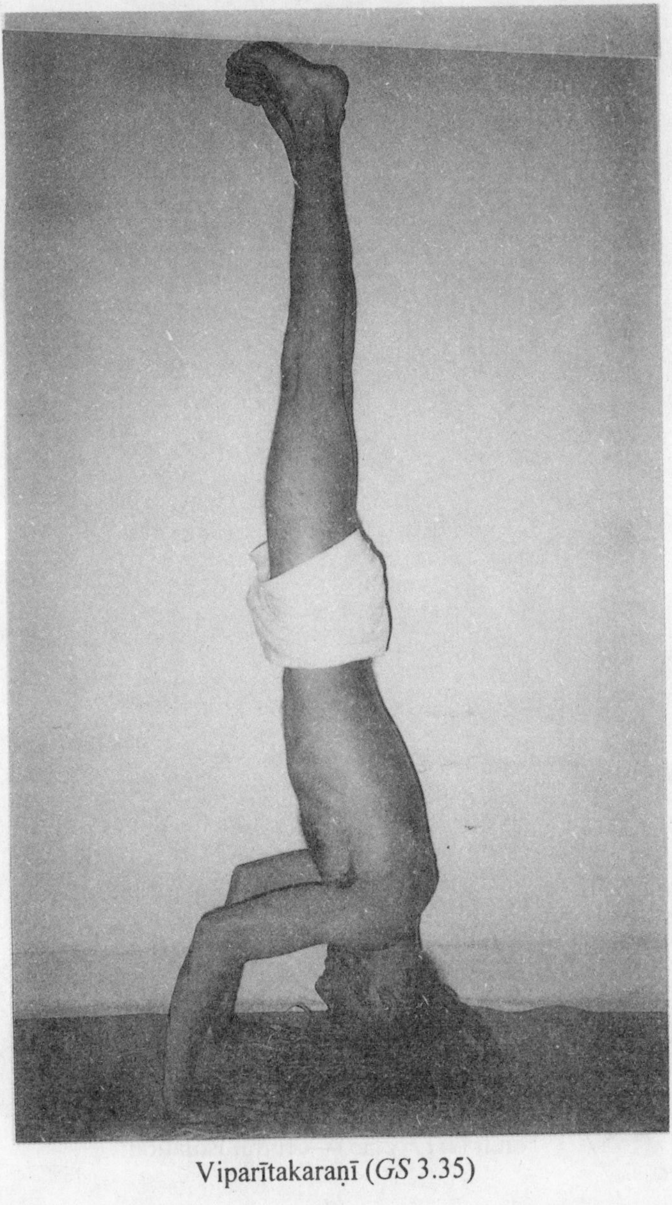

Viparītakaraṇī (*GS* 3.35)

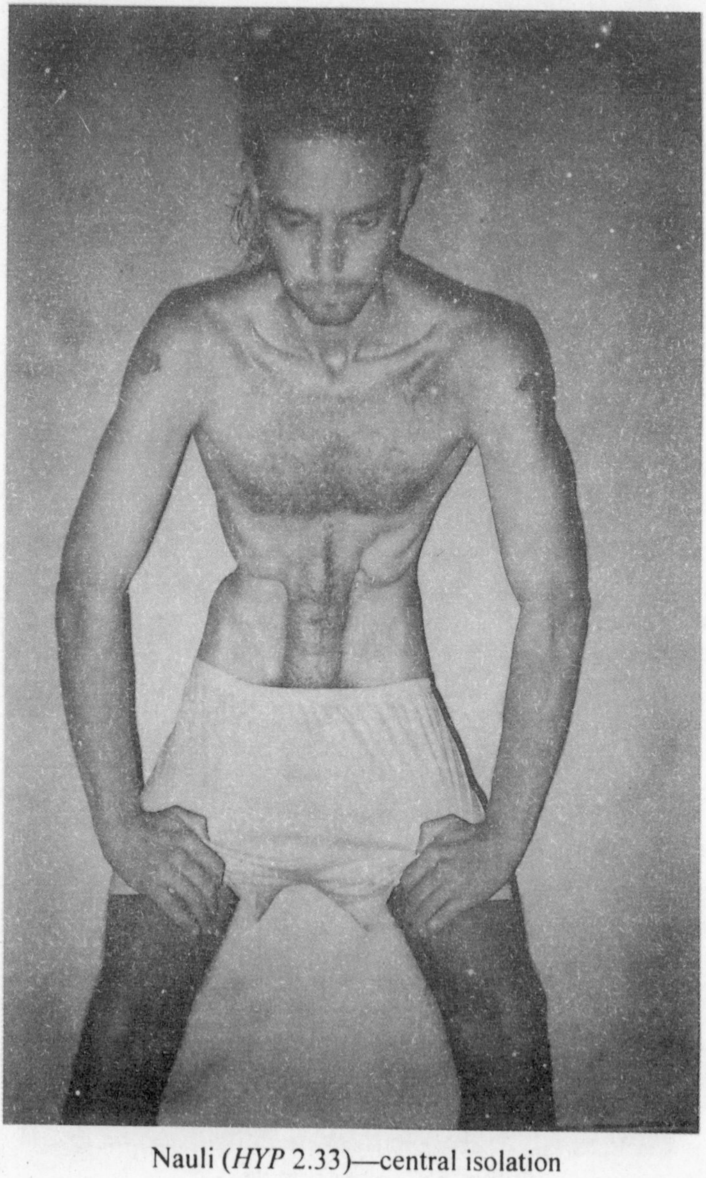

Nauli (*HYP* 2.33)—central isolation

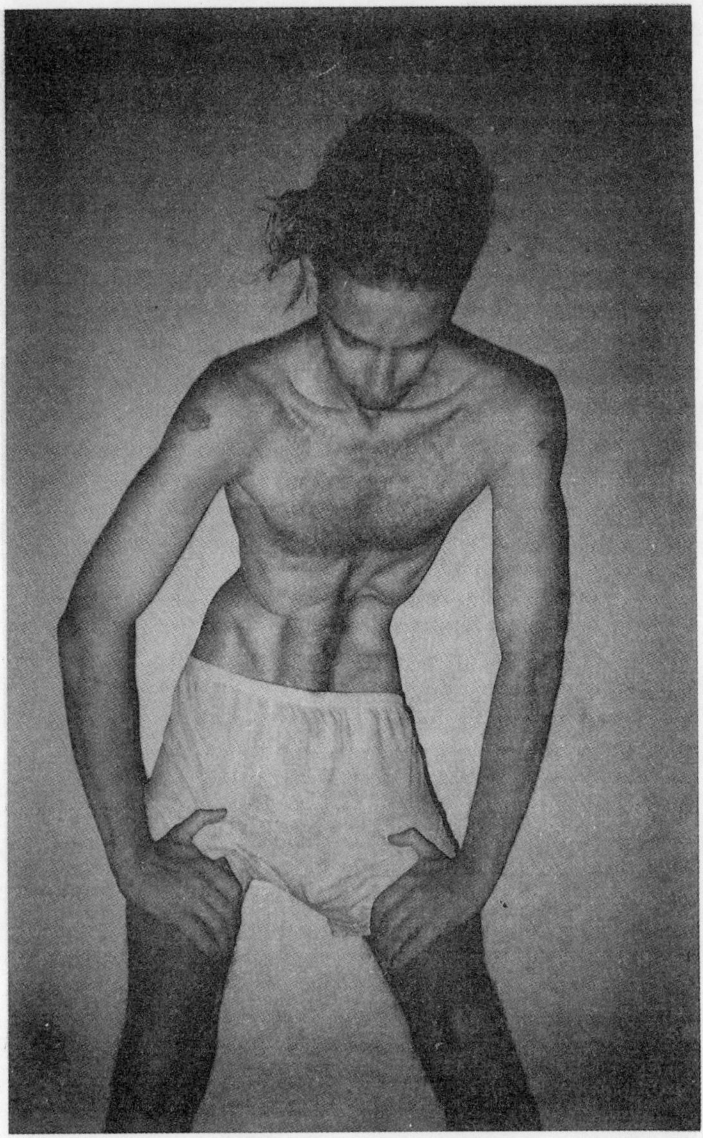

Nauli (*ib.*)—right isolation

Appendix B

Transliteration and pronunciation of Sanskrit* terms

For the purpose of this study, the more-or-less universally accepted system of transliteration from Devanāgarī to Roman script has been used. The table below shows the Sanskrit alphabet written in Roman script with appropriate diacritics, accompanied by a guide to the approximate phonemic value of each character.

Vowels

a	as in *around*, *organ*
ā	" " *father*, *jar*
i	" " *it*, *lily*
ī	" " *pique*, *ski*
u	" " *bush*
ū	" " *rude*
ṛ	a flapped 'r', produced by turning the tongue back on the hard palate and then flapping it forward
ṝ	as above, except more prolonged
ḷ	similar to *lry* in *revelry*
ḹ	as above, except more prolonged
e	as in *prey*; similar to French *été*, except longer
ai	" " *aisle*

* According to the transliteration system used in this study, *Sanskrit* should really be written *Saṃskṛta*, but the former spelling has been retained due to its having become so commonly recognised.

o	as in French *fausse*
au	" " *sauerkraut*
ṃ	indicates that the preceding vowel is nasalised
ḥ	indicates that the preceding vowel is aspirated

Consonants

k	as in ***sk**in*, French ***c**oup*
kh	an aspirated 'k', as in *pic**kh**andle*
g	as in ***g**o*, *do**g***
gh	an aspirated 'g', as in *do**gh**ouse*
ṅ	as in *si**ng***, *sku**n**k*
c	" " Italian *voce*
ch	" " ***ch**arm*
j	" " *jig*
jh	an aspirated 'j', as in *he**dgeh**og*
ñ	as in *hi**n**ge*
ṭ	" " *tip*, pronounced with retroflexion (i.e. striking the hard palate with the underside of the tongue)
ṭh	an aspirated 'ṭ'
ḍ	as in ***d**i**d*** (with retroflexion)
ḍh	an aspirated 'ḍ'
ṇ	as in *fu**n**d* (with retroflexion)
t	" " *water*, esp. Irish pronunciation
th	an aspirated 't', as in *an**th**ill* (*not* as in *that* or *thistle*)
d	as in ***d**isten**d***, *i**d**ea*
dh	an aspirated 'd', as in *a**dh**ere*
n	as in ***n**ot*, *ti**n***
p	" " *spin*
ph	an aspirated 'p', as in *u**ph**ill* (*not* as in *sphere* or *graph*)
b	as in ***b**i**b***
bh	an aspirated 'b', as in *a**bh**or*
m	as in ***m**en*, *s**m**ile*
r	" " *trip*
y	" " *yes*, *royal*
l	" " *lip*

v	midway between the 'v' in *veto* and the 'w' in ***wisp***
ś	as the 'sh' in ***shiver***
ṣ	as the 'sh' in ***flush*** (with retroflexion)
s	as in *sun* (never as the 'z'-sound in *is*, *resolve*, etc.)
h	" " ***hen***, ***aha!***

Appendix C

Texts on haṭha-yoga in Sanskrit and other Indian languages

Below is a list of texts belonging to the haṭha tradition, only a relatively small number of which have been translated into English. The list is unlikely to be exhaustive, but it at least gives an impression of the quantity of literature that exists on the subject.

If a work has traditionally been attributed to a particular author, the author's name is provided here after the title of the text. The majority of the texts' dates are uncertain, and have therefore not been included. None of them, however, are later than 1900 C.E. (A number of more recent texts can be found in the Bibliography.)

'Yoga Upaniṣads'
(all in Sanskrit)

Advaya-Tāraka-Upaniṣad
Amṛta-Nāda-Upaniṣad
Amṛta-(Nāda-)Bindu-Upaniṣad
Brahma-Vidyā-Upaniṣad
Darśana-Upaniṣad
Dhyāna-Bindu-Upaniṣad
Haṃsa-Upaniṣad
Kṣurikā-Upaniṣad
Mahā-Vākya-Upaniṣad
Maṇḍala-Brāhmaṇa-Upaniṣad
Nāda-Bindu-Upaniṣad
Pāśupata-Brāhmaṇa-Upaniṣad
Śāndilya-Upaniṣad
Tejo-Bindu-Upaniṣad
Triśikhi-Brāhmaṇa-Upaniṣad
Varāha-Upaniṣad
Yoga-Cūdāmaṇy-Upaniṣad
Yoga-Kuṇḍaly-Upaniṣad
Yoga-Rāja-Upaniṣad
Yoga-Śikhā-Upaniṣad
Yoga-Tattva-Upaniṣad

Other texts

In Sanskrit

Amanaskar-Yoga, Īśvara Vāmadeva
Amaraugha-Prabodha, Gorakṣa
Ānanda-Samuccaya
Ananta-Vākya, Carpata
Bṛhad-Yogi-Yājñavalkya-Smṛti, Yājñavalkya
Carpata-Mañjarī, Carpata
Carpata-Śataka, Carpata
Gheraṇḍa-Saṃhitā, Gheraṇḍa
Gorakṣa-Bhujaṅga, Lakṣmidhāra
Gorakṣa-Kalpa, Gorakṣa
Gorakṣa-Paddhati (a.k.a. *Gorakṣa-Saṃhitā*), Gorâkṣa
Gorakṣa-Śataka (a.k.a. *Jñāna-Śataka*, *Jñāna-Prakāśa-Śataka*), Gorakṣa
Gorakṣa-Śataka-Ṭīka, Śaṅkara
Gorakṣa-Śataka-Ṭippaṇa, Mathuranāth Śukla
Gorakṣa-Siddhānta-Saṃgraha, Gorakṣa
Gorakṣa-Vacana-Saṃgraha, Gorakṣa
Gorakṣa-Vijaya, Gorakṣa
Haṭha-Pradīpikā-Ṭīka, Rāmānanda Tīrtha
Haṭha-Pradīpikā-Ṭippaṇa, Umāpati
Haṭha-Ratna-Āvali, Śrīnivāsa Bhaṭṭa
Haṭha-Saṃketa-Candrikā, Sundara Deva
Haṭha-Tattva-Kaumudī, Sundara Deva
Haṭha-Yoga-Dhīrāya, Śiva*
Haṭha-Yoga-Dhīrāya-Ṭīka, Rāmānanda Tīrtha
Haṭha-Yoga-Pradīpikā, Svātmārāma Yogin
Haṭha-Yoga-Viveka, Īśvara Vāmadeva
Jñāna-Amṛta, Gorakṣa
Jñāna-Amṛta-Ṭippaṇa, Sadānanda
Jñāna-Yoga-Khaṇḍa
Jyotsnā, Brahmānanda
Kaula-Jñāna-Nirṇaya, Matsyendra
Nava-Śakti-Śataka, Gorakṣa
Sat-Karma-Saṃgraha, Cidghanānanda
Siddha-Siddhānta-Paddhati, Gorakṣa
Siddha-Siddhānta-Saṃgraha, Balabhadra
Śiva-Samhitā, Śiva
Yoga-Bīja, Śiva
Yoga-Cintāmaṇi, Śivānanda Sarasvatī
Yoga-Kārṇikā, Aghorānanda

* Many texts on haṭha-yoga are regarded as examples of divine revelation, and are thus traditionally ascribed to the deity Śiva himself.

Yoga-Mārtaṇḍa, Gorakṣa
Yoga-Śāstra, Dattātreya
Yoga-Siddhānta-Paddhati, Gorakṣa
Yoga-Viśaya, Matsyendra
Yoga-Yajñavalkya(-Saṃhitā) (a.k.a. *Yoga-Yājñavalkya-Gītā*), Yajñavalkya

In other languages

Amaranātha-Saṃvāda (Marāṭhī), Gorakhnāth
Gorakh-Bodh (Hindī), Gorakhnāth
Gorakhnāth-Ki-Vacan (Hindī), Banārsī Dās
Gorakh-Upaniṣad (Hindustānī and Rājastānī), Gorakhnāth

Appendix D

Traditional Hindu cosmological timetable

Brahman:	eternal
Brahmā:	emanating aspect
One lifespan of Brahmā:	100 Brahmic years = 3,110,400,000,000 human years
One year of Brahmā (*mahākalpa*):	360 days of Brahmā
One day of Brahmā (*kalpa*):	14 *manvantaras* (ages of Manu) = 1000 *mahāyugas* (great ages) = 4,320,000,000 human years
One night of Brahmā (*pralaya*):	one sixth of a kalpa
One mahāyuga:	4 yugas (kṛta + tretā + dvāpara + kali) = 4,320,000 human years
*Kṛta-yuga**:	1,780,000 human years
Tretā-yuga:	1,296,000 human years
Dvāpara-yuga:	864,000 human years
Kali-yuga:	432,000 human years

* *Kṛta* means 'fourth', especially with reference to dice, in which context it denotes the side of a die with four spots; similarly, *tretā* denotes the side with three spots, thus meaning

'third'; *dvāpara*, the side with two spots; and *kali*, the side with one ('the losing die' [Monier-Williams 1963: 261]). The yugas (ages), then, are counted in reverse order. The teachings of the Tantras, including those of haṭha-yoga, are traditionally believed to serve the requirements of spiritual aspirants in the present kali-yuga, which is held to have commenced with the death of the avatāra Kṛṣṇa in approximately 3102 B.C.E.

Glossary of key Sanskrit terms

abhyāsa persistent study, practice.
ācārya teacher.
ādhāra foundation, support.
adharma disorder, unrighteousness.
Ādinātha, Ādīśvara Primal Lord (a title of Śiva).
advaita non-dual, monist, singular.
Āgama 'coming near to'; a revealed text, particularly in the Śaiva tradition.
Agni fire; fire-deity; gastric fire.
ahaṃkāra 'I-maker'; faculty of egoity.
ahiṃsā non-injury, harmlessness.
ājñā order, command.
ākāśa space, sky, ether (cf. *kha*, *vyoman*).
aliṅga unmarked, undifferentiated.
amarī, amṛta undying, immortal; the nectar of immortality.
anāhata unstruck (sound).
ānanda unbroken bliss; happiness.
ananta unending, infinite.
aṅga limb, part; body.
aṅgula finger, toe; a finger's breadth.
antaḥkaraṇa inner instrument, inner activator, i.e. the mind, comprising buddhi, ahaṃkāra and manas.
antar, antara inner, internal.
apāna downward-flowing prāṇa.
aparigraha non-grasping, non-covetousness.
Āraṇyaka forest-text, the third portion of śruti.
ārya noble.
asaṃprajñāta-samādhi supracognitive samādhi, samādhi-without-cognitive-support (syn.: *nirvikalpa-samādhi*).
āsana posture; seat.
asmitā 'I-am-ness'; egoity.
aṣṭāṅga eight-limbed, eightfold.

asteya non-stealing.
āstika orthodox belief, i.e. in accordance with the Vedas (cf. *Vaidika*).
āśrama a dwelling or hermitage; stage of life.
ātman self or Self
ātma-samarpaṇa self-surrender.
avasthā abiding place; state; stage.
avatāra descended one, i.e. an incarnation of a deity.
avidyā non-seeing, spiritual ignorance (opposite of vidyā).
aviśeṣa undistinguished, unparticularised.
avyakta unmanifest prakṛti.

bahir*, *bāhya outer, external.
bandha lock, binding, bodily contraction.
Bhairava fierce, ferocious; a form of Śiva, or a son of Śiva and Pārvatī.
bhakti devotion, worship.
bhānu sun; solar plexus.
Bhārata India; a kingdom of ancient India; descendant of Bharata.
bhāṣya explication, commentary.
bheda*, *vedha piercing, penetration.
bīja seed; saṃskāra; sometimes a synonym of *bindu*.
bindu a point, dot, spot; seed; subtle essence of seminal fluid.
Brahmā the emanative or creative aspect of trimūrti.
brahmacārin 'one who moves in Brahman', is intent upon Brahman; a spiritual student.
brahmacarya 'moving in Brahman', being intent upon Brahman; chastity.
Brahman the Absolute, Reality.
Brāhmaṇa second portion of śruti, concerned with rituals and sacrifices, stories and explanations of Vedic Saṃhitās.
brāhmaṇa a member of the Vedic priestly caste.
Brahmānanda 'bliss of Brahman'; name of a sage, author of *Jyotsnā*.
brahmāṇḍa cosmos (macro- or microcosm).
brahmarandhra 'hollow of Brahman'; suṣumnā-nāḍī, or the apex thereof.
buddhi mind, intellect, reflective consciousness.

cakra wheel; vital centre.
Caṇḍakāpāli 'glowing skull', 'angry-faced'; an epithet of Śiva in his Bhairava form; name of a disciple of Gheraṇḍa.
candra moon; iḍā-nāḍī.

cela student, disciple (syn.: *śiṣya*).
cintāmaṇi thought-gem.
citra*, *citrā*, *citriṇī bright, variegated.
citta the entire mind-field, reflective screen of consciousness.
citta-vṛtti mental modifications.

dakṣiṇa south, southern; right side (of the body); gift, offering.
Dakṣiṇāmūrti 'South-facing' (a title of Śiva).
darśana true vision; spiritually uplifting gaze of a guru; philosophical viewpoint.
deha body (syn.: *kāya*, *piṇḍa*, *śarīra*).
deva being of light, deity, spirit.
Devī the Goddess, Śakti.
dhāraṇā fixing the mind on a point, concentration.
dharma law; nature; order; virtue; truth.
dhauti cleansing, purifying.
dhvani sound.
dhyāna meditation.
doṣa a humour of the body, constituent aspect of the personality.
draṣṭṛ the Seer, i.e. the Self.
duḥkha unsatisfactoriness, distress, pain.

Gaṅgā river that flows through northern India, or the guardian deity thereof; iḍā-nāḍī.
ghaṭa pot, vessel, container.
ghaṭastha-yoga yoga of the vessel (a synonym of *haṭha-yoga* used in *Gheraṇḍa-Saṃhitā* 1.2).
ghaṭikā a unit of time (24 minutes).
Gheraṇḍa the name of a sage, purported author of the *Gheraṇda-Saṃhitā*.
Gorakṣa(-nātha) (Hindī: Gorakhnāth) 'cow-protector'; the name of a legendary haṭha-yogin.
granthi knot.
guṇa strand, part, aspect, quality (cf. *triguṇa*).
guru 'weighty one', dispeller of darkness, spiritual teacher.

Hara Śiva.
Hari Viṣṇu.
haṭha forceful, firm, persistent; union of 'sun' (*ha*) and 'moon' (*ṭha*).

haṭha-yoga, -vidyā a specific soteriological system of physical and mental disciplines; the state (of being and knowledge) achieved by means of that system.
haṭha-yogin a practitioner of haṭha-yoga.
hṛd, hṛdaya heart; seat of emotion.

iḍā-nāḍī 'refreshing channel'; nāḍī to the left of suṣumnā.
Īśvara Lord, Śiva.
Īśvara-praṇidhāna devotion to Īśvara.

jala water.
jālaṃdhara net, snare; one of the three main bandhas.
japa repetition, recitation (of a mantra).
jīva life; living being.
jīvanmukta one who has attained jīvanmukti.
jīvanmukti living/embodied freedom.
jīvātman living/embodied self.
jñāna knowledge, wisdom, revelatory insight.

kaivalya, kevalatva absoluteness, aloneness, integration.
kalpa rule, regulation; investigation; a 'day of Brahmā'.
kanda bulb; root (of the nāḍīs).
kāṇḍa part, portion, section (of a text).
Kapālin 'skull-bearer'; an epithet of Śiva in his Bhairava form.
karma action, deed; ritual act.
karmāṇi [see *ṣaṭ-karmāṇi*].
kāya body (syn.: *deha, piṇḍa, śarīra*).
kāya-sādhana path towards bodily perfection.
kāya-siddhi bodily perfection.
kevala complete, total, absolute.
kha sky, space, atmosphere, ether (cf. *ākāśa*, *vyoman*).
khecarī 'moving in space'; a particular kind of mudrā.
khyāti vision, illumination.
kleśa affliction, obstacle.
kośa, koṣa sheath, covering.
kriyā action, performance; (cleansing) act.
Kṛṣṇa black, dark; name of an avatāra of Viṣṇu.
kumbhaka retention (of prāṇa).
Kuṇḍalinī(-śakti) 'she who is coiled'; serpent power.

laya, pralaya dissolution, absorption.
liṅga sign, mark, differentiation; phallus; symbol of Śiva.

loka world, plane, realm.

mahā great, supreme.
mahābhūta gross element.
mahat the great; universal aspect of buddhi.
manas mind, cognitive faculty.
maṇḍala circle, disc, sphere; world, realm.
maṇipūra, maṇipūraka jewel-filled.
mantra thought-power; sacred sound; chanted syllable, word or phrase.
maṭha, maṭhikā hermitage.
mātra measure; 'in its entirety', 'as such'.
Matsyendra(-nātha) 'Lord of fish'; name of a sage, reputed guru of Gorakṣa.
maya made of, produced by.
māyā (special) power; the phenomenal world (which 'veils' or 'masks' the ultimate reality, Brahman).
mokṣa, mukti liberation, release.
mudrā seal; circuit-forming gesture.
mūla root, base; one of the three main bandhas.
mūlādhāra root support, base, foundation.
muni sage.

nābhi navel.
nāda (inner) sound (cf. *śabda*, *vāk*).
nādānusandhāna contemplation of the nāda.
nāḍī (subtle) channel, flow, stream.
nāstika unbelieving, non-orthodox (cf. *Vedavāhya*).
Naṭarāja Dancing Lord (a form of Śiva).
nātha lord, master; an honorific; a particular sect of devotees of Gorakṣa.
nirvikalpa-samādhi samādhi-without-distinction (syn.: *asamprajñāta-samādhi*).
nirguṇa, niṣkala without parts, without attributes, indivisible (as distinct from *saguṇa*, *sakala*).
nirodha dissolution, harnessing, control.
nirūpaṇa exposition, examination.
nitya eternal, unending.
niyama lesser restraint; secondary ethical principle (cf. *yama*).

ojas vitality, life-energy, reservoir of prāṇa.

pāda foot; part, chapter (of a book).
padma lotus.
parama, parā highest, supreme.
paramātman supreme Self.
Pārvatī 'daughter of the mountain'; a name of Śakti, Śiva's consort.
Pātañjala-yoga, -darśana, Yoga darśana the yoga of Patañjali, as described in the *Yoga-Sūtra*; one of the six main āstika darśanas.
Patañjali 'fallen into the palm of a hand'; the name of a sage, purported author of the *Yoga-Sūtra*.
piṇḍa body (syn.: *deha, kāya, śarīra*).
piṅgalā-nāḍī 'tawny channel'; nāḍī to the right of suṣumnā.
pīṭha temple, shrine, place of pilgrimage.
pradhāna primal substance, extension; prakṛti.
pradīpikā 'that which sheds light', illumination.
prakṛti primal substance, the ground of all psychphysical manifestation, constituted by triguṇa.
prāṇa air, breath, vital force, organisational principle of life (syn.: *vāyu*).
praṇava word of praise, the syllable *om*.
prāṇāyāma extension of (the retention of) prāṇa, prāṇa-control.
prasāda grace, gift, blessing.
pratyāhāra withdrawal (of senses).
pratyakṣa visible, evident.
pṛthivī earth.
pūraka filling; inhalation.
Purāṇa eternal, ancient; mythico-philosophical treatise.
puruṣa male, person; self; true Self, principle of consciousness.
pūrva former, earlier; east.

rāga attachment.
rāja radiant, splendid; king, regal, royal.
rajas impulsion, movement; an aspect of triguṇa; also: space, void, sky; female sexual fluid.
rāja-yoga the 'royal yoga'; the final goal of haṭha-yoga.
Rāma an avatāra of Viṣṇu.
recaka exhalation.
ṛṣi seer, sage.
Rudra 'roarer'; a Vedic deity; an epithet of Śiva.
rūpa form; beauty.

śabda word, sound (cf. *nāda*, *vāk*).
śabda-brahman word/sound of the Absolute (i.e. *om*); a title of Kuṇḍalinī-śakti.
ṣaḍaṅga six-limbed, sixfold.
sādhana 'that which leads to the goal'; spiritual path.
saguṇa, sakala with parts, with attributes (as distinct from *nirguṇa*, *niṣkala*).
sahasrāra-padma thousand-petalled lotus, the crown cakra.
sahita supported.
Śaiva associated with Śiva; one who worships Śiva.
Śākta associated with Śakti; one who worships Śakti.
Śakti power; the consort of Śiva.
samādhi, samāpatti unity, identification, integration.
samarpaṇa surrender, giving (oneself) (cf. *ātma-samarpaṇa*)
Śāṃbhavī a name of Śakti, consort of Śaṃbhu (Śiva); a particular kind of mudrā.
Saṃhitā collection (of verses); the first portion of śruti.
Sāṃkhya enumeration, numbering; one of the six main āstika darśanas.
saṃnyāsa renunciation.
saṃnyāsin renunciant.
saṃprajñāta-samādhi cognitive samādhi, samādhi-with-cognitive-support (syn.: *savikalpa-samādhi*).
saṃsāra 'wandering'; the cycle of life, death and rebirth.
saṃskāra residual mental impression, subliminal activator; habit, custom.
saṃtoṣa contentment.
saṃyama intense concentrative meditation; the combined practice of dhāraṇā, dhyāna, and samādhi.
Sanātana-dharma Eternal law or truth, a name of the Vedic religion.
Sarasvatī 'the flowing one'; power and female consort of Brahmā; name of a river in ancient India; suṣumnā-nāḍī.
śāstra doctrine, teaching.
śataka one hundred.
ṣaṭ-karmāṇi six (cleansing) practices.
satsaṅga 'in the presence of truth'; assembly before a guru.
sattva 'realness'; illumination, purity, lucidity; an aspect of triguṇa.
sāttvika sattvic; pure, good, lucid, of the nature of sattva.
satya truth, truthfulness.
śauca purification, cleanliness.

savikalpa-samādhi samādhi-with-distinction (syn.: *saṃprajñāta-samādhi*)
siddha adept, one who has attained perfection.
Siddhānta 'the end of perfection'; the teachings of Vedānta.
siddhi attainment, perfection, special power.
śiṣya student, disciple, spiritual aspirant (syn.: *cela*).
Sītā female consort of Rāma.
Śiva the Absolute (according to Śaivism); a personification of the Absolute; the aspect of trimūrti responsible for dissolution or absorption.
śloka stanza.
smṛti memory, recollection; that which is remembered, i.e. teachings that are based upon śruti but are not themselves direct revelations of truth.
śodhana cleansing, purification.
Soma moon; moon-deity; divine nectar.
spanda vibration.
Śrī beautiful, radiant, splendid; name of Lakṣmī, consort of Viṣṇu; an honorific.
śruti 'that which is heard'; revealed scripture, comprising Saṃhitā, Brāhmaṇa, Āraṇyaka, and Upaniṣad.
sthira steady.
sthūla gross, physical.
sukha easy, pleasant, comfortable, agreeable.
sūkṣma subtle, refined.
śūnya space without form; void, empty.
Sūrya sun; sun-deity; piṅgalā-nāḍī.
suṣumnā-nāḍī 'gracious channel'; the central nāḍī in the spinal region, running from mūlādhāra-cakra to sahasrāra-padma.
sūtra thread; that which sews; a terse written statement; a text composed of such statements.
svadharma own duty, own nature.
svādiṣṭhāna ownmost abode.
svādhyāya study (of the scriptures).
svāmin owner, possessor; a spiritual master.
svara sound, breath, prāṇa.
Svātmārāma (Yogin, Yogīndra) the name of a sage, previously known as Cintāmaṇi; author of the *Haṭha-Yoga-Pradīpikā*.

tamas darkness; density; inertia; an aspect of triguṇa.
tāṇḍava dance.
tanmātra 'extension-as-such'; subtle element.
Tantra web, warp; ritual; doctrinal theory; literary exposition.
Tāntrika Tantric; related to, or in accordance with, the Tantras; one who follows such teachings.
tapas heat, heating, burning; zeal.
tarka contemplation (cf. *vitarka*).
tattva 'that-ness'; existent principle, truth.
tejas fire.
triguṇa the 'three strands' of prakṛti, namely *sattva*, *rajas* and *tamas*.
trimūrti 'three faces'; the three aspects of Brahman's power, represented as Brahmā, Viṣṇu and Śiva.

uḍḍīyāna 'flying up'; one of the three main bandhas.
ujjāyī uplifting; victorious.
upadeśa chapter, lesson.
upādhi limitation, veil, disguise, vessel.
Upaniṣad secret teaching; a text belonging to the fourth category of śruti.

vāda view, theory, doctrine.
Vaidika Vedic; related to, or in accordance with, the Vedas; one who follows such teachings (cf. *āstika*).
vairāgya non-attachment.
vajra thunderbolt; adamantine; diamond.
vajrolī mighty, adamantine; erect penis; a particular kind of mudrā.
vāk word, speech (cf. *nāda*, *śabda*).
vana forest, wood, garden.
vāta wind, air, one of the three doṣas; prāṇa.
vāyu air, wind, breath (syn.: *prāṇa*).
Veda revelation, true vision; ancient text, comprising hymns, ritual instructions, mystical and philosophical expositions, etc.
Vedānta 'end of (or final part of) the Veda', i.e. the Upaniṣads; one of the six main āstika darśanas.
vedāntin an adherent to, or proponent of, the Vedānta darśana.
Vedavāhya 'outside the Veda'; non-orthodox (cf. *nāstika*).
vibhūti special power, manifestation, gift, blessing.
vicāra refined vitarka; 'special movement' of the mind, subtle perception.
vidyā vision, knowledge.

vijñāna special or disciminatory knowledge (syn.: *viveka*); consciousness, intelligence.

viśeṣa particularised; distinction.

Viṣṇu the Absolute (according to Vaiṣṇavism); a personification of the Absolute; the aspect of trimūrti responsiblefor existence and preservation.

viśuddha, viśuddhi especially pure.

vitarka special or intense contemplation.

viveka discernment, discriminatory knowledge (syn.: *vijñāna*).

vṛtti whirl, vortex, wave, modification, distortion, turning, version.

vyakta manifest.

Vyāsa 'compiler'; the name of a sage, purported author of the *Yoga-Bhāṣya* and *Mahābhārata*.

vyoman space, sky, atmosphere, ether (cf. *ākāśa*, *kha*).

yama restraint; ethical precept (cf. *niyama*).

Yamunā a river in north Indian, or the guardian deity thereof; piṅgalā-nāḍī.

yantra device, machine, tool; symbol.

Yoga darśana [see *Pātañjala-yoga*].

yoga union, Self-realisation; the method of achieving that goal.

yogin a practitioner of yoga.

yoni womb, vulva; perineum; source, origin.

yuga age, epoch.

yukta joined, connected, united.

Bibliography

PRIMARY SOURCES

A. Editions and translations of principal haṭha-yoga texts

***Gheraṇḍa-Saṃhitā* of Gheraṇḍa**

Vasu, Śrīś Chandra, trans. 1895. *The Gheranda Saṁhitā: A Treatise on Haṭha Yoga.* Adyar: Theosophical Publishing House.

***Gorakṣa-Śataka* attributed to Gorakṣa**

Briggs, George Weston. 1973. *Gorakhnāth and the Kānphaṭa Yogīs* (Chapter 14). Delhi: Motilal Banarsidass.

***Haṭha-Yoga-Pradīpikā* of Svātmārāma Yogin**

Iyangar, Srinivasa, trans. 1972. *The Haṭhayogapradīpikā with the Commentary Jyotsnā of Brahmānanda and English Translation.* [Trans. revised by Radha Burnier and A. A. Ramanathan.] Adyar: The Adyar Library and Research Centre/The Theosophical Society.

Rieker, Hans-Ulrich. 1989. *The Yoga of Light: Hatha Yoga Pradipika.* New edn., trans. Elsy Becherer. London: Unwin.

Vishnudevananda, Swami, trans. 1997. *Hatha Yoga Pradipika.* New York: Om Lotus.

Śiva-Saṃhitā

Vasu, Rai Bahadur Srisa Chandra, trans. 1996. *The Siva Samhita.* New Delhi: Munshiram Manoharlal.

B. Other related Tāntrika material

***Ṣaṭ-Cakra-Nirūpaṇa* of Pūrṇānanda-Svāmī, and commentary by Kālīcaraṇa**

Avalon, Arthur (Sir John Woodroffe). 1974. *The Serpent Power: The Secrets of Tantric and Shaktic Yoga.* New York: Dover Publications. [This is a republication of the seventh edition. The first edition, published in 1919 by Luzac & Co., London, has also been referred to.]

Śiva-Svarodaya

Muktibodhananda Saraswati, Swami. 1984. *Swara Yoga: The Tantric Science of Brain Breathing.* Munger, Bihar: Bihar School of Yoga.

C. Principal Sāṃkhya and Yoga texts

***Sāṃkhya-Kārikā* of Īśvara Kṛṣṇa and its commentaries**

Jha, Ganganatha, trans. 1934. *Sāṁkhya-kārikā* of Īśvara Kṛṣṇa, with the *Tattva-kaumudī* of Vācaspati Miśra. 2nd edn. rev. Poona: The Oriental Book Agency.

Sastri, S. S. Suryanarayana, ed. and trans. 1935. *The Sāṅkhya-kārikā of Īśvara Kṛṣṇa.* Madras: University of Madras.

***Yoga-Sūtra* of Patañjali and its commentaries**

Arya, Pandit Usharbudh. 1986. *Yoga-sūtras of Patañjali with the Exposition of Vyāsa.* Trans. and commentary. Vol. 1: *Samādhi-pāda.* Honesdale, Pennsylvania: The Himalayan International Institute of Yoga Science and Philosophy.

Baba, Bangali. 1976. *The Yogasūtra of Patañjali with the Commentary of Vyāsa.* Trans. with additional notes. Delhi: Motilal Banarsidass.

Miller, Barbara Stoler. 1996. *Yoga: Discipline of Freedom.* Berkeley, California: University of California Press.

Satchidananda, Sri Swami. 1984. *The Yoga Sutras of Patanjali.* Revised edn. Yogaville, Virginia: Integral Yoga Publications.

Shastri, Dhundhiraja, ed. 1930. *Pātañjalayogadarśana*, with the *Rāja-Mārttaṇḍa* of Bhoja Rāja, *Pradīpikā* of Bhāvāgaṇeśa, *Vṛtti* of Nāgojī Baṭṭa, *Mani-Prabhā* of Rāmānanda Yati, *Pada-Cadrikā* of Ananta-Deva Pandit, and *Yoga-Sudhākara* of Sadāśivendra Sarasvatī. Varanasi: Chowkhambā.

SECONDARY SOURCES

Anand, B. K. and G. S. Chhina. 1961. 'Investigations on Yogis Claiming to Stop Their Heart Beats'. *Indian Journal of Medical Research* 49: 90-94.

Arya, Pandit Usharbudh. 1985. *Philosophy of Hatha Yoga.* 2nd edn. Honesdale, Pennsylvania: The Himalayan International Institute.

Aurobindo, Sri. 1956. *On the Veda.* Pondicherry: Sri Aurobindo Ashram.

———. 1970. *The Synthesis of Yoga.* Pondicherry: Sri Aurobindo Ashram.

———. 1970-76. *The Collected Works.* Pondicherry: Sri Aurobindo Ashram.

Bagchi, B. K. and M. A. Wenger. 1958. 'Simultaneous EEG and Other Recordings During Some Yogic Practices'. *Electroencephalography and Clinical Neuro-physiology* 10: 193.

Bagchi, Prabodha Chandra, ed. 1986. *Kaulajñāna-nirṇaya of the School of Matsyendranātha.* Trans. Michael Magee. Varanasi: Prachya Prakashan.

Balasubramanian, R. 1990. 'Advaita Vedānta: Its Unity with Other Systems and Its Contemporary Relevance'. *Indian Philosophical Systems* [various authors]. Calcutta: The Ramakrishna Mission Institute of Culture.

Banerjea, Akshaya Kumar. 1962. *Philosophy of Gorakhnath, with Goraksha-Vacana-Sangraha.* Delhi: Motilal Banarsidass.

Barnett, Lionel D. 1905. *Bhagavad-Gītā: or the Lord's Song.* London: J. M. Dent & Sons.

Bernard, Theos. 1968. *Hatha Yoga: the Report of a Personal Experience.* London: Rider & Company.

Bhole, M. V. and P. V. Karambelkar. 1971. 'Water Suction in Internal Cavities During Uddiyana and Nauli'. *Yoga-Mimamsa* 13.4: 26-32.

——— 1971. 'Effect of Yoga Training on Vital Capacity and Breath-Holding Time—A Study'. *Yoga-Mimamsa* 14.3,4: 19-26.

Birch, Beryl Bender. 1995. *Power Yoga: The Total Strength and Flexibility Workout.* New York: Simon & Schuster.

Brent, Peter. 1972. *Godmen of India.* Middlesex: Penguin.

Briggs, George W. 1938. *Gorakhnāth and the Kānphaṭa Yogīs.* Delhi: Motilal Banarsidass.

Buddhananda, Chela (under the guidance of Swami Satyananda Saraswati). 1984. *Moola Bandha: the Master Key.* 2nd edn. Munger, Bihar: Bihar School of Yoga.

Bühler, George. 1886. *The Laws of Manu.* Oxford: Clarendon Press.

Buhrman, Sarasvati. 1998. 'Leaving Depression Behind: The Yogic Way Out'. *Yoga International* 40: 26-33.

Conze, Edward. 1962. *Buddhist Thought in India.* London.

Das, Maya. 1990. 'Indian Philosophical Systems: Their Basic Unity and Relevance Today'. *Indian Philosophical Systems* [various authors]. Calcutta: Ramakrishna Mission.

Das, N. N. and H. Gastaut. 1955. 'Variations in the Electrical Activity of the Brain, Heart, Skeletal Muscles During Meditation and Trance'. *Electroencephalography and Clinical Neurophysiology* 6: 211-19.

Datey, K. K., S. Deshmukh, C. Dalvi and S. L. Vinekar. 1969. 'Shavasan: A Yogic Exercise in the Management of Hypertension'. *Angiology* 20: 325-33.

Dennett, Daniel C. 1991. *Consciousness Explained.* London: Penguin.

Desikachar, T. K. V. 1995. *The Heart of Yoga: Developing a Personal Practice.* Rochester, Vermont: Inner Traditions International.

Deussen, Paul. 1906. *The Philosophy of the Upanishads.* English trans. A. S. Geden. Edinburgh: T & T Clark.

Dimmitt, Cornelia and J. A. B. van Buitenen. 1978. *Classical Hindu Mythology: A Reader in the Sanskrit Purāṇas.* Philadelphia: Temple University Press.

Easwaran, Eknath. 1988. *The Upanishads.* London: Penguin.

Edgerton, Franklin. 1965. *The Beginnings of Indian Philosophy: Selections from the Rig Veda, Atharva Veda, Upani-ṣads, and Mahābhārata.* London: George Allen & Unwin.

Eliade, Mircea. 1969. *Yoga: Immortality and Freedom.* Trans. from the French by Willard R. Trask. London: Routledge & Kegan Paul.

———, ed. in chief. 1987. *The Encyclopedia of Religion.* Vol. 14. New York: Macmillan Publishing Company.

Feuerstein, Georg. 1974a. *Introduction to the* Bhagavad-Gītā*: Its Philosophy and Cultural Setting.* London: Rider and Company.

———. 1974b. *The Essence of Yoga: A Contribution to the Psychohistory of Indian Civilisation.* London: Rider and Company.

———. 1979. *The Yoga-Sūtra of Patañjali: An Exercise in the Methodology of Textual Analysis.* New Delhi: Arnold-Heinemann.

———. 1980. *The Philosophy of Classical Yoga.* Manchester: Manchester University Press.

———. 1990a. *Encyclopedic Dictionary of Yoga.* London: Unwin.

———. 1990b. *Yoga: The Technology of Ecstasy.* Wellingborough, Northamptonshire: Crucible/Thorsons.

———, trans. and ed. 1997. *Teachings of Yoga.* Boston & London: Shambhala.

———, Subhash Kak and David Frawley. 1995. *In Search of the Cradle of Civilization: New Light on Ancient India.* Wheaton, Illinois: Quest Books/Theosophical Publishing House.

——— and Jeanine Miller. 1971. *A Reappraisal of Yoga: Essays in Indian Philosophy.* London: Rider and Company.

Frawley, David. 1993. *Gods, Sages and Kings: Vedic Light on Ancient Civilization.* New Delhi: Motilal Banarsidass.

———. 1994. *The Myth of the Aryan Invasion of India.* New Delhi: Voice of India.

Funderburk, James. 1977. *Science Studies Yoga: A Review of Physiological Data.* Honesdale, Pennsylvania: The Himalayan International Institute.

Gandhi, Mohandas K. 1960. *Discourses on the Gita.* Ahmedabad: Navajivan Publishing House.

Garbe, Richard. 1900. 'On the Voluntary Trance of Indian Fakirs'. *The Monist* 10: 492-500.

Gelblum, Tuvia. 1992. 'On "the Meaning of Life" and the *Bhagavad Gītā*'. *Asian Philosophy* 2.2: 121-30.

Gerson, Scott. 1993. *Ayurveda: The Ancient Indian Healing Art.* Shaftesbury, Dorset: Element Books.

Gharote, M. L. 1973. 'Effect of Yogic Training on Physical Fitness'. *Yoga-Mimamsa* 15.4: 31-35.

Ghosh, Jajneswar. 1977. Introduction to: Swāmī H. Āraṇya, *The Sāṁkhya-sūtras of Pañcaśikha* and *The Sāṁkhyatattvāloka.* Delhi: Motilal Banarsidass.

Gopal, K. S., V. Anantharaman, S. Balachander and S. D. Nishith. 1973. 'The Cardiorespiratory Adjustments in "Pranayama," with and without "Bandhas," in "Vajrasana"'. *Indian Journal of Medical Science* 27.9: 686-92.

Govindan, Marshall. 1991. *Babaji and the 18 Siddha Kriya Yoga Tradition.* Montreal: Kriya Yoga Publications.

Goyandaka, Jayadaya, trans. 1943. *The Bhagavadgītā, or the Song Divine.* Gorakhpur: Gita Press.

Harshananda, Swami. 1981. *Hindu Gods and Goddesses.* Madras: Sri Ramakrishna Math.

Hewitt, James. 1987. *The Complete Yoga Book: The Yoga of Breathing, Posture, and Meditation.* London: Rider.

Hocking, M. G. 1993. *Exploring the Subconscious Using New Technology.* London: CMC Ltd.

Iyengar, B. K. S. 1981. *Light on Prāṇāyāma.* London: George Allen & Unwin.

———. 1988. *The Tree of Yoga.* London: Aquarian Press.

———. 1991. *Light on Yoga.* London: Aquarian Press.

Johari, Harish. 1986. *Tools for Tantra.* Rochester, Vermont: Inner Traditions India.

———. 1987. *Chakras: Energy Centers of Transformation.* Rochester, Vermont: Destiny Books/Inner Traditions.

Karambelkar, P. V., M. V. Bhole, and M. L. Gharote. 1969. 'Muscle Activity in Some Asanas'. *Yoga-Mimamsa* 12.1: 1-13.

Kirtan: Sivananda Chantbook. 1989. International Sivananda Yoga Vedanta Centres.

Koelman, Gaspar M. 1970. *Pātañjala Yoga: From Related Ego to Absolute Self.* Poona: Papal Anthenaeum.

Kramrisch, Stella. 1981. *The Presence of Śiva.* Princeton, New Jersey: Princeton University Press.

Krishna, Gopi. 1976. *Kundalini: Path to Higher Consciousness.* New Delhi: Orient Paperbacks.

———. 1992. *Kundalini – The Secret of Yoga.* New Delhi: UBSPD.

———. 1993. *The Purpose of Yoga.* New Delhi: UBSPD.

Larson, Gerald J. and Ram Shankar Bhattacharya, eds. 1987. *Encyclopedia of Indian Philosophies.* Vol. 4: *Sāṃkhya: A Dualist Tradition in Indian Philosophy.* Delhi: Motilal Banarsidass.

Leadbeater, C. W. 1968. *The Chakras: A Monograph.* 8th edn. Adyar: Theosophical Publishing House.

Lipner, Julius. 1998. *Hindus: Their Religious Beliefs and Practices.* London: Routledge.

Lott, Eric. 1980. *Vedantic Approaches to God.* London: Macmillan Press.

Marshall, P. J., ed. 1970. *The British Discovery of Hinduism in the Eighteenth Century.* Cambridge: Cambridge University Press.

Mitra, Vihári-Lála, trans. 1891. *The Yoga-Vásishtha-Maharamáyana of Válmiki.* 3 vols. Calcutta: Bonnerjee and Co.

Monier-Williams, Monier. 1963. *A Sanskrit-English Dictionary.* Delhi: Motilal Banarsidass.

Murphy, Michael. 1992. *The Future of the Body: Explorations Into the Further Evolution of Human Nature.* New York: G. P. Putnam's Sons.

Murray, Muz. 1986. *Sharing the Quest.* Shaftesbury, Dorset: Element Books.

Nikhilānanda, Swāmi, trans. 1944. *Māndūkyopanishad with Gauḍapada's Kārikā and Śaṅkara's Commentary*. Mysore: Sri Ramakrishna Ashrama.

O'Flaherty, Wendy D. 1973. *Śiva: The Erotic Ascetic*. Oxford: Oxford University Press.

Ozaniec, Naomi. 1990. *The Chakras*. Shaftesbury, Dorset: Element Books.

Potter, Karl H., gen. ed. 1977-96. *The Encyclopedia of Indian Philosophies*. Vol. 2: *Indian Metaphysics and Epistemology: The Tradition of Nyāya-Vaiśeṣika up to Gaṅgeśa*. Vol.6: *Indian Philosophical Analysis: Nyāya-Vaiśeṣika from Gaṅgeśa to Raghunātha Siromani*. Delhi: Motilal Banarsidass.

Radha, Swami Sivananda. 1993. *Kundalini Yoga for the West*. Spokane, Washington: Timeless Books.

Radhakrishnan, Sarvepalli. 1928. *The Vedānta According to Śaṁkara and Rāmānuja*. London: George Allen & Unwin.

———, trans. 1953. *The Principal Upaniṣads*. Delhi: Oxford University Press.

——— and Charles A. Moore, eds. 1957. *A Sourcebook in Indian Philosophy*. Princeton, New Jersey: Princeton University Press.

Rajaram, Navaratna S. 1993. *Aryan Invasion of India: The Myth and the Truth*. New Delhi: Voice of India.

Raju, P. T. 1985. *Structural Depths of Indian Thought*. New York: State University of New York Press.

Rama, Swami. 1986. *Path of Fire and Light*. Vol. 1: *Advanced Practices of Yoga*. Honesdale, Pennsylvania: The Himalayan International Institute.

———, R. Ballentine, and Swami Ajaya. 1976. *Yoga and Psychotherapy: The Evolution of Consciousness*. Honesdale, Pennsylvania: The Himalayan International Institute.

Śaṅkarācārya, Śrī. 1992. *Vivekacūḍāmaṇi*. 13th impression. Trans. Swāmī Mādhavānanda. Calcutta: Advaita Ashrama.

Sannella, Lee. 1987. *The Kundalini Experience: Psychosis or Transcendence?* Lower Lake, California: Integral Publishing.

Sastri, Dewan Bahadur K. S. Ramaswami. 1953. *Sivananda: A Modern World-Prophet*. Rishikesh: The Yoga-Vedanta Forest University.

Satyasangananda Saraswati, Swami. 1984. *Light on the Guru and Disciple Relationship*. Munger, Bihar: Bihar School of Yoga.

Scott, Mary. 1983. *Kundalini in the Physical World.* London: Routledge & Kegan Paul.

Schweizer, Paul. 1993. 'Mind/Consciousness Dualism in Sāṅkhya-Yoga Philosophy'. *Philosophy and Phenomenological Research* 53.4: 845-59.

Sharma, Chandrahar. 1960. *A Critical Survey of Indian Philosophy.* Varanasi: Motilal Banarsidass.

Shastri, D. C. B. 1990. 'The Indian Philosophical Systems: Their Basic Unity and Relevance Today'. *Indian Philosophical Systems* [various authors]. Calcutta: Ramakrishna Mission.

Singh, Jaideva. 1979. *Śiva Sūtras: The Yoga of Supreme Identity.* Delhi: Motilal Banarsidass.

Sivananda, Sri Swami. 1955a. *Tantra Yoga, Nada Yoga and Kriya Yoga.* Rishikesh: The Yoga-Vedanta Forest University.

———. 1955b. *The Yoga-Vedanta Sutras.* Rishikesh: The Yoga-Vedanta Forest University.

Svoboda, Robert E. 1998. 'A Question of Vision: The Relationship Between Ayurveda and Modern Medicine'. *Yoga International* 40: 34-41.

The Holy Bible, Containing the Old and New Testaments. 1901. Oxford: Oxford University Press.

Thomas, Edward J. 1927. *The Life of Buddha as Legend and History.* New York: Alfred A. Knopf.

Thoreau, Henry David. 1992. *Walden, or Life in the Woods: Selections from the American Classic.* Boston: Shambhala.

Udupa, K. N., R. H. Singh and R. M. Settiwar. 1971. 'Studies on Physiological, Endocrine and Metabolic Response to the Practice of Yoga in Young Normal Volunteers'. *Journal of Research in Indian Medicine* 6.3: 345-53.

Warren, H. C., trans. 1915. *Buddhism in Translations.* Harvard Oriental Series, Vol. 3, 6th edn. Cambridge, Mass.: Harvard University Press.

Wenger, M. A. and B. K. Bagchi. 1961. 'Studies of Autonomic Functions in Practitioners of Yoga in India'. *Behavioral Science* 6: 312-23.

Whicher, Ian R. 1992 [unpublished Ph.D. thesis]. *A Study of Patañjali's Definitions of Yoga: Uniting Theory and Practice in the* Yoga-Sūtras. University of Cambridge.

———. 1995. 'Cessation and Integration in Classical Yoga'. *Asian Philosophy* 5.1: 47-58.

———. 1998. *The Integrity of the Yoga Darśana: A Reconsideration of Classical Yoga.* New York: State University of New York Press.

Wood, Ernest. 1959. *Yoga.* Middlesex: Penguin.

Yogananda, Paramahansa. 1981. *Autobiography of a Yogi.* 12th edn. California: Self-Realization Fellowship.

Zaehner, R. C., ed. and trans. 1966. *Hindu Scriptures.* London: Dent.

———, trans. 1969. *The Bhagavad-Gītā.* Oxford: Clarendon Press.

Zvelebil, Kamil V. 1996. *The Siddha Quest for Immortality.* Oxford: Mandrake.

Index